The Garland Library
of Medieval Literature

General Editors
James J. Wilhelm, Rutgers University
Lowry Nelson, Jr., Yale University

Literary Advisors
Ingeborg Glier, Yale University
Guy Mermier, University of Michigan
Fred C. Robinson, Yale University
Aldo Scaglione, University of North Carolina

Art Advisor
Elizabeth Parker McLachlan, Rutgers University

Music Advisor
Hendrik van der Werf, Eastman School of Music

"Baths" (Courtesy of Wayland Picture Library)

The French Fabliau
B.N. MS. 837

Edited and translated by
RAYMOND EICHMANN
and JOHN DUVAL

Two Volumes
Vol. I

Volume 16
Series A
GARLAND LIBRARY OF MEDIEVAL LITERATURE

Garland Publishing, Inc.
New York & London
1984

Library of Congress Cataloging in Publication Data
Main entry under title:

The French fabliau.

(Garland library of medieval literature ; v. 16–   .
Series A)
Bibliography: v. 1, p.
1. Fabliaux. 2. French poetry—To 1500.
3. Fabliaux—Translations into English. 4. French poetry
—To 1500—Translations into English. 5. English poetry
—Translations from French. I. Eichmann, Raymond,
1943–   . II. DuVal, John, 1940–   . III. France.
Bibliothèque nationale. Manuscript. Français 837.
IV. Series: Garland library of medieval literature ;
v. 16, etc.
PQ1319.F7   1984   841'.1'08   83-48234
ISBN 0-8240-9419-0 (v. 1 : alk. paper)

196178

Printed on acid-free, 250-year-life paper
Manufactured in the United States of America

For our families
R.E. and J.D.

The Garland Library
of Medieval Literature

Preface of the General Editors

The Garland Library of Medieval Literature was established to make available to the general reader modern translations of texts in editions that conform to the highest academic standards. All of the translations are original, and were created especially for this series. The translations attempt to render the foreign works in a natural idiom that remains faithful to the originals.

The Library is divided into two sections: Series A, texts and translations; and Series B, translations alone. Those volumes containing texts have been prepared after consultation of the major previous editions and manuscripts. The aim in the editing has been to offer a reliable text with a minimum of editorial intervention. Significant variants accompany the original, and important problems are discussed in the Textual Notes. Volumes without texts contain translations based on the most scholarly texts available, which have been updated in terms of recent scholarship.

Most volumes contain Introductions with the following features: (1) a biography of the author or a discussion of the problem of authorship, with any pertinent historical or legendary information; (2) an objective discussion of the literary style of the original, emphasizing any individual features; (3) a consideration of sources for the work and its influence; and (4) a statement of the editorial policy for each edition and translation. There is also a Select Bibliography, which emphasizes recent criticism on the works. Critical writings are often accompanied by brief descriptions of their importance. Selective glossaries, indices, and footnotes are included where appropriate.

The Library covers a broad range of linguistic areas, including all of the major European languages. All of the important literary forms and genres are considered, sometimes in anthologies or selections.

The General Editors hope that these volumes will bring the general reader a closer awareness of a richly diversified area that

ix

has for too long been closed to everyone except those with precise academic training, an area that is well worth study and reflection.

James J. Wilhelm
Rutgers University

Lowry Nelson, Jr.
Yale University

Contents

Introduction

Origins and Problems

Joseph Bédier's century-old definition of the fabliaux, "*contes à rire en vers*" (comic verse tales; *Les Fabliaux*,* p. 30), has stood remarkably well, considering that the Middle Ages had no precise sense of *genre*, and the fableors themselves gave their creations a variety of names: *dit, ditié, fable, lai, example, proverbe, roman, risée*. Omer Jodogne notes that by the early fourteenth century, when the fabliaux were on the wane, the last known author, Jean de Condé, called them *truffes* (jokes) (1975, p. 24). Of the 160 surviving fabliaux, 56 are expressly called fabliaux; the fact that most of these end with some sort of moral, more or less appropriate to the tale, indicates that these authors might have thought of their *fabliaux* as mock-fables.

Scholars have accepted Bédier's definition with only minor adjustments. Attempts at structural definitions, such as Mary Jane Schenk's (1976) and Thomas Cooke's (1978) have never been meant to challenge Bédier's. Per Nykrog adds to Bédier's definition that the fabliau must belong to Medieval French literature, that it must be relatively short, and that it must restrict itself to the narration of one incident and its immediate consequences (1957, p. 13). Jodogne defines it as a "*conte en vers où, sur un ton trivial, sont narrées une ou plusieurs aventures plaisantes ou exemplaires, l'un et l'autre ou l'un ou l'autre*" (verse tales in a trivial tone that relate one or several incidents which are amusing or edifying or both; 1975, p. 23). He further points out that *Trubert*, which its author, Douin de Lavesne, called a fabliau, is not exactly "relatively short" with its 2,986 lines, and that, if we include it, a fabliau consists of several fables. Nykrog, however, did not accept *Trubert* as a

---

* See Select Bibliography for details for all authors cited here.

fabliau, calling it a novel. We agree, since its length and structure make *Trubert* vastly different from other poems in the fabliau canon. The disagreement over whether *Trubert* should be considered a fabliau, in spite of its author's claim, not only illustrates the loose nomenclature used by medieval authors but also emphasizes the necessity for a supple definition, one whose elements would not exclude obvious examples. This is why Bédier's "comic verse tales" has stood the test of time and is adequate for us.

Our primary source has been Henri Omont's 1932 facsimile reproduction of the late thirteenth century manuscript 837 in the Bibliothèque Nationale. The original manuscript is 362 pages of thick vellum, written on both sides, two fifty-line columns per page of close, virtually unpunctuated handwriting. Here romances, dramas, poems, translations, lais, dits, songs, moral tales and pious prayers, arranged with no great sense of order, keep company with our fabliaux.

This manuscript, formerly labeled Bibliothèque du Roi 7218, is rightfully considered the oldest and one of the two most important and complete collections of medieval literature. Containing sixty-two fabliaux, by far the largest representation per manuscript (Berne 254 has 41 fabliaux; Hamilton, 30; B.N. 1593, 24; B.N. 19.159, 26), it is the most widely consulted medieval manuscript since its compilation in the thirteenth century. It was already well known in the fifteenth century, when an unknown hand added titles at the beginnings of individual pieces, thereby facilitating its use, since the original copyist had put the titles only at the *explicit* following each poem. Later, sixteenth-century cataloguers at the royal library of François I attested to its venerability and worth by claiming that its composition went back to the time of Charlemagne. Claude Fauchet, president of the "Cour des Monnoyes," undoubtedly knew B.N. 837 and used it in the second volume of his anthology, *Recueil de l'origine de la langue et poésie française*, published in 1581. In the eighteenth century it acquired its present distinguished red binding, with a coat of arms and fleur-de-lis on the back, accentuating the rather sober title *Poésies* (Omont, p. v). Virtually every scholar of Medieval French literature is indebted to the manuscript for the wide range of subjects found among its two hundred fifty-two poems, all written in a clear, regular, gothic handwriting (Rychner, 1960, I. 136).

Beyond the manuscript, we may try to identify the scribe. Per Nykrog makes a good case that scribes in the libraries of wealthy amateur collectors copied down onto wax tablets the poems and stories recited by jongleurs who entertained there. Boivin in the fabliau *De Boivin de Provins* probably recited for such a scribe. He informs us that he was invited by the magistrate of Provins to stay there for three days, telling the story again and again. At some point a quantity of these wax tablets would accumulate and one scribe (as evidenced by a single handwriting) would set aside a few days to copy the materials from the wax tablets, in no discernible order, onto the expensive, durable parchment (Nykrog, 1957, pp. 45–48).

In addition, there were probably manuscripts of jongleurs, ephemeral and handy, like an actor's stage script, serving only as memory aids for an oral performance. One should, however, be very cautious with a genre like the fabliau, for which there exists a gap of sometimes one or two centuries between their performances and their actual *prise de forme* in the manuscript. As C.H. Livingston notes, "il est fort probable que seul un nombre restreint d'entre les fabliaux ont eu les honneurs de la copie sur parchemin et bien souvent, sans doute, longtemps après avoir été composés: (It is highly likely that only a select few of the fabliaux had the honor of being copied onto parchment, often, no doubt, long after being composed; Jongleur, 1951, p. 112). Since these jongleur manuscripts remain a mystery to us, we are woefully ignorant about the odyssey of a work from its author's imagination to its final written form.

The fabliaux must have existed for a long time in their elusive oral form before being finally received into the private library of a wealthy collector. Without this collector, our tales would have probably been lost, not because of their little worth or esteem but because of their oral nature and their brevity. As a matter of fact, this method of compilation probably insured the survival of the best and most popular poems of the genre, since the collectors must have elected to keep not only their personal preferences but also the ones considered classics. The jongleur of the tale *Des Deus Bordeors ribaus* boasts of his talent and the size of his repertoire, listing some fabliaux already close to one hundred years old (Nykrog 1957, p. 43) The poems he brags about are obviously the ones he considers the best, all of which have been preserved and have survived. Many fabliaux have come down to us in several manuscripts: *De la Coille noire* (mentioned in *Des Deus Bordeors*) in seven; *De la Dame escoillee* in six: *Aristote, Du Bouchier d'Abevile, Du Chevalier qui fist les cons parler, De Cele qui se fist fourtre,* and *Du Vilain qui conquist* in five. These multiple occurrences not only attest to the popularity of the individual pieces, but also of the genre in general, which is represented in well over thirty manuscripts.

In summary, the survival of the fabliau can be attributed to the following process, well explained by Nykrog. The original poet was conscious that he was composing according to high artistic, as well as popular, standards. He sent his work out to the public, where, if it was good enough, it would circulate from castle to castle, from private houses to inns, taverns and fair-markets, by the mouths of jongleurs or be written down on wax tablets or on parchment (Nykrog, 1957, p. 44). Finally, sometimes over a century later, if it survived the test of popularity, a fabliau would find its way into a handsome bound book of an amateur collector of good tales.

Beyond the manuscript, we look for the fabliaux in their most intense existence, in the mouths and gestures of the jongleurs, or *ménestrels,* as they often called themselves, and in the ears and eyes of their audience. What a wonderful one-man (or sometimes one-woman) show the jongleurs must have been! Economy demanded that they travel alone. They could not afford to share the small profits—except perhaps with a dancing bear. They were jugglers, acrobats, animal trainers, and reciters of war and love poetry. And whenever the audience was getting weary, they could always get a good laugh with a fabliau. Note what happens at a great feast where a count gives orders to the minstrels to show off their talents, promising his scarlet coat for the one who tells the best tale or does the best trick:

> One minstrel after another labored
> To do his trade as best he could.
> One played the drunk, another the fool.
> One sang, another played music
> And others recited a debate,
> And another told jokes.
> Those who knew the art of the jongleur
> Played the fiddle before the count.

> There were some who recited fabliaux
> Where many funny things were told . . .
>
> (*Du Vilain au buffet*, 138–147)

The fabliau circulated in its multiversion form thanks to the jongleurs' memory and talent for recomposing. The occasional written reproductions of oral performances which we possess must be considered diachronic samples of different levels of development of a tale. For example, in the manuscript B.N. 24432 (P: Nykrog's siglum, 1957, pp. 310–11), a variant of *De Boivin de Provins* instructs the audience: "So as to be able to hear, please keep quiet for a while" (Appendix, lines 36–37). This call to the audience for attention is not found in A, our manuscript, and must refer to a different set of performing circumstances. The fabliau is therefore a multiversion genre whose multiplicity is not, as Jean Rychner explains, the result of faulty memories or scribal interferences (Rychner, *Contribution*, 1960, passim; Eichmann, 1978) but of the part played by the jongleurs in spreading and recomposing the tales. As Roy Pearcy has reasoned, a cross-fertilization of fabliaux is at the base of the multiplicity of versions because the jongleur could isolate and recombine from his repertoire common elements, borrowing from several to produce an original tale ("Structural Models," 1974, p. 113), and similarities among fabliaux do not account for a written relationship, but attest to a vibrant, ever-changing, malleable, oral genre.

Were the jongleurs also the composers of their repertoire? Textual evidence is not clear. As Nykrog points out (1957, p. 38), many authors of fabliaux predicted that their works would travel from place to place performed by others. They were proud of their creations and, wishing to continue to be recognized as the authors, often integrated their signatures into the tales. The performers, too, were proud of the original authors, for they preserved the signatures through many versions and in at least one case, *Du Chevalier qui fist parler*, gave credit to the original author whose work he had changed considerably. Noting that the same fabliaux may recur in widely diverse manuscripts, sometimes written over a hundred years apart, and that virtually every fabliau cited elsewhere still exists in manuscript form, Nykrog amply demonstrates that the average jongleur was not a composer of fabliaux, but a mere reciter and performer of older, popular tales (1957, p. 440).

Several jongleurs, however, were indeed composers of their own material, being thus at the same time *trouvères* and jongleurs. Such are, for instance, Gautier le Leu and Jean Bodel. The former composed his own works in order to perform them himself: "Since I want to set myself to rhyming and telling fabliaux . . ." (*Du Sot Chevalier*, 1–2). The latter, with a great deal of pride, takes credit for his fabliaux:

> The man who did the tale of the gruel
> And the one about the dead peasant of Bailluel
> Who was never sick or failing,
> And the one about Gombert and the two clerks
> Whom he wickedly kept in his house,
> And about Brunain, the priest's cow,
> Who led Blerain away I believe,
> And told the tale of the dream of the pricks
> Which the lady had to handle,
> And the one about the wolf whom the goose deceived,
> And about the two envious jerks,
> And about Barat and Travers
> And their friend Haimet,
> Takes on another fabliau . . .
>
> (*Des II Chevaus*, 1–14)

Did these performer-authors compose with a stylus and wax tablet, or did they work the verses out in their heads between performances, or did they actually compose during the performance in the same manner as the Yugoslavian epic singers (Eichmann, "Oral Composition," 1979)? There are arguments against every one of these possibilities. It is unlikely that many jongleurs could afford enough parchment for all their scripts.

Since, on the other hand, wax tablets would have been too cumbersome either to carry from place to place or to use during a performance, the jongleur would have had to recite from memory, a difficult task for anyone with a sizable repertoire; or else he would have had to compose during narration, also difficult, since, unlike the Yugoslavian epic singers, the fableors had to find a rhyme every sixteen syllables. Also, did the authors freely give their creations to other jongleurs, or did they charge a fee? Did they perhaps teach their art and poems to apprentice jongleurs? Or were the tales simply pirated by jongleurs with exceptionally good memories? We have no certain answers to these questions.

Where did the stories come from before they were put into their definitive form? Attempts, none of them entirely successful, have been made to identify their origins through geographical location, through social class, and through previously existing genres. The earliest theories proposed that the fabliaux are remnants of Aryan mythology or belong to the anthropological heritage still in evidence in modern popular tales. Joseph Bédier effectively refutes these hypotheses but reserves most of his energies for his assault on the Orientalist theories of Theodor Benfey (1814) and Reinhold Köhler (1865). In almost two hundred pages of densely documented and cleverly reasoned arguments, Bédier demonstrates the total absence of evidence for a mass migration, via the crusades or the Spanish Moors, of tales from India to Western Europe. Nykrog (1957, pp. xx–xxxviii), points out that Bédier's attack was misdirected, since he aimed it at German Indianists instead of at John Dunlop and Gaston Paris, Bédier's former professor, to whom he dedicated his study.

Bédier proposed his own theory to explain the presence of the fabliaux in medieval literature: while the subjects of the fabliaux are part of the legacy of mankind, it was a specifically Gallic genius that shaped these universal tales into their forms. Having noted the simultaneous emergence of the fabliaux and of the bourgeois class during the Middle Ages, Bédier equated the two, thus making the same *post hoc ergo propter hoc* mistake he had earlier accused the Orientalists of making: "Il est exact que les fabliaux sont ordinairement l'oeuvre des bourgeois. Le genre naquit le jour où se fut vraiment constituée une classe bourgeoise: il fleurit concurremment à toute une littérature bourgeoise" (The genre was born at the very moment the bourgeois class was established: it flourished along with a whole bourgeois literature; pp. 371–72). Despite admitted evidence that the fabliaux were also enjoyed by the aristocracy, Bédier boldly stated that they were written by and for the bourgeoisie, from bourgeois source material. "A chacun sa littérature propre: ici la poésie des châteaux, là celle des carrefours" (To each his own literature: here we have the poetry of the chateaux; there the poetry of the street corners; p. 371).

To limit a genre to a certain class is indeed bold. If Bédier had meant *bourgeois* to refer only to an attitude, he should have said so. If, as is likely, he meant that the fabliaux belonged to the city, although enjoyed in the castles, he was in error. On the basis of vocabulary analysis, Charles Muscatine has demonstrated that the fabliaux have more of a rural character than an urban one and that, in view of the mobile nature of medieval social classes, it would be wrong to make the fabliaux the property of a particular locality (Muscatine, 1976). Marie-Thérèse Lorcin has pointed out that while approximately forty fabliaux locate their events in what were considered cities in the Middle Ages (eight hundred inhabitants or more), forty-five occur in villages or hamlets and the rest are impossible to locate accurately. She concludes that the identification of fabliau settings with towns is basically fruitless: both the Parisian Rutebeuf and the urban Jean Bodel situate their tales in rural areas (1979, p. 18).

The most convincing arguments against Bédier's theory of the fabliau as a bourgeois genre come from the Danish scholar Per Nykrog, who sees the fabliaux as deliberate parodies of courtly subjects and manners:

> Le fabliau est très souvent une parodie de la courtoisie, mais loin de viser l'aristocratie, cette parodie se moque des classes qui lui sont inférieures. Le fabliau paraît donc être le genre par lequel les nobles s'amusent au dépens de la courtoisie des vilains!
> (The fabliau is very often a parody of courtly behavior, but far from aiming at the aristocracy, this parody pokes fun at the lower classes. Thus, the fabliau seems to be the genre that the nobility uses to make fun of the courtliness of commoners!; 1957, p. 104)

In Nykrog's theory, the questions of nature, destination, and origins of the fabliau seem to be confused. While establishing the nature of the fabliau to be an aristocratic parody of courtly genres, he hesitates to draw the easy conclusion that its nature and origin are the same. Later on in his work, he proposes that the fabliau has its origin in the fable, a theory that is supported by other scholars such as Johnston and Owen (hereafter J.O.) and R. Guiette. For etymological and thematic reasons, a link between the fable and the fabliau does seem likely. It is also reasonable to believe that after the fabliaux had their start, they began to feed on courtly genres (Busby, "Courtly Literature"), using them as a backdrop to generate or intensify laughter. Undeniably, such famous passages as the fight scenes in *D'Aloul* (560–719; 864–924) and *De Sire Hain et*

Dame Anieuse (166–230) are clear references to courtly and epic confrontations.

The controversies over the fabliau public, destination and connections with epic and courtly genres point to a very real medieval phenomenon, the interdependency among genres. Medieval authors did not share our consuming concern for categorizing and defining. They gathered their material wherever they found it: the author of *Des braies le prestres* claims that people who had witnessed a funny story told him about it (272, 279–290), whereas the author of *Des Braies le prestres* claims that people who had witnessed a funny story told him about it (272, 279–290), whereas the author of *D'Aloul* boasts an *escriture*, something written, as his source. Having gathered the material, the fableor put it to rhyme and recited it to whoever was likely to enjoy it. In *Du Prestre qui ot mere a force*, he tells us that "A cest mot finist cis fabliaus / que nous avons en rime mis / por conter devant nos amis" (Here ends this fabliau, which we have put into rhyme to recite before our friends; 200–202), while in the *Des .III. Avugles de Compiegne*, the tale was meant for dukes and counts (6). Some fabliaux were undoubtedly recited in taverns by jongleurs, such as the one in *Du Povre Mercier*, who cries, "Done moi boire si t'agree" (Give me something to drink, please; Montaiglon and Raynaud, 2, 122; hereafter, M.R.); others at the house of an individual, as we have seen in *De Boivin de Provins* (52). C. H. Livingston cites a fabliau told at a peasant's house (1951, pp. 128–29, note 4.) Some fabliaux were told to a seated audience (*Du Prestre et des .II. ribaus*, 6); other fableors felt the need to hail passers-by, asking them to stop and listen (*Des .III. Boçus*, 1–3). In *De la Demoisele qui ne pooit oïr*, as well as in *Du Pescheor de pont seur Saine* (line 214), the audience was mixed. In general, it is safe to say that the fabliaux were collected from a variety of sources and repeated throughout the land to a variety of audiences, such as the ones whom the jongleur in *Du Jugemant des Cons* goes "seeking throughout the land to find out whether the judgment is well done" (162–63).

The variant versions of tales also attest to a fableor's concern for a varied public, as he changed and adapted the poems to suit the particular needs of the performance or the taste of his audience. Jean Rychner, however, is not very convincing in his claim that the style of a certain fabliau reveals the social class of the audience for whom a certain fabliau was composed. In his analysis of the variants of several fabliaux, Rychner assumes that the ones written in the most elevated style were destined for an audience of a higher social level, and that unfortunate revisions and adaptations were made for a less demanding public of a lower social status (1960, I, 58). As Roy Pearcy has noted, such a methodology is fallacious because it reduces "the history of redaction . . . to a history of corruption and degradation" (1972, p. 117). Robert Harrison probably best describes the vicissitudes of oral tales from performer to performer and audience to audience:

> It is possible that in the fabliaux we see the emergence into written literature of a body of folklore that has always been with us, living a scurrilous underground life in the bawdy joke and the tavern tale, and constantly transmitted and enriched by local wags and visiting firemen who, knowing how to make a good story better, kept intact the general theme and punch lines while revising superficial details to suit the local audience.
> (p. 5)

In short, the fabliaux, universal and timeless, gained esteem and were deemed artistically worthy of being put down on parchment in the thirteenth century, a time of literary, social, and economic revival, and a time when they satisfied the need of one class to laugh at another one or at itself.

Style

In the scant sixteen pages (341–357) that Joseph Bédier devotes to the style of the fabliaux, the best he can say about them is that they are brief and unpretentious. (Bédier calculates that the fabliaux average between 300 and 400 lines per fabliau). What he fails to observe is that these qualities are not accidental, but the very essence of a skillfully developed art. R. Guiette puts it succinctly:

> Ces contes sont menés à la française, tambour battant, droit devant eux. La composition en est toute linéare, et en pleine clarté. Pas de détours, pas d'ombres troubles, pas de mystères. L'atmosphère est pure et nette. On respire librement. Les couleurs sont fraîches, comme chez les anciens peintres que l'on dit primitifs.

> (These tales march along, French style, with the drum beating
> ahead of them. The composition is entirely linear and clear.
> No detours, no disturbing ambiguities, no mysteries. The
> atmosphere is pure and neat. We can breathe freely. The colors
> are fresh as with the old, so-called primitive painters; *Fabliaux
> et contes*, 1960, pp. 24–25)

Spoken before live audiences, they cannot afford the trappings of
the literary works—elaborate settings, deep examinations of character, rich, realistic details of contemporary life. Instead, they provide masterful sketches, silhouettes, brush-strokes which allude to
more than they describe. Hundreds of scenes take place in banquet
halls, bedrooms or along the road, ordinary places requiring little
description but resonant with possibility because they are places
where people meet.

With little time for elaboration, the fabliaux often draw upon
existing familiar genres and use them as backdrops. Thus, the
fabliaux, are dotted with "signals," to use Keith Busby's term
("Courtly Literature"), which allude to other genres, such as the
Roman de Renart, lyric poetry, the Bible (Helsinger, pp. 98–103),
but mostly to courtly novel situations, for which the fabliaux often
propose humorous or even obscene solutions, obviously different
from the ones proposed by the works they parody. With a few
words, these connections, or "signals," can summon a whole com-
plex of emotions and attitudes. Courtly expressions such as
fin'amors place a character securely in a context that has already
been established in the courtly tradition. Honeycutt shows that the
very fact that the character is a knight is a signal for a whole set of
courtly expectations and that humor rises from the disappointment
of these expectations (1974, pp. 90–91).

The fabliaux, however, do not rest solely on courtly literature.
Many signals refer to situations in other fabliaux; the genre often
feeds on itself. The ten-line explanation of how the husband in *Du
Pescheor de Pont seur Saine* (87–96) finds the penis can be effectively brief because the pattern is familiar. Likewise, the mention of
the goose which the lover brings for dinner and the bath which his
mistress prepares for him alerts the audience to many other situations where the unexpected (but not for the public) return of the
husband interrupts the bath. In the same manner, fabliau characters
arouse certain expectations. Thus when a lecherous monk or priest

arrives on the scene, we get the signal that his attempts at seduction will not be successful, for, as Nykrog notes, his success ratio is only five out of twenty-two (1957, p. 110). On the other hand, the introduction of a clerk or squire signals a chance for successful love play.

The quality of a story, whether parodic or not, still depends on the manner of telling. The verse form clearly distinguishes the fabliaux from their source material: as prose tales, these stories would not have been written down at all. The fabliaux give a feeling of freshness, energy and rhythm, much of which is due to the flexible octosyllabic couplet. Nykrog notes that it was the fabliau that most fully freed the octosyllabic couplet from the heavy so- briety of saints' lives and historical chronicles and allowed the form to display the full range of its capabilities in comic action and dialogue (1957, pp. 245–48). Avoiding long descriptive passages, the authors move rapidly to the most dramatic element of the tale, the dialogue. The quick-paced octosyllabic couplet is ideal for the give-and-take of dialogue. Whenever possible, the narrator, aware of the dramatic potential in the binary movement of verbal con- frontation, steps aside and leaves the stage to his protagonists. Quoted directly or indirectly, the characters come alive in their scenes, often revealing more of themselves than their description does. The repartees sparkle when two or sometimes three charac- ters face off, usually answering each other mid-couplet or even mid- line, as in the confrontation between the priest, his mistress, and the servant girl in *Du Bouchier d'Abevile* (369–494).

These tales are not without faulty lines and tiring line-fillers, which Bédier points out (pp. 342–43), weaknesses probably due to the oral nature of the genre, although they also occur in other, respectable "literary" ones. But the line-fillers are often appropriate (Honeycutt, 1975). The characterization, though rarely deep, is vivid, and the tales are told economically and energetically.

Influences

The fabliaux, although extinct as a genre after Jean de Condé in the middle of the fourteenth century, have continued to leave a remark- able impression on the literature of the following centuries. It would indeed be impossible here to cite every influence and adaption of each fabliau. We must refer for evidence to Joseph Bédier's bibliographic notes (pp. 442–76) and to Victor Leclerc's "Fabliaux" (pp. 69–215). The influences of the fabliau can be noticed either in its subject matters or in its artistic achievement, or in both. Chaucer, the *Nouvelles*, and Jean de La Fontaine, to name three, seem to be indebted to the fabliau. Influences must of course be computed not by how many times the fabliaux as a genre or individual tales have been repeated through the centuries but by what degree they have kept themselves alive under new forms.

It is as hard to determine precisely any direct influence of the fabliaux on Boccaccio, Chaucer, and La Fontaine as it is to trace the origins of the fabliaux. All three authors devote considerable talent to writing their own variations on the genre, yet none of them credits any fabliaux as sources. It may be that the tales were so widespread, not only throughout France but through all Europe, that any talk of one particular tale's influencing another is meaningless, and that the fabliaux, Boccaccio's tales, and Chaucer's tales are three parallel responses to a common folk source. It is very likely that the artistic skill of the jongleurs, as they spread the fabliaux through all levels of society in the French-speaking world, left its mark on popular story-telling throughout Europe after the jongleurs were gone.

To the south the emergence of the Tuscan *novella* may at least be seen as part of the same story-telling tradition as the fabliau. The term itself, meaning *story*, is French; it had already been used by Chrétien de Troyes and in the *Roman de Renart* (Dubuis, 1973, p. 31). Nykrog conjectures that Boccaccio's tales, which derived from early fable-like prose Italian tales, evolved parallel to the fabliaux from "la mine inépuisable des exemples" (the inexhaustible mine of *exempla*; Nykrog, 1957, pp. 259–60). Like the fabliaux, the novellas retain the clear narrative style of oral delivery, uncluttered by long descriptive passages of philosophical digressions (Sempoux, p. 15). Part of Boccaccio's genius, Sempoux explains, is to highlight these oral characteristics with a frame tale that identifies the stories as oral entertainment (pp. 15–16). (Chaucer gives even greater oral life to his stories where the relationship between tale and teller is much more intimate.) The one oral characteristic which did not descend to Boccaccio is the verse. Nykrog reasons that this is because of the early development of prose in

Italy, even when the novella was still at the *exemplum* stage (1957, p. 260).

One of Boccaccio's great contributions is that he gathered fabliaux, lais, *exempla* and Oriental tales in one unified volume, thus recognizing implicitly that these genres are really sub-genres of the novella, the forerunner to the fifteenth-century French *nouvelle*, whose nature, says Roger Dubuis, is above all a structural one, dictated by the need to be brief (1973, p. 31). Dubuis, however, denies that the French *nouvelles* owe any significant debt to Boccaccio's novellas. Another contribution by Boccaccio is to *actualize*, that is, to give the tales the authority of current events: "La nouvelle" says J.-Ch. Payen (1975, p. 51), "actualise le fabliau ou l'anecdote édifiante, en les situant dans un cadre historique et géographique précis." (The novella *actualizes* the fabliau or the moral tale by situating it in a precise, historical and geographical framework.) In his novellas, particularly the comic ones, Boccaccio frequently gives specific, realistic names to characters and sets them in recognizable European locations.

For instance, Boccaccio's close analogue to the fabliau *Des Tresces* (M.R. IV, 67), the eighth tale of the seventh day, begins, "*Dovete dunque sapere che nella nostra città fu già un ricchissimo mercatante chiamato Arriguccio Berlinghieri*" (You probably know that in our city [Florence] there was a very rich merchant named Arriguccio Berlinghieri; p. 477). This Arriguccio, we are told, married a young lady of the nobility named Sismonda, who fell in love with a young man named Ruberto. The effect of all this specificity is to give the illusion of recent history rather than fiction. Setting the story in Florence is particularly effective and daring; since the narrator, Neifile, is Florentine and she is telling her tale to a group of young Florentines, we can assume that her information is reliable and that most of her young friends recognize the people involved. In fact, we know that Boccaccio's primary audience was also Florentine, people who could have easily checked out the truth of this bit of town gossip. Furthermore, the Florentine narrators of the *Decameron* tell other tales about Florentines whom, even from our great distance, we recognize: Giotto, the painter; Guido Calvalcante de Calvalcanti, the poet and philosopher; and fat Ciacco, the last two of whom are residents of Dante's Hell. Such local precision would make us want to accept Neifile's tale of the tresses as historically accurate, if we didn't already know that the same story was being told a century earlier in France, anonymously about anonymous characters in no specified locale.

Yet Dubuis claims that this actualizing process is original with the fifteenth-century French nouvelles. In fact, if we take Nykrog's and Dubuis' views of literary history together, we have an interesting symmetry: Nykrog's view that Boccaccio's comic tales, though later, developed independently of the fabliaux, and Dubuis' view that the French nouvelles, though later, developed independently of Boccaccio's novellas. Without documented credit, we cannot prove otherwise, but France and Italy are close, and stories travel easily. Besides, many plots are similar, and some are extremely close: *Des Tresces* to Day 7, Tale 4 of the *Decameron*; *De la Borgoise d'Orliens* to Day 7, Tale 7; *De la Nonnette* (*Romania*, XXXIV, 279) to Day 4, Tale 2; *De Gombert et des deus clers* (M.R., V, 60), and *Du Clerc qui fu repus derriere l'escrin* (M.R., IV, 47) are all retold in *Les Cent Nouvelles Nouvelles*. More important still, Boccaccio's comic novellas and the later comic nouvelles share such a kindred spirit, with their deceptions and reversals, their lecherous clerks and clerics, their lusty wives, their rich old cuckolds and their quick race to comic conclusion, that they can reasonably be classed as prose fabliaux.

Of the twenty-four tales (six of which are incomplete) in Chaucer's *Canterbury Tales*, six and a half are fabliaux: the tales of the Miller, the Reeve, the Cook (incomplete), the Shipman, the Summoner, the Merchant, and the Wife of Bath. This gives the fabliau a preponderance over any other type of tale. Of these, all but the *Cook's Tale* have analogues among the French fabliaux. The *Reeve's Tale* is quite close in plot to two surviving fabliaux, *Du Meunier et des deux clers* (M.R., V, 83) and *De Gombert et des deus clers* (M.R., I, 283). Can we assume that Chaucer went to school with the fabliaux? Did a fabliau such as *Du Prestre qui abevete* (M.R., III, 54) first teach him that Damion and May might get away with adultery before her husband's eyes in *The Merchant's Tale*? Was it from fabliaux such as *De la Vescie a prestre* (M.R., III, 106) and *Du Bouchier d'Abeville* that he learned to develop the simple contrivances of jokes into full stories, such as the *Summoner's Tale* and the *Man of Law's Tale*? The *Reeve's* and *Miller's Tales* rush impetuously through deceptions, mistakes, and misunderstandings to the reestablishment of an illogically based order. Did Chaucer learn to aim for that effect from such fabliaux as *Du Meunier et des deux clers, D'Estula,* and *Des Trois Boçus*? Were such creative, energetic wives as the Wife of Orleans and the wives in *D'Aloul* and *De Berangier au lonc cul* forerunners of the Wife of Bath? And did the cunning old tramp in *De la Viele Truande* contribute to the looks and character of the heroine of the *Wife of Bath's Tale*?

The only reason we might have to doubt Chaucer's debts to these tales is that he was born approximately the same year that the last of the fableors, Jean de Condé, died: 1340 or 1341. But if we look for possible English antecendents to Chaucer's fabliaux, we find very little. No doubt popular jokes were circulating through English taverns just as they always do everywhere, but the only English comic tale written down before Chaucer, except for a tale from the *Roman de Renart,* is *Dame Sirith* (Benson and Anderson, p. 372) composed in jingly stanzas rhyming *aabccb*, with nothing of the elasticity of the French octosyllabics or Chaucer's pentameter verse. On the other hand, Chaucer was intimately familiar with French culture and literature. The English upper classes around the court at London were still bilingual. Chaucer traveled in France, read the literature, borrowed some of the verse forms, and translated such works as the thirteenth-century *Roman de la rose,* so it is very likely that he was reading French manuscripts with fabliaux in them. Since the heyday of the fabliaux was past, he would not have heard them performed—except possibly in out-of-the-way places where the news hadn't gotten out that the genre was dead; England, however, might have been just such a place, since several fabliaux had been composed in the Anglo-Norman dialect.

If, as the evidence suggests, Chaucer's sources for his comic tales are French, he does his best to disguise the fact. He never uses the French word *fabliau* to describe any of his works, despite its fairly frequent use by the French authors: the six and a half tales which we call fabliaux would certainly be numbered among those which, according to Chaucer's *Retraction* "sownen into synne" (Robinson, Fragment X, Group I, 1085), but so would most of the other tales, since Chaucer also retracts many non-fabliaux, including the lovely *Book of the Duchess* and the romance-novel *Troilus and Criseyde,* which itself ends with a fine Christian retraction of worldly vanities.

Instead of *fabliaux*, Chaucer designates some of his tales *churl's tales*. With variations on this term, Chaucer as pilgrim–narrator makes a show of being embarrassed by the *Miller's Tale*, saying, "This Millere . . . told his cherles tale" [I(A)3170], and with the *Reeve's Tale*, "The Miller is a cherl. . . . So was the Reve eek and othere mo" [I(A)3182–83], and the Reeve himself is embarrassed to stoop to the level of the Miller in telling his tale, "Right in his cherles termes wol I speke" [I(A)3917]. The Cook, with his back-clawing approval of the *Reeve's Tale*, is plainly determined to continue with another churl's tale: "But God forbede that we stynte heere. . . ."[I(A)4339]. From the term *churl*, from the social position of the tellers, and from the stories themselves, Chaucer would have us infer that these tales arise from the native English lower classes. The term *churl* (as opposed to *peasant* or *villain*) is decidedly English; the Miller blames his own "misspeaking" on "the ale of Southwerk" [I(A)3140], the Reeve seasons his tale with the North English accents of his student clerks, and the *Miller's*, *Reeve's* and *Cook's Tales* all have decidedly English settings (Oxford, Trumpington near Cambridge, and London, with references to Cheapside and Newgate). Chaucer gives little indication what "othere mo" churls he has in mind among his pilgrim narrators. Certainly the Summoner is a churl, in more ways than one. His tale of farting, inspired by a quarrel parallel to the one between the Miller and the Reeve, would be churlish by any standards. Unlike the remaining three Chaucerian fabliaux, the "*Summoner's Tale*" is set in contemporary England.

However much they may also "sownen into synne," the *Wife of Bath's*, the *Merchant's* and the *Shipman's Tales* seem more literary, courtly, cosmopolitan, and perhaps, from the point of view of Englishmen looking toward the culture and civilization across the channel, more French. They are about knights and ladies of the high bourgeoisie, told by pilgrims who regularly travel beyond the confines of England. The *Wife of Bath's* takes place in Britain, it is true, but in the fairy land of King Arthur which had been resurrected in French literature by writers such as Chrétien de Troyes. The *Merchant's Tale* takes place in Lombardy. Unlike the fabliaux, it is heavy with Biblical and classical quotations and interlaced with Roman mythology, and the bitter disillusion of the teller brings it closer to tragedy than any fabliau ever came. The one Chaucerian fabliau which is actually set in France, the *Shipman's Tale*, has been called the most typically French of Chaucer's fabliaux. (Cooke, 1978, p. 172). Even so, for all its admirable cleverness, the *Shipman's Tale* lacks a quality typical of many of the fabliaux, liveliness. The lover is neither poetic, frantic nor precipitous in his desire. The wife is neither passionate nor energetic in her manipulation. The character who is most often the liveliest of the triangle, wonderfully vital in his stupidity, the cuckold, is here a minor figure, a ledger-keeper. From this point of view, the delightful *Miller's Tale* is closer to the "typical" fabliau.

In the English-speaking world, the French tales have suffered and continue to suffer unfavorable comparison with Chaucer's tales. Nevill Coghill's is an extreme example of this attitude: "These fabliaux were for the most part written down in the thirteenth century and for their clumsiness and lack of gaiety seem dull and dirty by comparison with Chaucer, whose style is as clean and as sharp as a whistle" (p. 99). Any comparison between the work of a single great writer and a type is bound to be unfair. Although a few of the fableors, such as Jean Bodel and Rutebeuf, are highly acclaimed in other genres, none approaches Chaucer in stature, and most of the authors whose names we know are no more than that— just names. The great majority of the fabliaux, as we have seen, are anonymous. Chaucer, on the other hand, is a whole corpus in himself. Any single work of his draws all the others to it to complement it and be complemented by it. This is especially true of the *Canterbury Tales*, which not only reflect upon each other, but tell about their tellers and about the other pilgrims and the trip they are making. This above all is Chaucer's great contribution to the universe of storytelling. It is hardly fair to compare a Chaucerian tale with an individual French fabliau, because what is individual in Chaucer has been weighed and measured and reexamined and reinterpreted, but there is so little English criticism of the French fabliaux that Chaucer's original touches are usually interpreted as his successes in doing what the French fabliaux "failed" to do, without regard to what is fresh or original in the French works.

La Fontaine's *Contes* are a little further in time from the fabliaux than we are from La Fontaine. With him the comic tales return to verse, but are much more varied and carefully wrought. Most are in regular decasyllabics with unpredictable rhyme schemes rather than couplets. A few are octosyllabic and about a fourth are *vers libre*, the irregular verse of unpredictable rhyme and line length that La Fontaine uses so successfully in the *Fables*. He even introduces *La Coupe enchantée* (Marnier, p. 230) and *Pâté d'anguille* (p. 274) with refrains for a rondeau effect. Instead of the anonymous jongleur calling his audience to come and listen, we have La Fontaine, poet, scholar, and man of his time, addressing us intimately as an *ami lecteur* (friend reader; *L'Abbesse*, p. 258; *Le Roi Candaule et le maitre en droit*, p. 270). Like many of the fabliau narrators, he doesn't mind sticking his nose into the tale and commenting on the action, making judgments about social customs and marriage in *Le Calendrier des vieillards* (p. 208) and *Mazet de Lamporechio* (p. 222), defending himself against antifeminism in *Les Oies de Frere Philipe* (p. 224), or commenting on sources in *La Servante justifiée* (p. 203). He acknowledges many sources: Rabelais, Machiavelli, Ariosto, *Les Cent Nouvelles Nouvelles*, and above all, Boccaccio. What is remarkable is that the stories themselves have changed so little. Again we have analogues and reworkings of the familiar plots, again the same spirit of fun and the same fabliau characters that we observed in Boccaccio and Chaucer. As a matter of fact, Göran Bornäs has shown that one of the *Contes*, "Le Cocu battu et content," is closer stylistically to the fabliau *La Borgoise d'Orliens* than to its Boccaccian model. In Boccaccio's Tale 7, 7, certain courtly elements seem to clash with the raucous plot, causing improbable motivation and violations against the unities of action and tone. What Bornas suggests is not that La Fontaine was aware of *La Borgoise d'Orliens*, but that his revisions, in accord with seventeenth-century Neoclassical standards, brought his tale closer to the spirit of the medieval genre, where unnecessary complications are usually rejected.

That the stories have changed so little in four hundred years is probably testimony to the conservativeness of the genre as much as to recurring literary styles. What has been least stable is the form that the artists molded the stories to: octosyllabic couplets, iambic pentameter couplets, prose, or in the case of La Fontaine, a dazzling variety of verse. But the stories remain simple, direct, amusing, for artists throughout the centuries to adapt to their own forms.

Editorial Policy For This Translation

Using Per Nykrog's inventory of fabliaux (1957, pp. 311-24) as our base, we have chosen forty fabliaux that are peculiar to B.N. 837 and not found in the Berne 354 to make up the first two volumes of the series, *The French Fabliau*. We have also used his siglum system (pp. 310–311) in our references to variant manuscripts in our notes. In establishing the original Old French text, we have been concerned with giving an accurate rendition of our manuscript. Since the version of a fabliau represents one state in the multiple existence of one tale, its faithful transcription, as far as good sense will allow, seems most appropriate. Significant variants are given in the notes to enable the reader to judge the other states of the tale. Only when absolutely necessary for purposes of clarity did we correct the original or add to it. All such interventions on our part are indicated either by brackets in the text or by an explanation in the notes.

Generally, we have followed the editorial recommendations of Alfred Foulet and Mary Blakely Speer, *On Editing Old French Texts* (Lawrence: Kansas, 1979). Missing syllables in a faulty line are identified by a negative number in parentheses in the notes; extra syllables, by a positive number. In keeping with the precedent set by other volumes in the Garland Medieval Library, we have aimed for clear prose translations which stay as close as possible to the original idiom. In the few instances where we have had to interpret a meaning from a garbled text or from an unclear idiomatic usage, we provide a literal translation in the Translation Notes.

Also in keeping with Garland precedent, we have adhered to logical English tense sequence. Thus, where Old French often combines the future with the past for indirect discourse (*jura un serement/ qu'ele le fera mencongier; Saineresse*, II, 6–7), we have translated the future as the conditional (she swore an oath that she *would make* a liar out of him). In the Old French, narrative tense shifts from past to present and back again are frequent and arbitrary, sometimes occurring within a compound predicate. The only rules seem to have been the demands of rhyme and meter. Following ordinary English usage, we have kept the narration in the past tense.

One remarkable fact about the tense shifts is that they are limited to the narration. The fact that they almost never occur in dialogue indicates that the authors felt good tense sequence was necessary for realistic and forceful conversation. The only poem in this collection which seems to use these tense shifts for stylistic purposes is Rutebeuf's *De Frere Denise* (Volume II), where shifts from past to present are usually reserved for an increase in excitement (lines 66, 217–218, 233–234), psychological description and authorial comment (89, 95–99, 101, 117–123, 129–133, 142–43, 202).

The ideal purpose of a dual-language text is to introduce the reader to the pleasures of the original work in the original language by way of the new language. This is particularly important in verse, where the sound of the original is an integral part of the work. Since thirteenth-century French is no more different from modern French than Chaucerian English is from modern English, readers with even a slight knowledge of French should take advantage of that knowledge to let the English lead them back to the original poems.

Manuscripts

In the notes to our edition and to our translation, we refer to variant manuscripts by using Nykrog's siglum system (1957, pp. 310–311):

Siglum	Manuscript
A	B.N. 837 (anc. 7218)
B	Berne 354
C	Berlin Hamilton 257
D	B.N. 19 152 (anc. St. Germ. 1830)
E	B.N. 1593 (anc. 7615)
F	B.N. 12 603 (anc. suppl. fr. 180)
G	Middleton (Wollaton Hall)
H	B.N. 2168 (anc. 7989)
I	B.N. 25 545 (anc. N.-D. 274)
J	B.N. 1553 (anc. 7595)
K	B.N. 2173 (anc. 7991)
L	B.N. 1635 (anc. 7633)

M	Brit. Mus. Harl. 2253
N	Rome Casanatensis
O	Pavia U.B. 130 E 4
P	B.N. 24 432 (anc. N.-D. 198)
Q	B.N. nouv. acq. 1104
R	Arsenal 3524 (anc. BLF 317)
S	Arsenal 3525 (anc. BLF 318)
T	Chantilly Condé 1578
U	Turin L.V. 32
V	Genève 7 fr. 179
Vbis	Lyon, Bibl. Munic. 5495
W	B.N. 1446 (anc. 7834)
X	B.N. 12581
Y	Brit. Mus. add. 10289
Z	Oxford Digby 86
a	B.N. 375 (anc. 6987)
b	B.N. 1588 (anc. 7609)
c	B.N. 12 483
d	B.N. 14 971
e	Arsenal 3114
f	Chartres 620
g	Rotschild 2800
h	Cambridge Corp. Chr. 50
i	Puy-de-Dôme (fragment)
k	Arsenal 3516

    Grateful acknowledgment is made to the trustees of the Bibliothèque Nationale in Paris for permission to reproduce materials from the 837 manuscript. Special thanks go to the University of Arkansas for the Research Incentive Grant which helped to cover the typing costs and to Susan Stiers, Debbie Wilson, and Kay DuVal for long hours of extremely difficult typing. Thanks also to the Garland General Editor, James J. Wilhelm, for a thorough and perceptive reading of this text, with many helpful suggestions.

Select Bibliography

I. Editions

Barbazan, Etienne. *Fabliaux et contes des poètes françois des XII, XIII, XIV, et XVes siècles, tirés des meilleurs auteurs.* 3 vols. Paris: Chez Vincent, 1756.

Barbazan, Etienne, and Dominique M. Méon, *Fabliaux et contes des poètes français.* 4 vols. Paris, 1808–23; rpt. Geneva: Slatkine, 1975.

Christmann, H.H. *Zwei altfranzösische Fablels.* Tübingen: Niemeyer, 1963.

Delbouille, Maurice. *Le Lai d'Aristole de Henri d'Andeli.* Paris: Société d'Edition "Les Belles Lettres," 1951.

Ebeling, Georg. *"Auberée": Altfranzösische Fablel mit Einleitung und Anmerkungen.* Halle: Niemeyer, 1895.

Faral, Edmond. *Le Manuscrit 19152 du fonds français de la Bibliothèque Nationale.* Paris: Singer-Polignac, 1934.

Faral, Edmond, and Julia Bastin. *Rutebeuf: Oeuvres complètes.* 2 vols. Paris: A. and J. Picard, 1959–1960; I, 256–265; II, 281–308.

Flutre, Louis Fernand. "Un Manuscrit inconnu de la Bibliothèque de Lyon, 'Le Vilain qui n'iert pas de son hostel,'" *Romania,* 62 (1936), 2–16.

Förster, Wendelin. "'Du Valet qui d'aise a mesaise se met,' altfranzösische Fabliau zum ersten Male hgg." *Jahrbuch für Romanische und Englische Literatur,* 13 (1873), p. 288.

Gougenheim, Georges. *Cortebarbe, Les Trois Aveugles de Compiègne,* Paris: Champion, 1932.

Héron, Alexandre. *Le Lai d'Aristote,* Rouen: L. Gy, 1901.

Hilka, Alfons, and Werner Söderhjelm. *Petrus Alfonsus. Disciplina Clericalis: III Französische Versbearbeitungen.* Acta Societatis Scientiarum Fennicae, 49. Helsinki: Finnischen Litteratuur-Gesselschaft, 1922.

Johnston, Ronald C., and D.D.R. Owen. *Fabliaux.* Oxford: Blackwell, 1965.

Jubinal, Achille. *Nouveau Recueil de Contes, dits, fabliaux et antres contes . . .* 2 vols. Paris: E. Pannier, 1839–42.

Langfors, Arthur. "'Le Dit de Dame Jouenne': Version Inédite du Fabliau du 'Pré Tondu.'" *Romania,* 45 (1918–19), 99–107.

——————. *Huon Le Roi: Le Vair Palefroi avec deux versions de la Male Honte.* Paris: Champion, 1927.

Levy, B.J. *Selected Fabliaux, Edited from the B.N. Fonds Français 837 Fonds Français 191152 and Berlin Hamilton 257.* University of Hull: Department of French, 1978.

Livingston, Charles H. *Le Jongleur Gautier le Leu: Etude sur les fabliaux.* Cambridge, Mass.: Harvard University, 1951.

Malatesta, Henri, illustr. *Le Moine Sacristain, fabliau du XIIIe siècle.* Paris: Glomeau, 1912.

Manfellotto, Annalisa Landolfi. *I "Fabliaux" di Jean de Condé. Edizione critica, con introduzione, note e glossario.* L'Aquila: Japadre, 1981.

Ménard, Philippe. *Fabliaux français du Moyen Age.* Vol. I. Textes Littéraires Français, 270. Geneva: Droz, 1979.

Méon, Dominique M. *Fabliaux et contes des poètes françois des XIe, XIIe, XIIIe, XIVe et XVe siècles tirés des meilleurs auteurs.* 4 vols. Paris: B. Warée oncle, 1808.

——————. *Nouveau Recueil de fabliaux et contes inédits des poètes français des XIIe et XVe siècles.* 2 vols. Paris: Chasseriau, 1823.

Meyer, Paul. "Le Chevalier, la dame et le clerc." *Romania,* 1 (1872), 69–87.

——————. "Le Fabliau du héron ou la fille mal gardée." *Romania,* 26 (1897), 85–91.

Montaiglon, Anatole de, and Gaston Raynaud. *Recueil général et complet des fabliaux des XIIIe et XIVe siècles.* 6 vols. Paris: Librairie des Bibliophiles, 1872–1890; rpt. New York: Burt Franklin, n.d.,; also rpt. Geneva: Slatkine, 1973.

Morawski, J. "Le Fabliau du Prestre Pelé." *Romania,* 55 (1925), 542–48.

Nardin, Pierre. *Jean Bodel: Fabliaux.* Paris: Nizet, 1965.

Omont, Henri. *Fabliaux, dits et contes en vers français du XIII siècle; facsimile du manuscrit français 837 de la Bibliothèque nationale.* Paris: E. Leroux, 1932; rpt. Geneva: Slatkine, 1973.

Raynaud, Gaston. "Une Nouvelle Version du Fabliau de 'La Nonnette.'" *Romania*, 34 (1905), 279–83.

Reid, T.B.W. *Twelve Fabliaux.* Manchester: Manchester University Press, 1968.

Robert, A.C.M. *Fabliaux inédits tirés du ms. de la Bibliothèque du Roi, no. 1830 ou 1239.* Paris: Rignoux, 1834.

Rohlfs, Gehrard. *Sechs altfranzösische Fablels, nach der Berliner Fablelhandschrift.* Sammlung Romanischer Uebungstexte, *1.* Halle: Niemeyer, 1925.

Rostaing, Charles, ed. "Constant du Hamel." *Edition critique avec commentaire et glossaire.* Paris: Louis-Jean, GAP, 1947.

Rychner, Jean. *Du Bouchier d'Abevile: Fabliau de XIIIe siècle (Eustache d'Amiens).* Geneva: Droz, 1975.

Scheler, Auguste. *Trouvères belges du XIe au XIIe siècles: chansons d'amour, jeux partis, pastourelles, dits et fabliaux.* Brussels: M. Clossen, 1876.

——————. *Dits et contes de Beaudouin et Jean de Condé.* 2 vols. Brussels: n.p., 1866; II, 121–31, 271–79.

——————. *Dits de Watriquet de Couvin.* Brussels: V. Devaux, 1868, pp. 373–90.

Väänänen, Veikko. *Du Segretain moine, fabliau anonyme du XIIIe siècle.* Helsinki: n.p., 1949.

Walters-Gehrig, M., *Trois Fabliaux.* Tübingen: Niemeyer, 1961.

Zipperling, Carl. *Das altfranzösische Fablel "Du Vilain Mire."* Halle: Niemeyer, 1912.

II. *Translations*

Benson, Larry D., and Theodore M. Andersson, eds. and trans. *The Literary Context of Chaucer's Fabliaux.* Indianapolis and New York: The Bobbs-Merrill Co., Inc., 1971.

Brandin, Louis. *Lais et Fabliaux du XIIIe siècle.* Poèmes et récits de la Vieille France, *15.* Paris: E. de Boccard, 1932.

Brians, Paul. *Bawdy Tales from the Courts of Medieval France.* New York: Harper & Row, 1972.

Brusegan, Rosanna, ed. and trans. *Fabliaux, raconti francesi medievali.* Torino: Einaudi, 1980.

Caullot, Nelly. *Fabliaux et contes du moyen âge.* Paris: Hatier, 1957.

DuVal, John. "The Villager and His Two Asses." In *Intro 7,* ed. George Garrett, Garden City, N.Y.: Doubleday Anchor Books, 1975, pp. 273–275.

——————. "Les Tresces: Semi-Tragical Fabliau, Critique and Translation." *Publications of the Missouri Philological Association,* 3 (1979), 7–16.

——————. "Medieval French Fabliaux." *Lazarus,* 1 (1980), 8–49.

Eichmann, Raymond, ed., and John DuVal, trans. *Cuckolds, Clerics and Countrymen. Medieval French Fabliaux.* Fayetteville: University of Arkansas Press: 1982.

Fabliaux et contes du moyen âge. Paris: Hatier, 1967.

Flutre, Louis Fernand. *Fabliaux du moyen âge.* Lyon: Editions du Fleuve, 1958.

Guerrand, Roger Henri. *Fabliaux, contes, et miracles du moyen âge.* Paris: Livre Club du Libraire, 1964.

Guiette, Robert. *Fabliaux et contes.* Paris: Le Club du Meilleur Livre, 1960; rpt. Paris: Stock, 1981.

Harrison, Robert. *Gallic Salt.* Berkeley: University of California Press, 1974.

Hellman, Robert, and Richard O'Gorman. *Fabliaux: Ribald Tales from the Old French.* New York: Crowell, 1965.

Lee, Charmaine, ed. and trans. *Il Falcone desiderato: Poemetti erotici francesi.* Milan: Bompiani, 1980.

Le Grand d'Aussy, S.J., Pierre Jean Baptiste. *Fabliaux ou contes du XIIe et du XIIIe siècle, traduits ou extraits d'après divers manuscrits du tems.* 4 vols. Paris: E. Onfroy, 1779; rpt. Geneva: Slatkine, 1973.

Limentani, Alberto, ed. and trans. *Rutebeuf: I Fabliaux.* Venezia: 1976.

Orr, John, ed. and trans. *Eustache d'Amiens: "Le Boucher d'Abbeville."* London: Oliver and Boyd, 1947.

Ott, Jean. *"Les Trois Bossus," d'après le fabliau du trouvère Durand, XIIIe siècle.* Limoges, 1911.

Rickard, Peter et al. *Medieval Comic Tales.* Cambridge, Eng.: D.S. Brewer Ltd., 1973.

Rouger, G. *Fabliaux.* Paris: Gallimard, 1978.

Scott, N. *Contes pour rire? Fabliaux des XIIIe et XIVe siècles.* Paris: Ed. de Minuit, 1977.

Teissier, Maurice and Henry Nicholas. *Les Fabliaux.* Paris: Fernand Lanore, 1958.

III. *Critical Works*

Aubailly, Jean-Claude. "Du Narré au joué, le motif du faux confesseur." In *Mélanges . . . offerts à P. Jonin.* Aix-en-Provence: Cuerma, Université de Provence, 1979, pp. 49–61.

Baird, Joseph L., and Lorrayne Y. Baird. "Fabliau Forms and the 'Hegge Joseph's' Return." *Chaucer Review,* 8 (1973), 159–69.

Bar, Francis. "A Propos de Saint Pierre et le jongleur." *Romania,* 46 (1940–41), 532–37.

Barth, Albert. "Le Fabliau du Buffet." In *Festschrift zur 49 Versammlung deutscher Philologen.* Basel: E. Birkhäuser, 1907, pp. 148–80.

Barth, Bruno. *Liebe und Ehe im Altfranzösischen Fabel und in der Mittelhochdeutschen Novelle.* Berlin: Mayer & Müller, 1910.

Bausinger, Hermann. "Schwank und Witz." *Studium Generale,* 11 (1958), 699–710.

Beach, Charles Ray. *Treatment of Ecclesiastics in the French Fabliaux of the Middle Ages.* Modern Language Series, 34. Lexington: University Press of Kentucky, 1960.

Bédier, Joseph. *Les Fabliaux.* 6th ed. Paris: Champion, 1964.

Bercescu, Sorina. "Le vilain mire si le Médecin malgré lui." *Analele Universitatii Bucuresti. Literatura universala si comparata,* 21, No. 1 (1972), 87–95.

Bergerfurth, Wolfgang. "'Des Fables fait on les fabliaus,'" Zum Verhaltnis von Fabel und Fablel." In *Festschrift für Rupprecht Rohr zum 60. Geburstrag.* Ed. Wolfgang Bergerfurth, et al. Heidelberg: Gross, 1979, pp. 61–63.

Bertoni, Giulio. "Il Fabliau detto 'De Pré tondu.'" *Zeitschrift für Romanische Philologie,* 36 (1912), 488–489.

Beyer, Jürgen. *Schwank und Moral: Untersuchungen zum altfranzösischen Fabliau und verwandten Formen.* Heidelberg: C. Winter: 1969.

―――――. "The Morality of the Amoral." In *The Humor of the Fabliaux: A Collection of Critical Essays.* Ed. Thomas D. Cooke and Benjamin L. Honeycutt. Columbia: University of Missouri Press, 1974, pp. 15–42.

Bianciotto, Gabriel. "Le Fabliau et la ville." In *Third International Beast Epic, Fable and Fabliau Colloquium, Münster i. W., 1979.* Köln-Wien: Bohlau, 1981. pp. 43–65.

Blankenburg, Wilhelm. *Der Vilain in der Schilderung der altfranzösischen Fabliaux.* Greifswald: J. Abel, 1902.

Bloch, Howard R. "The Fabliaux, Fetishism, and Freud's Jewish Jokes." *Representations,* 4 (1983), 1–26.

Boccaccio, G. *Il Decamerone.* Milan: Editrice Lucchi, 1969.

Bornäs, Görnas. "Le cocu battu et content," *Studia Neophilogica,* 44 (1982), 37–61.

Brewer, D.S. "The Fabliaux." In *Companion to Chaucer Studies.* Ed. Beryl Rowland. New York: Oxford University Press, 1968, pp. 247–267.

Brunetière, Ferdinand. "Les Fabliaux du moyen âge et l'origine des contes." *Revue des Deux Mondes 112* (1893), 184–213.

―――――. "Les fabliaux du Moyen Age et l'origine des contes." In *Etudes critiques sur l'histoire de la littérature française.* Paris, 1899, vol. VI, 37–77.

Burbridge, Roger T. "Chaucer's 'Reeve's Tale' and the Fabliau 'Le Meunier et les .II. clers.'" *Annuale Medievale,* 12 (1971), 30–36.

Busby, Keith. "Fabliau et roman breton: le cas de 'Bérenger au long cul.'" In *Actes du IVᵉ Colloque Epopée Animale, Fable et Fabliau. Paris-Evreux, 4-11 Septembre 1981.* (forthcoming)

―――――. "Courtly Literature and the Fabliaux: Some Instances of Parody." Section 131, International Congress on Medieval Studies, Kalamazoo, Michigan, May 1982.

Canby, Henry S. "The English Fabliau." *Publication of the Modern Language Association,* 21 (1906), 200–214.

Caylus, Anne Claude Phillipe. "Mémoire sur les fabliaux." In *Mémoires de littérature, tirés des registres de l'Académie Royale des Inscriptions et Belles-Lettres,* Paris: r.p., 1746; Vol. XX, 352–76.

Chênerie, Marie-Luce. "Ces Curieux Chevaliers tournoyeurs . . . ." *Romania,* 97 (1976), 327–68.

Clouston, W.A. "The Lady and Her Suitors." In *Popular Tales and Fiction,* Edinburgh, 1887; II, 289–316.

Cluzel, Irénée. "Le Fabliau dans la littérature provençale du moyen âge.: *Annales du Midi,* 66 (1954), 317–26.

Coghill, Nevill. *The Poet Chaucer.* London: Oxford University Press, 1967.

Cooke, Thomas D. "Formulaic Diction and the Artistry of 'Le Chevalier qui recovra l'Amor de sa Dame.'" *Romania,* 94 (1973), 232–40.

——————. "Pornography, the Comic Spirit, and the Fabliaux." In *The Humor of the Fabliaux: A Collection of Critical Essays.* Ed. Thomas D. Cooke and Benjamin L. Honeycutt. Columbia: University of Missouri Press, 1974, pp. 137–62.

Cooke, Thomas D., and Benjamin L. Honeycutt, eds. *The Humor of the Fabliaux: A Collection of Critical Essays.* Columbia: University of Missouri Press, 1974.

——————. *The Old French and Chaucerian Fabliaux: A Study of Their Comic Climax.* Columbia: University of Missouri Press, 1978.

Crist, Larry, and James A. Lee. "L'Analyse fonctionnelle des fabliaux." In *Etudes de Philologie romane et d'histoire littéraire offertes à Jules Horrent.* Ed. Jean Marie D'Heur and Nicoletta Cherubini. Tournai: Gedit, 1980, pp. 85–104.

Cross, Tom Peete. "Notes on the Chastity-testing Horn and Mantle." *Modern Philology,* 10 (1912–13), 289–99.

De Cesare, Raffaele. "Di nuovo sulla leggenda di Aristotele cavalcato." In *Miscellanea del Centro di Studi Medievali.* Università Cattolica del Sacro Cuore. Milan: Vita e pensiero, 1956, pp. 181–247.

Delbouille, Maurice. "Problèmes d'attribution et de composition III. Le Fabliau du 'Prestre teint,' est-il l'oeuvre de Gautier le Leu?" *Revue Belge de Philologie et d'Histoire,* 11 (1932), 591–97.

——————. "Le Fabliau du 'Prestre teint,' conservé dans le manuscrit

Hamilton 257 de Berlin n'est pas de la main de Gautier le Leu." *Revue Belge de Philologie et d'Histoire,* 32 (1954), 373–94.

—————. "Les Fabliaux et Le Roman de Renart." In *Histoire illustrée des lettres françaises de Belgique.* Ed. Gustave Charlier and Joseph Hanse. Brussels: La Renaissance du Livre, 1958, pp. 45–51.

Diekmann, Erwin. *Die Substantivbildung mit Suffixen in den Fabliaux.* Tübingen: Niemeyer, 1969.

Di Stefano, Giuseppe, "Fabliaux." In *Dizionario critico dela letteratura francese.* Ed. Franco Simone. Torino: Union Tipografico, 1972; Vol. I, 419–23.

Dronke, Peter. "The Rise of the Medieval Fabliau: Latin and Vernacular Evidence." *Romanische Forschungen,* 85 (1973), 275–97.

Dubuis, Roger. "La Genèse de la nouvelle en France au moyen âge." In *Cahiers de l'Association Internationale des Etudes Françaises,* 18 (1966), 9–20.

—————. *Les Cent Nouvelles Nouvelles et la tradition de la nouvelle en France au moyen âge.* Grenoble: Presses Universitaires de Grenoble, 1973.

—————. "Notes Complémentaires sur la nouvelle françaises." In A. Sempoux, *La Nouvelle.* Typologie des sources du Moyen Age occidental, 9. Turnhout: Brepols, 1973, 31–35.

Eichmann, Raymond. "The Question of Variants and the Fabliaux.: *Fabula,* 17 (1976), 40–44.

—————. "The Search for Originals in the Fabliaux and the Validity of Textual Dependency." *Romance Notes,* 19 (1978), 90–97.

—————. "The Anti-Feminism of the Fabliaux." In *French Literature Series: Authors and Philosophers,* 6 (1979), 26–34.

—————. "Oral Composition: A Recapitulatory View of its Value and Impact." *Neuphilologische Mitteilungen,* 80 (1979), 97–109.

—————. "The Artistry of Economy in the Fabliaux." *Studies in Short Fiction,* 17 (1980), 67–73.

Faral, Edmond. *Les Jongleurs en France au moyen âge.* Paris: Champion, 1910; rpt. New York: Burt Franklin, 1970.

—————. "Le Fabliau latin au moyen âge." *Romania,* 50 (1924), 321–85.

Flutre, Louis Fernand. "Le Fabliau, genre courtois?" *Frankfurter Universithätsreden*, 22 (1960), 70–84.

Foulon, Charles. "Le Thème du berceau dans deux contes populaires du moyen âge." In *Littérature savante et littérature populaire. Congrès national de littérature comparée*. Paris: Didier, 1965, pp. 183–87.

Frosch-Freiburg, Frauke. *Schwankmären und Fabliaux. Ein Stoff und Motivvergleich*. Göppinger Arbeiten zur Germanistik, 49. Göppingen: Kummerle, 1971.

Goodall, Peter. "The Reeve's Tale, Le Meunier et les II Clercs, and the Miller's Tale." *Parergon*, 27, 13–16.

Guerlin de Guer, Charles. "Le Comique et l'humour à travers les âges: les fabliaux." *Revue des Cours et des Conférences*, 28 (1926–27), 325–50.

Guiette, Robert. "Note sur le fabliau du 'mari-confesseur'." *Revue Belge Philologie et d'Histoire*, 20 (1941), 117–26.

————————. "Fabliaux: Divertissement sur le mot 'fabliau.' Notes conjointes. Note sur le fabliau du 'mari confesseur.'" *Romanica Gandensia*, 8 (1960), 61–86, also in *Forme et senefiance*. Geneva: Droz, 1978, pp. 84–100.

Hart, Walter Morris. "The Fabliau and Popular Literature." *Publications of the Modern Language Association*, 23 (1908), 329–74.

————————. "The Narrative Art of the Old French Fabliaux." In *Anniversary Papers by Colleagues and Pupils of George Lyman Kittredge*. Boston: Ginn and Company, 1913, pp. 209–16.

Helsinger, Howard. "Pearls in the Swill: Comic Allegory in the French Fabliaux." In *The Humor of the Fabliaux: A Collection of Critical Essays*. Ed. Thomas D. Cooke and Benjamin L. Honeycutt. Columbia: University of Missouri Press, 1974, pp. 93–105.

Henry, Charles. "The Grip of Winter in 'Des Trois Bossus,' an Old French Fabliau." *Comparative Literature Studies*, 6 (1979), 26–34.

Herrman, F. *Schilderung und Beurteilung der gesellschaftlichen Verhältnisse Frankreichs in der Fabliaudichtung*. Leipzig, 1900.

Hilka, Alfons. "Zum Fablel von den drei Bückeligen." *Zeitschrift für französische Sprache und Literatur*, 47 (1924), 70–72.

Holbrook, Richard. "The Printed Text of Four Fabliaux in the Receuil Général . . . Compared with the Readings in the Harleian Ms. 2253," *Modern Language Notes*, 20 (1905), 193–97.

Holmes, Urban T. "Notes on the French Fabliau." In *Middle Ages, Reformation, Volkskunde: Festschrift for John G. Kunstmann*. Chapel Hill: University of North Carolina Press, 1959, pp. 39–44.

Honeycutt, Benjamin L. "The Knight and His World as Instruments of Humor in the Fabliaux." In *The Humor of the Fabliaux: A Collection of Critical Essays*. Ed. Thomas D. Cooke and Benjamin L. Honeycutt. Columbia: University of Missouri Press, 1974, pp. 75–92.

——————. "An Example of Comic Cliché in the Old French Fabliaux." *Romania*, 96 (1975), 245–55.

Jauss, Hans-Robert. "Littérature médiévale et théorie des genres." *Poétique*, 1 (1970), 79–101.

Jodogne, Omer. "Des fragments d'un nouveau manuscrit de 'Constant du Hamel', fabliau du XIIIᵉ siècle." *Moyen Age*, 69 (1963), 401–15.

——————. "Considérations sur le fabliau." In *Mélanges offerts à René Crozet à l'occasion de son soixante-dixième anniversaire*. Ed. Pierre Gallais and Yves-Jean Rious. 2 vols. Poitiers: Société d'Etudes Médiévales, 1966; II, 1043–55.

——————. "Le Caractère wallon de 'La Vessie au prestre,' Fabliau de Jacques de Baisieux." *Bulletin de la Commission Royale de Toponymie et de Dialectique*, 44 (1970), 29–42.

——————. *Le Fabliau*. Typologie des sources du Moyen Age occidental, *13*. Turnhout: Brepols, 1975.

Joly, Aristide. "De la condition des vilains au moyen âge d'après les fabliaux." In *Mémoires de l'Académie nationale des sciences, arts et belles-lettres de Caen*. Caen: n.p., 1882, pp. 445–92.

Kahane, Henry, and Renée Kahane. "Herzeloyde." In *Mélanges de linguistique romane et de philologie médiévale offerts à M. Maurice Delbouille*. 2 vols. Gembloux, Belgium: J. Duculot, 1964; II, 329–35.

Kasprzyk, Krystyna. "Pour la sociologie du fabliau: Convention, tactique et engagement." *Kwartalnik Neofilologiczny*, 23 (1976), 153–61.

Kiesow, Reinhard. *Die Fabliaux*. Rheinfelden: Schauble, 1976.

Krömer, Wolfram. "Das Fabliau," in his *Kurzerzählungen und Novellen in den romanischen Ländern bis 1700*. Grundlagen der Romanistik, *3*. Berlin: Erich Schmidt Verlag, 1973, pp. 47–59.

Lacy, Gregg F. "Augustinian Imagery and Fabliau 'Obscenity.' " In *Studies on the Seven Sages of Rome and Other Essays in Medieval Literature:*

Dedicated to the Memory of Jean Misrahi. Ed. Henri Niedzielski et al. Honolulu: Educational Research Associates, 1978, pp. 219–30.

——————. "Fabliau Stylistic Humor." *Kentucky Romance Quarterly*, 26 (1979), pp. 349–59.

Lacy, Norris. "Types of Esthetic Distance in the Fabliaux." In *The Humor of the Fabliaux: A Collection of Critical Essays*. Ed. Thomas D. Cooke and Benjamin L. Honeycutt. Columbia: University of Missouri Press, 1974, pp. 107–17.

——————. "The Fabliaux and Comic Logic." *Esprit Créateur, 16* (1976), 39–45.

Ladd, A. "Classification of the Fabliaux by Plot Structure." In *University of Glasgow, International Beast Epic Colloquium, 23rd–25th September 1975*. Glasgow: K. Varty, 1976, pp. 92–107.

Lange, Marius. *Vom Fabliau zu Boccaccio und Chaucer. Ein Vergleich zweier Fabliaux mit Boccaccio "Decamerone IX, 6" und mit Chaucer's "Reeve's Tale."* Hamburg: Friederichsen, de Gruyter & Co., 1934.

Langfors, Arthur. "Le Fabliau découvert à Lyon et le ms. 354 de Berne," *Romania, 62* (1936), 392–95; 64 (1938), 252–55.

Langlois, Charles-Victor. "La société du moyen-âge d'après les fabliaux," *Revue Bleue, 48* (1981), 227–236, 289–297.

Lanson, Gustave. "Les Fabliaux." In *Histoire de la littérature française*. 9th ed. Paris, 1906, pp. 101–105.

LeClerc, Victor. "Fabliaux." In *Histoire littéraire de la France*. 39 vols. Paris: Imprimerie Nationale, 1895; XXIII, 69–215.

Lecoy, Felix. "Note sur le fabliau de 'Prêtre au Lardier'." *Romania, 82* (1961), 524–35.

——————. "A propos du fabliau de Gautier Le Leu 'De Dieu et dou pescour.'" In *Mélanges de linguistique romane et de philologie médiévale offerts à M. Maurice Delbouille*. 2 vols. Gembloux: J. Duculot, 1964; II, 367–79.

——————. "Analyse thématique et critique littéraire. Le cas du 'Fabliau.'" In *Actes du 5ème Congrès des romanistes scandinaves. Turku (Abo) du 6 au 10 août 1972*. Annales Universitatis Turkuensis, Ser. B, 127. Turku: Turum Yliopisto, 1973, pp. 17–31.

Lee, Charmaine, Anna Riccadonna, Alberto Limentani, and Aldo Miotto. *Prospettive sui fabliaux, contesto, sistema, realizzazioni*. Padova, 1976.

Legry-Rosier, Jeanne. "Manuscrits de contes et de fabliaux." *Bulletin d'Information de l'Institut de Recherche et d'Histoire des Textes,* 4 (1955), 37–47.

Lejeune, Rita. "La Patrie de Gautier le Leu," *Moyen Age,* 47 (1937), 1–21.

—————. "Hagiographie et grivoiserie. A propos d'un dit de Gautier Le Leu." *Romance Philology,* 12 (1958–1959), 355–56.

Lian, A.P. "Aspects of Verbal Humour in the Old French Fabliaux." In *Australasian Universities Language and Literature Association: Proceedings and Papers at the Twelfth Congress.* Sydney: AULLA, 1970, pp. 235–61.

Liebrecht, Felix. "Von den Drei Frauen," *Germania,* 21 (1876), 385–99; rpt. *Zur Volkskunde,* Heilbronn: Grebr. Henninger, 1879, 124–41.

Limentani, Alberto. "Qualche Precisazione sui 'fabliaux' di Rutebeuf." *Studi Francesi,* 24 (1980), 485–86.

Lindgren, Laru. "Courtebarbe, auteur des 'Trois Aveugles de Compiègne,' est-il aussi l'auteur du fabliau du 'Chevalier à la robe vermeille?' " In *Mélanges de philologie et de linguistique offerts à Tauno Nurmela,* Turku, Finland, 1967, pp. 91–102.

Livingston, Charles H. "Le Jongleur Gautier Le Leu. A Study in the Fabliaux," *Romanic Review,* 15 (1924), 1–67.

—————. "The Fabliau des Deux Anglois et de l'anel." *Publications of the Modern Language Association,* 40 (1925), 217–24.

—————. "Explication d'une allusion littéraire dans un texte du XIIIᵉ siècle," *Romanic Review,* 31 (1940), 112–13.

Lorcin, Marie-Thérèse. "Quand les princes n'épousaient pas les bergères ou mésalliance et classes d'âge dans les fabliaux." *Medioevo Romanzo,* 3 (1976), 195–228.

—————. "Les Voyages ne forment que la jeunesse, ou le voyageur et l'étranger dans les fabliaux." In *Voyage, quête, pélérinage dans la littérature et la civilisation médiévales. Actes du colloque . . . d'Aix en Provence.* Senefiance 2. Aix en Provence: Ed. CUERMA, 1976.

—————. *"La prostituée des fabliaux est-elle intégrée ou exclue?" Exclus et systèmes d'exclusion dans la littérature et la civilisation médiévales.* Senefiance 5. Aix-en-Provence, 1978, pp. 105–118.

—————. *Façons de sentir et de penser: les fabliaux français.* Paris: Champion, 1979.

Loth, Johannes. *Die Sprichwörter und Sentenzen der altfranzösischen Fabliaux*. 2 vols. Greifenberg: C. Lemcke, 1885–96.

Lukasik, Stanislaw. "Fabliau." *Zagadnienia Rodzajow Literackick*, 4 (1961), 217–221.

Marnier, Jean, ed. *Jean de La Fontaine: Oeuvres complètes*. Paris: Editions du Seuil, 1965.

McClintock, Michael W. "Games and the Players of Games: Old French Fabliaux and the 'Shipman's Tale.'" *Chaucer Review*, 5 (1970), 112–36.

McGalliard, John C. "Chaucerian Comedy: The Merchant's Tale, Jonson and Molière." *Philological Quarterly*, 25 (1946), 343–70.

McGillavry, K. "Le Jeu de dés dans le fabliau de 'Saint Pierre et le Jongleur.'" *Marche Romane*, 28 (1978), 175–79.

Ménard, Philippe. *Les fabliaux, contes à rire du moyen-âge*. Paris: PUF, 1979.

Merl, Hans-Dieter. *Untersuchungen zur Struktur, Stilstik und Syntax in den Fabliaux Jean Bodels*. Europäische Hochschulschriften *13*; Französische Sprache und Literatur, *16*. Bern: Lang, 1972.

——————. *Untersuchungen zur Struktur, Stilistik und Syntax in den Fabliaux Rutebeufs, Gautier Le Leus und Jean de Condés*. Bern: Lang, 1976.

Meyer, Paul. "Le Chevalier, la dame et le clerc." *Romania*, *1* (1871), 69–87.

Micha, Alexandre. "A Propos d'un fabliau, 'Du Preudomme qui rescolt son compere de noier.'" *Moyen Age*, 55 (1949), 17–20.

Muscatine, Charles. *Chaucer and the French Tradition*. Berkeley: University of California Press, 1957.

——————. "The Wife of Bath and Gautier's 'La Veuve.'" In *Romance Studies in Memory of Edward Bilings Ham*. Ed. Urban T. Holmes. Hayward, California: California State College, 1967, pp. 109–14.

——————. "The Social Background of the Old French Fabliaux." *Genre*, 9 (1976), 1–19.

Morawski, Jean, ed. *Proverbes français antérieurs au XVe siècle*. Paris: E. Champion, 1925.

Nardin, Pierre. *Lexique comparé des fabliaux de Jean Bodel*. Paris: Droz, 1942.

Noomen, Willem. "Structures narratives et force comique: Les fabliaux." *Neophilologus*, 62 (1978) 361–73.

──────────. "Qu'est-ce qu'un fabliau?" In *XIV. Congresso di Linguistica e Filologia Romanza: Acti V*. Ed. Alberto Vàrvaro. Naples: Macchiaroli, 1981; Amsterdam: Benjamins, 1981, pp. 431–32.

Nykrog, Per. *Les Fabliaux: Etude d'histoire littéraire et de stylistique médiévale*. Copenhagen: Ejnar Munksgaard, 1957; rpt. with Postscript, Geneva: Droz, 1973.

──────────. "Courtliness and the Townspeople: The Fabliaux as a Courtly Burlesque." In *The Humor of the Fabliaux: A Collection of Critical Essays*. Ed. Thomas D. Cooke and Benjamin L. Honeycutt. Columbia: University of Missouri Press, 1974, pp. 59–73.

Ocheret, Iu. V. "K voprosu ob opredelenii zhanra fablio." Moskovskii Gosvdarstevennyi Pedagogischeskii Institut Imeni V.I. Lenina. *Uchenye Zapiskii*, 382 (1970), 219–45.

Olevskaia, V. "La nouvelle en France au XVe siècle et les fabliaux" (in Russian). *Annales Scientifiques de l'Institut Pédagogique Lénine à Moscou*, 324 (1969), 108–24.

Olsen, Michel. *Les Transformations du triangle érotique*. Copenhagen: Akademisk, 1976.

Olson, Glending. "'The Reeve's Tale' and 'Gombert.'" *Modern Language Review*, 64 (1969), 721–25.

──────────. "The Medieval Theory of Literature for Refreshment and Its Use in the Fabliau Tradition." *Studies in Philology*, 71 (1974), 291–313.

──────────. "'The Reeve's Tale' as a Fabliau." *Modern Language Quarterly*, 35 (1974), 219–30.

Owen, D.D.R. "The Element of Parody in 'Saint Pierre et le Jongleur.'" *French Studies*, 9 (1955), 60–63.

Ott, Jean. "*Les Trois Bossus*," *fabliau en 1 acte, en vers d'après le trouvère Durand de Douai*. Paris: O. Dousset, 1931.

Patzer, Otto. "The Wealth of the Clergy in the Fabliaux." *Modern Language Notes*, 19 (1904), 195–196.

Payen, Jean-Charles. "Lai, fabliau, exemplum, roman court: pour une typologie du récit bref aux XIIe et XIIIe siècles." in *Le Récit bref au moyen-âge*. Ed. D. Buschinger. Amiens: Univ. of Picardy, 1980, pp. 7–23.

————. "Goliardisme et Fabliaux, Interférences ou similitudes? Recherches sur la fonction idéologique de la provocation en littérature." In *Third International Beast Epic, Fable and Fabliau Colloquium, Münster i.W., 1979*. Köln-Wien: Bohlau, 1981, pp. 267–89.

Payen, Jean-Charles, and F.N.M. Diekstra. *Le Roman*. Typologie des sources du Moyen Age occidental, 12. Turnhout: Brepols, 1975.

Pearcy, Roy J. "A Minor Analogue to the Branding in 'The Miller's Tale.'" *Notes and Queries, 16* (1969), 333–335.

————. "A Classical Analogue to 'Le Preudome qui rescolt son compere de noier.'," *Romance Notes, 12* (1971), 422–27.

————. "Realism and Religious Parody in the Fabliaux: Watriquet de Couvin's 'Les Trois Dames de Paris.'" *Revue Belge de Philologie et d'Histoire, 50* (1972), 744–54.

————. "Relations between the D and A Versions of 'Berengier au long Cul.'" *Romance Notes, 14* (1972), 1–6.

————. "'Le Prestre qui menga les meures' and Ovid's 'Fasti, III, 745–760.'" *Romance Notes, 15* (1973), 159–63.

————. "Modes of Signification and the Humor of Obscene Diction in the Fabliaux." In *The Humor of the Fabliaux: A Collection of Critical Essays*. Ed. Thomas D. Cooke and Benjamin L. Honeycutt. Columbia: University of Missouri Press, 1974, pp. 163–96.

————. "Structural Models for the Fabliaux and the 'Summoner's Tale's' Analogues." *Fabula, 15* (1974), 103–13.

————. "An Instance of Heroic Parody in the Fabliaux." *Romania, 98* (1977), 105–07.

————. "Chansons de geste and Fabliaux: 'La Gageure' and 'Berenger au long cul.'" *Neuphilologische Mitteilungen, 79* (1978), 76–83.

Pelen, Marc M. "Form and Meaning of the Old French Love Vision: The 'Fabliau dou Dieu d'Amors' and Chaucer's 'Parliament of Fowls.'" *Journal of Medieval and Renaissance Studies, 9* (1979), 277–305.

Pfeffer, Peter. *Beiträge zur Kenntnis des altfranzösischen Volkslebens, meist auf Grund der Fabliaux*. 3 vols. Karlsruhe: n.p., 1898–1901.

Pillet, Alfred. *Das Fableau von den "Trois Bossus" und verwandte Erzählungen früher und später Zeit*. Halle: Niemeyer, 1901.

————. "Ueber den Gegenwärtigen Stand der Fabliaux-Forschung." *Neuphilologische Centralblatt, 17* (1904), 98–104.

Pilz, Oscar. *Beiträge zur Kenntnis der altfranzösischen Fabliaux, I: Die Bedeutung des Wortes Fablel.* Stettin: Grassman, 1889; II: *Die Verfasser der Fabliaux.* Görlitz, 1889.

Pitcher, Edward W. "A Note on the Source of 'The Child of Snow' and 'The Son of Snow.'" *Early American Literature, 13* (1978), 217–18.

Pollain, Jean. "Les Falbiaux." In *Tableau de la littérature française.* Ed. A. Adamov. Paris: Gallimard, 1962; I, 84–88.

Preime, August. *Die Frau in den altfranzösischen Schwänken,* Cassel: T.G. Fisher, 1901.

Raynaud, Gaston. "Trois Dits tirés d'un nouveau manuscrit de fabliaux," *Romania, 12* (1883), 209–229.

Rhaue, Hans. *Ueber das Fabliau "Des Trois Aveugles de Compiègne" und verwändte Erzählungen,* Braunsberg: Heyne, 1914.

Ribard, Jacques. *Un Ménestrel du XIVe siècle: Jean de Condé.* Geneva: Droz, 1969.

Richardson, Janette, *Blameth Not Me: A Study of Imagery in Chaucer's Fabliaux.* The Hague: Mouton, 1970.

Robinson, F., ed. *The Words of Geoffrey Chaucer.* Cambridge, Mass.: Houghton Mifflin Press, 1957.

Robbins, Rossell Hope. "The English Fabliau: Before and After Chaucer." *Moderna Sprak, 64* (1970), 231–44.

Rostaing, Charles. "A Propos de 'Constant du Hamel.' Additions et corrections." *Revue des Langues Romanes, 71* (1953), 324–329.

Rowland, Beryl. "What Chaucer Did to the Fabliaux." *Studia Neophilologica, 51* (1979), 205–13.

Ruelle, P. "Les Fabliaux." In *La Wallonie, le pays et les hommes, lettres, arts, culture.* Ed. Rita Lejeune and Jean Stiennon. 3 vols. Brussels: La Renaissance du livre, 1977; I, 151–55.

Rychner, Jean. "Fabliaux" in *Dictionnaire des lettres françaises.* Vol. I: *Le Moyen Age.* Paris: Fayard, 1951.

—————. *Contribution à l'étude des fabliaux: Variantes, remaniements, dégradations.* 2 vols. Geneva: Droz; Paris: Minard, 1960.

—————. "Les Fabliaux: genre, styles, publics." In *La Littérature narrative d'imagination.* Ed. Faculté des Lettres de l'Université de Strasbourg. Paris: Presses Universitaires de France, 1961, pp. 41–54.

Schaar, Claes. "The Merchant's Tale," "Amadas et Ydoine," and "Guillaume au Faucon." *Bulletin de la Soc. Royale des Lettres de Lund,* 2 (1952–1953) 87–95.

Schenck, Mary Jane. "The Morphology of the Fabliau." *Fabula,* 17 (1976), 26–39.

——————. "Functions and Roles in the Fabliaux." *Comparative Literature,* 30 (1978), 22–24.

Schofield, W. Henry. *The Source and History of the Seventh Novel of the Seventh Day in the Decameron.* Harvard Studies and Notes in Philology and Literature, 2. Cambridge, Mass.: Harvard University Press. 1893.

Schulze-Busacker, Elizabeth. "Proverbs et expressions proverbiales dans les fabliaux." *Marche Romane,* 28 (1978), 163–74.

Serper, Arié. "Le Monde culturel des fabliaux et la réalité sociale." In *Third International Beast Epic, Fable and Fabliau Colloquium, Münster i.W.,* 1979. Köln-Wien: Bohlau, 1981, pp. 392–403.

Sempoux, A. *La Nouvelle.* Typologie des sources du Moyen Age occidental, 9. Turnhout: Brepols, 1973.

Sinclair, K.V. "Anglo-Norman Studies: The Last Twenty Years." (Section 8: "Fabliaux-Satirical and Humorous Pieces"). *Australian Journal of French Studies,* 2 (1965), 225–26.

Söderhjelm, Werner. "Hugues le Roi de Cambrai," *Romania,* 25 (1896), 449–55.

Spencer, Richard. "The Courtois-Vilain Nexus in 'La Male Honte.'" *Medium Aevum,* 37 (1968), 272–292.

——————. "Who Is the King of La Male Honte?" In *Gallica: Essays Presented to J. Heywood Thomas by Colleagues, Pupils and Friends.* Cardiff: University of Wales Press, 1969, pp. 41–51.

——————. "Generic Characteristics of the Fabliaux: A Critique of Nykrog." In *University of Glasgow, International Beast Epic Colloquium,* 23–27 September 1975. Glasgow: K. Varty, 1976, pp. 81–91.

——————. "The Treatment of Women in the 'Roman de la Rose', the 'Fabliaux' and the 'Quinze Joyes de Mariage.'" *Marche Romane,* 28 (1978), 207–14.

Stearns-Schenck, Mary Jane. "Les Structures narratives dans le 'Cuvier.'" *Marche Romane,* 28 (1978), 185–92.

──────────. "Narrative Structure in the Exemplum, Fabliau and the Nouvelle." *Romanic Review,* 72 (1981), 367–82.

Steppuhn, August. *Das Fablel vom "Prestre comporté," Ein Beitrag zur Fablelforschung und zur Volksunde.* Königsberg: Hartung, 1913.

Stillwell, Gardiner. "The Language of Love in Chaucer's Miller's and Reeve's Tales and in the Old French Fabliaux." *Journal of English and Germanic Philology,* 44 (1955), 693–99.

Storost, Joachim, "Zur Aristoteles—Sage im Mittelalter. Geistesgeschichtliche, folkloristiche und literarische Grundlagen zu Iher Erforschung." In *Monumentum Bambergense: Festgabe fur Benedikt Kraft.* Munich: Kosel-Verlag, 1955, pp. 298–348.

──────────. "Femme chevalchat Aristotte." *Zeitschrift für Französische Sprache und Literatur,* 66 (1956), 186–201.

Subrenat, Jean. "Notes sur la tonalité des fabliaux. A propos du fabliaux: 'Du Fevre de Creeil.'" *Marche Romane,* 25 (1975), 83–93.

Suchier, Walter. "Der Schwank von der viermal getöten Leiche in der Literatur des Abend und Morgenlandes." *Zeitschrift für Romanische Philologie,* 42 (1922), 561–605.

──────────. "Fablelstudien." *Zeitschrift für Romanischen Studien,* 42 (1922), 561–605.

Theiner, Paul. "Fabliau Settings." In *The Humor of the Fabliaux: A Collection of Critical Essays.* Ed. Thomas D. Cooke and Benjamin L. Honeycutt. Columbia: University of Missouri Press, 1974, pp. 119–36.

Thouvenin, Georges. "Le Fabliau de l'Oue au Chapelain et une légende orientale." *Romania,* 49 (1923), 417–22.

Tiemann, Hermann. "Bemerkungen zur Entstehungsgeschichte der Fabliaux." *Romanische Forschungen,* 72 (1961), 406–22.

Togeby, Knud. "The Nature of the Fabliaux." In *The Humor of the Fabliaux: A Collection of Critical Essays.* Ed. Thomas D. Cooke and Benjamin L. Honeycutt. Columbia: University of Missouri Press, 1974, pp. 7–13.

──────────. "Les Fabliaux," *Orbis Litterarum,* 12 (1957), 85–98.

Toldo, Pietro. "Pel Fabliau di Constant du Hamel," *Romania,* 32 (1903), 552–64.

──────────. "Die Geschichte von dem in speckschranke versteckten Priester." *Zeitschrift des Vereins für Volkskunde,* 13 (1903), 412–20.

Valentini, Giuseppe. *Les Fabliaux de l'espace.* Naples: G. Scalabrini, 1965.

Van den Boogaard, Nico. "Amplification et abréviation: les contes de Hais-
eau." In *Mélanges . . . offerts à Léon Geschiere*, Amsterdam: 1975, pp.
55–69.

—————. "Les Fabliaux: versions et variations." *Marche Romane, 28*
(1978), 149–61.

—————. "Le Fabliau anglo-normand." In *Third International Beast
Epic, Fable and Fabliau Colloquium, Münster i.W.*, 1979. Köln-Wien:
Bohlau, 1981, pp. 66–77.

Vàrvara, Alberto. "I fabliaux e la societa." *Studi Mediolatini e Volgari, 8*
(1960), 275–99.

—————. "Il Segretain Moine ed il realismo dei Fabliaux." Studi
Mediolatini e Volgari, 14 (1966), 195–213.

Verulsdonck, J. Th. "Le Manuscrit B.N. 25545." *Marche Romane, 28*
(1978), 193–95.

Wailes, Stephen L. "The Unity of the Fabliau 'Un Chivalier et sa Dame et
un Clerk.'" *Romance Notes, 14* (1972), 593–96.

—————. "Fortuna and Social Anomaly: Principles of Medieval
Humour in 'Asinarius and Rapularius.'" *Seminar, 9* (1973), 87–96.

—————. "Vagantes and the Fabliaux." In *The Humor of the
Fabliaux: A Collection of Critical Essays.* Ed. Thomas D. Cooke and
Benjamin L. Honeycutt. Columbia: University of Missouri Press, 1974,
pp. 43–58.

—————. "Role-Playing in Medieval *Comaediae* and Fabliaux." *Neuphilologische Mitteilungen.* 75 (1974), 640–49.

—————. "Students as Lovers in the German Fabliau." *Medium
Aevum*, 46 (1977), 196–211.

Walkley, M.J. "The Fabliau as a Guide to Lifemanship in Medieval
France," *Parergon, 25* (1979), 33–38.

Warnhagen, Herman. "Die Erzählung von der Wiege." *English Studies, 9*
(1885–86), 240–66.

Werner, Jacob. "Liber furum ovvero il 'fabliau de Barate et Haimet.'" *Studi
Medievali, 3* (1911), 509–513.

Williams, Harry F. "French Fabliau Scholarship." *South Atlantic Review,*
46 (1981), 76–82.

Wilson, Geoffrey. *A Medievalist in the Eighteenth Century, Legrand
d'Aussy and the Fabliaux ou Contes.* The Hague: Nijhoff, 1975.

The French Fabliau
B.N. MS 837
v. I

D'ESTORMI

par

Hues Piaucele

1.

Por ce que je vous ai molt chier,
vous vueil un fablel commencier
d'une aventure qui avint.
C'est d'un preudomme, qui devint
povres entre lui et sa fame.   5
Non ot Jehans, et ele Yfame.
Riches genz avoient esté,
puis revindrent en povreté;
mais je ne sai par quoi ce fu,
quar onques conté ne me fu;   10
por ce ne le doi pas savoir.
        Troi prestre par lor mal savoir
covoitierent dame Yfamain.
Bien la cuidierent a la main
avoir prise, por la poverte   15
qui la feroit a descouverte.
De folie se porpensserent,
quar parmi la mort en passerent,
issi com vous m'orrez conter
se vous me volez escouter,   20
et la matere le devine,
qui nous raconte la couvine
de la dame et des .III. prelaz.
Chascuns desirre le solaz
de dame Yfamain a avoir.   25
Por ce li promistrent avoir,
je cuit, plus de .IIII.XX. livres.
Ainsi le tesmoingne li livres
et la matere le raconte,
si com cil furent a grant honte   30
livré par lor maleürtez,
mes ce fist lor desleautez,
de lor crupes et de lor rains.
Bien l'orrez dire au daarains,
por que vous vueilliez tant atendre.   35
Ainz Yfame ne vout entendre

2.

ESTORMI

by

Hues Piaucele

1.

Since I consider you very dear,
I would like to begin a fabliau for you
About an adventure which happened.
It is about a gentleman who became
Poor, both he and his wife.   5
His name was John and hers, Yfame.
They had been rich people;
But they fell into poverty again;
But I don't know how it happened,
Because it was never told to me--   10
That's why I shouldn't be expected to know it.
 Three priests, with evil intentions,
Coveted Lady Yfame.
They really thought she was theirs
For the taking, because poverty   15
Was clearly persecuting her.
They were intending a foolish act,
And they died because of it,
As you will hear me tell
If you listen to me,   20
For the story makes it clear
And tells what happened
Between the lady and the three prelates.
Each one desired to have
The solace of Lady Yfame.   25
To this end, they promised her money,
I think more than eighty pounds.
That's what the book says
And how the story tells it,
How, by their misfortune,   30
They were delivered to great shame,
But their treachery is what did this--
By their haunches and by their loins.
You will hear it all to the end,
Provided you wait that long.   35
But Yfame didn't wish to hear

3

lor parole ne lor reson,
ainz a tout conté son baron
l'afere tout si comme il va.
Jehans li respondit: "Diva,   40
bele suer, me contes tu voir?
Te prometent il tant d'avoir
com tu me vas ci acontant?"
"Oïl, biaus frere, plus que tant,
mes que je vueille lor bons fere."   45
"Dehez ait qui en a que fere,"
fet Jehans, "en itel maniere!
Miex ameroie en une biere
estre mors et ensevelis
que ja eüssent lor delis   50
de vous a nul jor de ma vie!"
"Sire, ne vous esmaiez mie,"
fet Yfame, qui molt fu sage.
"Povretez, qui molt est sauvage,
nous a mis en molt mal trepeil.   55
Or feroit bon croire conseil
par quoi nous en fussons geté;
li prestre sont riche renté;
s'ont trop dont nous avons petit.
Se vous volez croire mon dit,   60
de povreté vous geterai
et a grant honte meterai
ceus qui me cuident engingnier."
"Va donc, pensse du hamoingnier,"
fet Jehans, "bele douce suer;   65
mes je ne voudroie a nul fuer
qu'il fussent de vous au desus."
"Tesiez! Vous monterez la sus
en cel solier tout coiement.
Si garderez apertement   70
m'onor et la vostre et mon cors;
les prestres meterons la fors,
et li avoirs nous remaindra.
Tout issi la chose avendra
se vous le volez otrier."   75
"Alez tantost sanz detrier,"
fet Jehans, "bele douce amie,
mes, por Dieu, ne demorez mie!"
    Au moustier s'en ala Yfame,
qui molt par estoit bone fame.   80
Ainz que la messe fust chantee
fu assez tost amonestee
de ceus qui quierent lor anui.
Yfame chascun a par lui
tout belement l'un aprés l'autre,   85
qu'ainc n'en sot mot li uns de l'autre,
mist lieu de venir a son estre.
Tout avant au premerain prestre

Their speech or their argument;
Instead, she told her husband the whole
Business just as it had happened.
John answered her, "Hold on!   40
Dear sister, are you telling me the truth?
Are they promising you as much money
As you say they are?"
"Yes, dear brother, more than that,
Provided I do their pleasure."   45
"Curses on anyone who has anything to do with it
In such a way," said John.
"I would rather be dead
On a bier and buried
Than for them to have their pleasure   50
With you any day of my life!"
"My lord, don't worry,"
Said Yfame, who was very wise;
"Poverty, which is very cruel,
Has gotten us in very bad trouble.   55
Now it would be good to heed counsel
On how we might be released from it:
Priests are richly endowed;
They have too much of what we lack.
If you will trust my word,   60
I will release you from poverty
And will put to great shame
Those who expect to seduce me."
"Go ahead then--figure out how to do it,"
Said John, "dear, sweet sister,   65
But I wouldn't want at any price
For them to get on top of you."
"Quiet! You get up there
Very quietly in that loft.
And you will watch over   70
My honor, and yours, and my body;
We will throw the priests out,
But the money will stay with us.
The whole thing will take place here
If you agree to it."   75
"Go right ahead without delay,"
Said John, "my beautiful, sweet friend,
And, for God's sake, don't wait!"
Off to church went Yfame,
Who was a very good woman.   80
Before the mass was fully sung,
She had everything planned
For those who were seeking their own downfall.
Very skillfully, one after the other,
With each one individually,   85
So that no one knew a word about the other,
Yfame set up an appointment for them at her house.
First of all the good lady made

5

a mis la bone dame leu
que il viengne entre chien et leu,   90
et si aport toz ses deniers:
"Dame," fet cil, "molt volentiers,"
qui molt est pres de son torment,
ne porquant va s'en liement.
Estes vous venu le secon,   95
qui voloit avoir du bacon.
Molt par avoit chaude la croupe!
Devant dame Yfame s'acroupe,
puis li descuevre sa penssee.
Et cele, qui s'est porpennssee   100
de sa grande male aventure,
li a mis leu par couverture
qu'il venist quant la cloche sone.
"Dame, ja n'aurai tant d'essoine,"
fet li prestres, "par saint Amant,   105
que je ne viegne a vo commant,
que pieça que je vous convoite."
"Aportez moi donc la queilloite
que vous me devez aporter."
"Volentiers, je les vois conter,"   110
fet cil, qui de joie tressaut.
Et li autres prestres resaut,
puis li demande de rechief:
"Dame, vendrai je ja a chief
de ce dont je vous ai requise?"   115
Et la dame, qui fu porquise
de sa grant honte et de son mal,
li dist: "Biaus sire, il n'i a al.
Vostre parole m'a atainte,
et povretez qui m'a destrainte   120
me font otroier vo voloir.
Or venez sempres a prinsoir
trestout belement a mon huis,
et si ne venez mie vuis
que vous n'aportez ma promesse."   125
"Ja ne puisse je chanter messe,
dame, se vos n'avez vostre offre!
Je les vois metre hors du coffre,
et les deniers et le cuiret."
Atant a la voie se met   130
cil qui est molt liez de l'otroi.
Or se gardent bien de lor roi,
qu'il ont porchacié laidement
lor mort et lor definement!
      Oublié avoie une chose   135
qu'a chascun prestre a la parclose
fist Yfame entendre par guile
que Jehans n'ert pas en la vile;
si s'en refist chascuns plus jois,
mes cele nuit a granz conjois   140

An appointment with the first priest
For him to come at sunset   90
And bring all his money.
"Lady, very willingly," said he,
Who was very near to his death,
But went off to it joyfully.
Here came the second one,   95
Who wanted to get some bacon.
He was very hot in the haunches!
He crouched in front of Lady Yfame,
Then he laid bare his thoughts to her.
And she, who had meditated   100
On her great, wicked venture,
Made a secret appointment with him
To come when the bell rang.
"Lady, there will be no obstacle great enough,"
Said the priest, "by Saint Amant,   105
To keep me from coming at your command,
Because for a long time I have coveted you."
"Then bring me the fee
That you are supposed to bring me."
"Gladly. I'm going to count it out,"   110
Said he, who was jumping for joy.
And the third priest popped up
And immediately asked her,
"Lady, am I to achieve
The thing I asked you for?"   115
And the lady, who was pursuing
His great shame and his misfortune,
Told him: "Good lord, it must be so.
Your words have touched me,
And so does poverty, which goads me on.   120
They make me agree to your will.
Now come soon, right after nightfall,
Very nicely to my door,
And don't come empty-handed,
Without bringing what you've promised me."   125
"May I never sing mass again,
Lady, if you don't get your promise.
I'm going to get them out of the safe,
Both the money and the purse."
Finally one man, being very happy with the agreement,   130
Set out on the road.
Now let them look out for the trap,
For they have vilely pursued
Their deaths and their destructions!
    I have forgotten one thing: 135
That on concluding the agreement,
Yfame had guilefully led each priest
To believe that John was not in town;
Each one rejoiced the more at that,
And they dedicated that night   140

jurent, ce sachiez vraiement.
Et dame Yfame isnelement
est revenue a sa meson;
son baron conte la reson.
Jehans l'oï, molt liez en fu.   145
A sa niecete a fet le fu
alumer et la table metre.
Cele, qui ne se vout demetre
qu'ele ne face son commant,
a mis la table maintenant,   150
qu'ele savoit bien son usage.
Et Yfame qui molt fu sage,
li dist: "Biaus sire, la nuit vient;
or sai je bien qu'il vous covient
repondre, qu'il en est bien poins."   155
Et Jehans, qui ot .II. porpoins,
en avoit le meillor vestu.
Biaus hom fu et de grant vertu.
En sa main a pris sa coingnie;
une maçue a empoingnie,   160
qui molt ert grosse, de pommier.
      Estes vous venu le premier,
tout carchié de deniers qu'il porte.
Tout belement hurte a la porte;
il ne veut mie c'on l'i sache.   165
Et dame Yfame arriere sache
le veroil, et l'uis li desfarme.
Quant cil a veü dame Yfame,
si la cuide avoir deceüe.
Et Jehans, qui tint la maçue   170
qui molt ot grosse la cibole,
Felonessement le rebole,
si que li prestres n'en sot mot.
Tout coiement, sanz dire mot,
avala Jehans le degré.   175
Et cil, qui cuide avoir son gré
de la dame, tout a estor,
vint a li, se li fet un tor
si qu'en mi la meson l'abat.
Et Jehans, qui sor eus s'embat,   180
tout belement et sanz moleste,
le fiert a .II. mains en la teste
si durement de la coingnie:
la teste li a si coingnie
li sans et la cervele en vole.   185
Cil chiet mors, si pert la parole.
Yfame en fu molt esmarie;
Jehans jure sainte Marie,
se sa fame noise fesoit,
de sa maçue la ferroit.   190
Cele se test, et cil embrace
celui qui gist mors en la place;

To great joy, be assured of that.
And Lady Yfame immediately
Came back home.
She told her husband about the developments.
John heard and was overjoyed.   145
He had his niece light
The fire and set the table.
She did not want to fail
To do his command,
But set the table right away,   150
For she knew her job well.
And Yfame, who was very wise,
Told him, "My good lord, night is coming;
Now I know very well that you
Must hide, because it is really time."   155
John, who had two doublets,
Put on the better one.
He was a fine man and very stout-hearted.
He took his stick in hand;
He grasped a club, which was very big,   160
Made of apple wood.
        Well, here came the first,
All loaded down with the money he was carrying.
He knocked very lightly at the door;
He didn't want anyone to know he was there.   165
And Lady Yfame pulled back
The bolt and opened the door.
When he saw Lady Yfame,
He thought he had seduced her.
John, who held the club,   170
Which had a very big head,
Brandished it wickedly,
So that the priest didn't know a word about it.
Very quietly, without saying a word,
John went down the stairs,   175
And the other man, who thought he was getting
His way with the lady at the first attack,
Came to her, turned her around
And threw her down in the middle of the house.
Then John, who threw himself upon them,   180
Very neatly and without any noise,
Using both hands, struck him in the head
Very hard with the club:
He hit his head so hard
That the blood and brains flowed out.   185
The man fell dead speechless.
Yfame was very much distressed by this.
John swore by Holy Mary
That if his wife made a sound,
He would strike her with the club.   190
She quieted down, and he got hold of
The man who was lying dead in the room.

9

en sa cort l'enporta errant,
si l'a drecié tout maintenant
a la paroi de son bercil,   195
et puis repere du cortil;
dame Yfame reconforta.
    Et li autres prestres hurta,
qui queroit son mal et sa honte;
et Jehans el solier remonte.   200
Et dame Yfame l'uis li oevre,
qui molt fu dolente de l'uevre,
mes fere li estuet par force.
Et cil entre carchiez el porce,
les deniers mist jus qu'il portoit.   205
Et Jehans, qui la sus estoit,
par la treillie le porlingne,
felonessement le rechingne;
aval descent tout coiement.
Et cil embraça esraument   210
celi por avoir son delit,
si l'abati en un biau lit.
Jehans le vit, molt l'en pesa.
De la maçue qui pesa
le fiert tel cop en la caboce,   215
ce ne fu pas por lever boce,
ainz esmie quanqu'il ataint!
Cil fu mors, la face li taint,
quar la mort l'angoisse et sousprent.
Et sire Jehans le reprent,   220
si le va porter avoec l'autre,
puis a dit: "Or estes vous autre!
Je ne sai s'il vous apartient,
mes miex vaut compaignon que nient!"
Quant ot ce fet, si s'en retorne;   225
son afere molt bien atorne;
les deniers a mis en la huche.
    Ez vous le tiers prestre, qui huche
tout belement et tout souef.
Et Yfame reprent la clef,   230
maintenant l'uis li desferma;
et cil, qui folement ama,
entra en la meson carchiez.
Et sire Jehans est muciez
souz le degré et esconssez.   235
Et cil, qui cuide avoir son sez
de la dame, l'a embrachié
et sus un biau lit l'a couchié.
Jehans le vit, molt s'en corece;
la maçue qu'il tint adrece,   240
tel cop il done lez la temple
que toute la bouche li emple
de sanc et de cervele ensamble.
Cil cheï mors, li cors li tramble,

He hastily carried him into the yard
And at once straightened him up
Against the wall of his sheepfold,   195
And then he returned from the yard
And comforted Lady Yfame.
    Then the next priest knocked,
In search of his evil and his shame;
And John climbed back up into the loft.   200
Lady Yfame opened the door for him
Feeling very miserable about the business,
But she was forced to go through with it.
And he, loaded down, entered the door,
And put down the money he was carrying.   205
John, who was up above,
Kept his eye on him through the railing.
He snarled at him wickedly,
Then came down very quietly.
The other man immediately embraced   210
Her to have his pleasure
And threw her down on a fine bed.
John saw him; it upset him very much.
With the heavy club
He dealt him such a blow in the head   215
That it was not to raise a bump,
But shattered whatever it touched!
The man was dead; his face changed color,
Because death tormented and overtook him.
Then Master John took him up again   220
And went to carry him near the other one,
Saying, "Here's another!
I don't know if he belongs to you,
But a companion is better than nothing!"
When he had done this, he returned;   225
His business was turning out very well;
He put the money in the bin.
    Then came the third priest, who knocked
Very nicely and very softly.
Yfame took the key again.   230
She opened the door immediately;
And he, who was madly in love with her,
Came into the house loaded down.
Master John stayed hidden
And concealed underneath the steps,   235
And the other, who expected to get his satisfaction
With the lady, embraced her
And laid her down on the fine bed.
John saw it and was very angry about it;
He lifted the club he held   240
And gave him such a blow on the temple
That his whole mouth filled
With blood and brains together.
He fell over dead; his body quivered

quar la mort l'angoisse et destraint.   245
Et sire Jehans le restraint,
maintenant le prestre remporte,
si le dreça delez la porte:
Quant ce ot fet, si s'en revient.
    Or sai je bien qu'il me covient   250
dire par quel reson Jehans,
qui molt ot cele nuit d'ahans,
remist les .II. prestres ensamble.
Se ne le vous di, ce me samble,
li fabliaus seroit corrompus.   255
Jehans fust a mal cul apus,
ne fust uns sien niez, Estormis,
qui adonc li fu bons amis,
si com vous orrez el fablel.
    Yfame ne fu mie bel   260
de l'afere, mes molt dolante.
"Se je savoie ou mes niez hante,"
fet Jehans, "je l'iroie querre.
Il m'aideroit bien a conquerre
a delivrer de cest fardel,   265
mes je cuit qu'il est au bordel."
"Non est, biaus Sire," fet sa niece,
"encor n'a mie molt grand piece
que je le vi en la taverne
la devant chies dame Hodierne."   270
"Ha!" fet Jehans, "por saint Grigore,
va savoir s'il i est encore."
Cele s'en torne molt corcie;
por miex corre s'est escorcie.
A l'ostel vient, si escoutoit   275
se son frere leenz estoit.
Quant el l'ot, les degrez monta;
delez son frere s'acosta,
qui getoit les dez desouz main.
Ne li vint mie bien a main   280
la cheance, quar il perdi.
A poi que tout ne porfendi
de son poing trestoute la table!
Voirs est, c'est chose veritable,
qui ne m'en croit demant autrui,   285
que cil a sovent grant anui
qui jeu de dez veut maintenir.
Mes ne vueil mie plus tenir
ceste parole, ainçois vueil dire
de celi qui son frere tire,   290
qui de li ne se donoit garde.
    Estormis sa seror regarde,
puis li demande d'ont el vient:
"Frere," fet ele, "il vous covient
parler a moi par ça desouz."   295
"Par foi, je n'irai mie sous,

12

Because death tormented and gripped him.   245
Master John grabbed on to him;
Then he carried the priest
Over and set him beside the door:
When he had done this, he came back.
 Now I know very well   250
That I should tell how John,
Who had a lot of work that night,
Got rid of the two priests together.
If I don't tell you, it seems to me
That the fabliau would be deficient.   255
John would have been in a bad fix
If it hadn't been for his nephew, Estormi,
Who was a good friend of his then,
As you will hear in the story.
 Yfame was not at all pleased   260
With the business, but was very unhappy.
"If I knew where my nephew was hanging out,"
Said John, "I would go look for him;
He would help me arrange
To get rid of this burden,   265
But I think he's at the whorehouse."
"No, he isn't, good lord," his niece said.
"Just a little while ago
I saw him at the tavern,
Over at Lady Hodierne's establishment."   270
"Ha!" said John, "by Saint Gregory,
Go find out if he's still there!"
She left in a great hurry;
She strained to run as well as she could.
She came to the house and listened   275
To hear if her brother was inside.
When she heard him, she went up the steps;
She walked over to her brother,
Who was throwing dice underhanded.
Luck wasn't coming to his hand,   280
Because he was losing.
It's a wonder he didn't break
The whole table with his fist!
This is true; it's a veritable fact.
Whoever doesn't believe me should ask someone else,   285
Because whoever wants to keep up a game of dice
Often has great distress.
But I don't want to continue
This discourse any more; instead, I want to tell
About the woman, who was tugging at her brother,   290
Who was not paying any attention to her.
 Estormi looked at his sister,
Then asked her where she had come from:
"Brother," she said, "you must
Speak to me over there downstairs."   295
"By faith, I won't go down,

13

que je doi ja ceenz .V. saus."
"Tesiez vous, que bien seront saus,
que je les paierai molt bien.
Biaus ostes, dites moi combien   300
mes freres doit ceenz par tout."
".V. saus." "Vez ci gage por tout:
je vous en lerai mon sorcot.
A il bien paié son escot?"
"Oïl, bien avez dit reson."   305
Atant issent de la meson.
Li vallés a non Estormis,
atant s'est a la voie mis.
Estormis sa seror demande
se c'est ses oncles qui le mande.   310
"Oïl, biaus frere, a grant besoing."
        Li osteus ne fu mie loing;
a l'uis vienent, enz sont entré,
et quant Jehans a encontré
son neveu, molt grant joie en fet.   315
"Dites moi qui vous a mesfet,
por le cul Dieu," fet Estormis.
"Je te conterai, biaus amis,"
fet sire Jehans, "tout le voir.
Uns prestres par son mal savoir   320
vint dame Yfamain engingnier;
et je le cuidai mehaingnier;
si l'ai ocis; ce poise mi.
Se cil le sevent d'entor mi,
je serai mors isnel le pas."   325
"Ja ne me mandiiez vous pas,"
fet Estormis, "en vo richece,
mes ja ne lerai por perece,
par le cul Dieu," fet Estormis,
"puis que tant m'en sui entremis,   330
que vous n'en soiez delivrez.
Fetes tost, un sac m'aportez,
quar il en est huimés bien eure!"
Et sire Jehans ne demeure,
ainz li a le sac aporté.   335
Au prestre, qu'il ot acosté,
d'une part son neveu enmaine;
mes ainçois orent molt grand paine
qu'il li fust levez sor le col.
Estormis en jure saint Pol   340
qu'ainz ne tint si pesant fardel.
Ses oncles li baille un havel
et use pele por couvrir.
Cil s'en vait, s'a fet l'uis ouvrir,
qui ne demanda pas lanterne.   345
Parmi une fausse posterne
vait Estormis, qui le fais porte:
ne veut pas aler par la porte.

Since I owe five sous in here."
"Keep quiet for they will be satisfied,
Because I will pay them very well.
Good host, tell me how much   300
In all my brother owes you here."
"Five sous." "Here is a pledge note for all of it.
I'll leave you my jacket for it.
Now has he paid his bill?"
"Yes, you've really spoken rightly."   305
Finally they left the house.
The young man who was named Estormi
Set out on the road.
Estormi asked his sister
If it was his uncle sending for him.   310
"Yes, good brother, he is in great need."
    The house wasn't far off;
They came to the door and went in,
And when John met
His nephew, he was very happy.   315
"Tell me who has done you wrong,
By God's ass," said Estormi.
"Good friend," said Master John,
"I'll tell you the whole truth.
A priest with evil intentions   320
Came to seduce Lady Yfame;
And I only meant to hurt him;
But I killed him; this distresses me.
If the people in my neighborhood find out about it,
I'll be dead in an instant."   325
"You never used to send for me,"
Said Estormi, "when you were rich,
But by God's ass," said Estormi,
"Since I'm this far into it
I won't, out of laziness, allow   330
You not to be freed from him.
Bring me a sack at once,
Because it's still pretty early!"
Master John did not wait,
But brought him the sack.   335
He took his nephew over
To the priest, whom he had propped up;
But they had a lot of trouble
Getting him lifted to Estormi's neck.
Estormi swore by Saint Paul   340
That he had never held such a heavy weight.
His uncle handed him a pick
And a shovel for covering over.
Without even asking for a lantern,
He started out and got the door opened.   345
Through a small door in the back,
Went Estormi, carrying his load.
He didn't want to go through the front door.

15

Et quant il est aus chans venus,
si a le prestre geté jus; 350
el fons d'un fosse fet la fossé.
Celui, qui ot la pance grosse,
enfuet, et puis si l'a couvert.
Son pic et sa pele rahert,
et son sac; atant s'en repere. 355
    Et Jehans ot si son afere
atiré qu'il ot l'autre prestre
remis et el lieu et en l'estre
dont cil avoit esté getez
qui enfouir estoit portez: 360
bien fu parfont en terre mis.
Atant est venuz Estormis
a l'uis, et il li est ouvers.
"Bien est enfouiz et couvers,"
fet Estormis, "li dans prelas." 365
"Biaus niez, ainz me puis clamer las,"
Fet Jehans, "qu'il est revenuz!
Jamés ne serai secoruz
que je ne soie pris et mors."
"Dont il a le[s] deable[s] el cors, 370
qui l'ont raporté ça dedenz!
Et s'il i en avoit .II. cenz,
si les enforrai je ainz le jor!"
A cest mot a pris son retor,
son pic et son sac et sa pele, 375
puis a dit: "Ainz mes n'avint tele
aventure en trestout cest monde.
A foi, dame Diex me confonde
se j'enfouir ne le revois!
Je seroie coars renois 380
se mon oncle honir lessoie!"
Atant vers le prestre s'avoie,
qui molt estoit lais et hideus;
et cil, qui n'ert pas peüreus
nient plus que s'il ert toz de fer, 385
li dist: "De par toz ceus d'enfer
soiez vous ore revenuz!
Bien estes en enfer connuz
quant il vous ont ci raporté!"
Atant a le prestre acosté, 390
si l'en porte, a tout lui s'en cort
parmi le sentier de la cort;
ne le veut mie metre el sac.
Estormis sovent en somac
le regarde, si le ramposne: 395
"Restiiez ore por la dosne
revenuz si novelement?
Ja por nul espoentement
ne lerai que ne vous enfueche."
Atant de la haie s'aprueche, 400

16

When he came to the fields,
He threw the priest down;   350
He dug the grave at the bottom of a ditch,
Buried the fat-bellied fellow,
And then covered him over.
He grabbed his pick and his shovel
And his sack again; then he went back.   355
    John had managed his affairs in such a way
That he had the other priest
Set down in the same place and position
From which the other one had been removed
Who had been carried out for burial: 360
He had been put very deep into the ground.
Then Estormi came to the door,
And it was opened for him.
"The lord prelate is buried
And covered up," said Estormi.   365
"Good nephew, look how unlucky I am,"
Said John, "because he's come back!
I'll never be saved
From being caught and killed."
This body is possessed   370
By devils, who brought it back!
But if there were two hundred of them,
I would bury them before daybreak!"
At these words, once again he took
His pick, his sack, and his shovel.   375
Then he said, "Never before did anything
So strange happen to me in the whole world.
In faith, may the Lord God destroy me
If I don't go back and bury him again!
I'd be a renegade coward   380
If I left my uncle to be shamed!"
Then he headed toward the priest,
Who was very ugly and hideous;
And he who was no more frightened
Than if he'd been made all out of iron,   385
Said to him, "Go ahead
And rejoin all the people of Hell!
You must be well-known in Hell,
Since they brought you back here!"
Finally he got the priest up   390
And carried him out. With all his strength
He ran down the path of the yard.
He didn't trust putting him in the sack.
Estormi often looked sideways
At him, and he jeered at him: 395
"Is it because of the lady
You've come again?
No amount of fear
Will ever make me give up burying you."
At last he reached the hedge.   400

celui qu'il portoit i apuie;
sovent garde qu'il ne s'en fuie.
La fosse a fete molt parfonde,
le prestre prent, dedenz l'afonde,
si lons comme il estoit, le couche,   405
puis li a les iex et la bouche
et le cors tout couvert de terre;
puis jure les sainz d'Engleterre,
ceus de France et ceus de Bretaingne,
que molt avera grant engaingne   410
se li prestres revient huimés.
Mes de cestui est il bien pes,
que il ne porra revenir!
Mes du tiers soit au convenir,
que il trovera ja tout prest,   415
mestier li est qu'il se r'aprest,
quar on li jue de bondie.
      Or est resons que je vous die
de Jehan, qui mist, c'est la voire,
el lieu le daarain provoire   420
ou li autre dui furent pris
qui ja erent fors du porpris
enfoui par lor grant mesfet.
Et, tantost qu'Estormis ot fet,
a son ostel est reperiez.   425
"He! Las! Com je sui traveilliez,"
fet Estormis, "et eschaufez!
Molt estoit cras et esfossez
li prestres que j'ai enfoui;
molt longuement i ai foui   430
por lui metre plus en parfont.
Se deable ne le refont
revenir, ja ne revendra."
Et Jehans dist ja ne verra
l'eure qu'il en soit delivrez: 435
"J'en serai a honte livrez
ainz demain a l'avesprement."
Estormis li respont: "Comment
serez vous livrez a tel honte?"
"Ha! biaus douz niez, ci n'a nul conte   440
que je ne soie en grant peril.
Revenuz est en no cortil
li prestres que vous enportastes."
"Par foi, onques puis ne parlastes,"
fet Estormis, "que vous mentistes,   445
quar orainz a voz iex veistes
que je l'enportai a mon col:
je n'en croiroie pas saint Pol,
oncles, que vous deïssiez voir."
"Ha! biaus douz niez, venez veoir   450
le prestre qui revenuz est."
"Par foi, tierce foie droiz est!

He leaned the man he was carrying up against it.
He kept looking at him to make sure he didn't run away.
He made the grave very deep,
Took the priest, put him deep in it,
Laid him down lengthwise,   405
Then covered the eyes and the mouth
And the body completely with dirt;
Then he swore by the saints of England,
France, and Brittany
That he would be very much deceived   410
If the priest came back today.
He was sure about this one.
He wouldn't be coming back!
But as for the third,
Which he would find nearby,   415
He would have to be prepared,
Because they were playing him for a fool.
     Now I must tell you
About John, who put (this is the truth)
The last priest in place,   420
Where the other two had been taken,
Who were now outside the fenced-in yard,
Buried, because of their great misdeed.
And as soon as Estormi had finished,
He went back to his house.   425
"Ha! Oof! How overworked
And heated up I feel," said Estormi.
"The priest I buried
Was very fat and stout;
I had to dig for a long time   430
To get him in deeper.
Unless devils make him
Come back, he never will.
John replied that he would never see
The hour when he would be free of this!   435
"I will be delivered up to shame
Before tomorrow evening."
Estormi answered: "Why
Should you be delivered to shame?"
"Ha! Dear, good nephew, there is no doubt   440
But that I am in great danger.
The priest you carried out
Has come back into our yard."
"By faith, then, you never did say anything
Without lying," said Estormi,   445
"Because just now with your own eyes you saw
Me carry him out on my neck:
Uncle, I wouldn't even believe Saint Paul
If he said you were telling the truth."
"Ha! Dear nephew, come look   450
At the priest, who has come back."
"In faith, this is actually the third time!

19

Ne m'i leront a nuit mengier!
Par foi, bien se cuide vengier
li deables qui le raporte;   455
mes de rien ne me desconforte,
Ne pris .II. oes lor granz merveilles!"
Au prestre vint; par les oreilles
l'aert, et puis par le goitron;
puis en a juré le poistron   460
que le provoire renforra,
ne ja por ce ne remaindra,
s'il a les deables el ventre.
A cest mot en grant paine rentre
Estormis, qui le prestre encarche.   465
Sovent va maudissant sa carche;
n'en puet mes, quar forment li grieve.
"Par le cuer Dieu, cis fais me crieve,"
fet Estormis, "je m'en demet!"
Atant a la terre le met,   470
que plus avant ne le porta.
Delez une saus acosta
le prestre, qui ert cras et gros;
mes ainçois li sua li cors
que il eüst sa fosse fete.   475
Et, quant il l'ot molt bien parfete,
au prestre vint, et si l'embrace.
Cil fu granz, et Estormis glace:
En la fosse chieent anduit.
"Par foi, or ai je mon pain cuit,"   480
fet Estormis, qui fu desous.
"Las! Or morrai je ci toz sous,
quar je sui ci en grant destrece."
Et la mains au prestre radrece,
qui del bort de la fosse eschape,   485
puis li a doné tel soupape,
por poi les denz ne li esmie.
"Vois, por le cul sainte Marie,"
fet Estormis, "je suis matez!
Cist prestres est resuscitez!   490
Com m'a ore doné bon frap!
Je ne cuit que mes li eschap,
que trop me foule et trop me mate."
Atant l'aert par la gargate,
si le torne, et li prestres chiet.   495
"Par foi," fet il, "il vous meschiet!
Quant je sui deseure tornez,
malement serez atornez."
Atant est saillis a sa pele;
au prestre en a donee tele   500
qu'aussi la teste li esmie
com fust une pomme porrie.
Atant est de la fosse issus.
Celui, qui cras ert et fessus,

They won't let me eat tonight!
In faith, the devil who is bringing him back
Really thinks he's getting vengeance;   455
But I don't worry about anything,
And I don't give two eggs for their great miracles!"
He went to the priest and seized him by
The ears and by the throat;
Then he swore by his ass   460
That he would bury the priest again,
And he'd never stop, even
If he had a devil in his belly.
At that word Estormi came back in
Very painfully and hoisted the priest up.   465
He went cursing his burden;
He couldn't help it, because it grieved him greatly:
"By God's heart this load is killing me,"
Said Estormi; "I give up!"
At that he put him down   470
Because he couldn't carry him any farther.
He set up the priest, who was fat and big,
Beside a willow tree;
But his body was sweating
Before he had finished the grave.   475
And when he had completed it,
He came to the priest and took him in his arms.
This one was big, and Estormi slipped.
Both of them fell into the grave.
"In faith, now my goose is cooked,"   480
Said Estormi, who was underneath;
"Alas! Now I shall die here all alone,
For I am in deep trouble here."
And the priest's hand straightened out
And slipped from the edge of the grave   485
And gave him such a whack
That his teeth almost shattered.
"Look, by Saint Mary's ass,"
Said Estormi, "I'm killed!
This priest has come back to life!   490
What a big blow he gave me just now!
I don't think I'll ever get away from him,
Because he is crowding me and beating me too much."
Then he grabbed him by the throat
And turned him, and the priest fell.   495
"In faith," said he, "it's too bad for you!
When I've gotten back on the top,
You'll get yours then!"
Finally he jumped up to get his shovel;
He gave the priest such a good one   500
That it shattered his head
Like a rotten apple.
Then he climbed out of the grave.
He covered all over with dirt

a tout de terre acouveté; 505
assez a sailli et hurté
por la terre sor lui couchier.
Puis jure le cors saint Richier
que il ne set que ce puet estre
se li prestres revient en l'estre; 510
ja n'ert mes enfouiz par lui,
quar trop li a fet grant anui.
Ce dist, puis s'en vait a cest mot.
    N'ot gueres alé quant il ot
un prestre devant lui aler, 515
qui de ses matines chanter
venoit par sa male aventure;
par devant une devanture
d'une meson est trespassez.
Estormis, qui molt fu lassez, 520
le regarda a la grant chape:
"Vois," fet il, "cil prestres m'eschape!
Par le cul Dieu, il s'en reva!
Qu'est ce, sire prestres? Diva,
me volez vous plus traveillier? 525
Longuement m'avez fet veillier,
mes certes noient ne vous vaut."
Dont hauce ce havel en haut,
le prestre fiert si lez l'oreille
que ce fust une grant merveille 530
se li prestres fust eschapez,
quar il fu du havel frapez
que la cervele en cheï jus.
"Ha!" fet il, "Trahitres parjurs,
com m'avez fet anuit de honte!" 535
Que vous feroie plus lonc conte?
Estormis le prestre reporte
par une bresche lez la parte,
si l'enfuet en une marliere.
Trestout en si fete maniere 540
fist Estormis com j'ai conté,
et, quant il (l')ot acouveté
le prestre, si repere atant.
Du revenir se va hastant,
por ce que li jors apparoit. 545
    Jehans estoit a la paroit
dedenz sa meson apuiez.
"Diex," fet il, "quant ventra mes niez?
Molt sui engranz que je le voie."
Estes vous celui par la voie 550
que molt ot eü de torment;
a l'uis vient, et cil esraument
li ouvri l'uis, et si le baise,
puis li dist: "Molt dout la malaise
que vous avez eü por mi. 555
Mort vous ai trové bon ami

The man, who was fat and big in the rump.   505
He jumped and beat the earth a lot
To lay it down on the top of him.
Then he swore by Saint Richier's body
That he did not know what would happen
If the priest came back to the house;   510
He would never more be buried by him,
Because he had given him too much trouble.
He said this; then he left with that word.
He had scarcely left when he heard
A priest walking in front of him,   515
Coming from singing
His Matins, through his own bad luck;
He passed by
In front of the house.
Estormi, who was very tired,   520
Looked at him in his great cloak:
"Look," he said, "this priest is getting away from me!
By God's ass, he's going back!
What is this, Sir Priest? Look here,
Do you want to keep on making me work?   525
You've kept me awake for a long time,
But it certainly won't do you any good."
Then he lifted the pick on high.
He struck the priest so hard beside the ear
That it would have been a great wonder   530
If the priest had escaped,
Because he was struck with the pick
So that his brains poured down.
"Ha!" said Estormi, "perjured traitor,
What shame you have done me tonight!"   535
Why should I make the story longer for you?
Estormi carried the priest back
To a gap in the hedge beside the door
And buried him in a marl pit.
Estormi did everything exactly   540
In the way that I have told,
And when he had covered up
The priest, then he went back.
He was in a hurry to return,
Because day was breaking.   545
        John was leaning by the wall
Inside his house.
"God," said he, "when will my nephew come?
I am very eager to see him."
Here he came down the road,   550
Having suffered a great deal of anguish.
He came to the door, and the other at once
Opened the door for him and kissed him.
Then John told him: "I greatly regret the trouble
You have had on account of me.   555
I have found you to be a good friend

anuit, foi que doi saint Amant.
Or pues bien fere ton commant
de mon cors et de mon chatel."
Dist Estormis: "Ainz n'oï tel!   560
N'ai soing de deniers ne d'avoir.
Mes, biaus oncles, dites moi voir
se li prestres est revenuz."
"Nenil! Bien [i] sui secoruz;
Jamés aperçuz n'en serai."   565
"Ha! Biaus oncles, je vous dirai
une bone chetiveté.
Quant j'oi le prestre acouveté,
or escoutez que il m'avint:
li prestres devant moi revint   570
quant je dui entrer en la vile;
eschaper me cuida par guile,
et je li donai du havel
si durement que le cervel
li fis espandre par la voie.   575
Atant le pris, si me ravoie
par la posterne la aval.
Si l'ai geté en contreval;
en une rasque l'ai bouté."
Et, quant Jehanz ot escouté   580
la reson que li dist ses niez,
si dist: "Bien en estes vengiez!"
Aprés dist bas tout coiement:
"Par foi, or va plus malement,
que cil n'i avoit riens mesfet;   585
mes teus compere le forfet
qui n'i a pas mort deservie.
A molt grant tort perdi la vie
li prestres qu'Estormis tua,
mes deables grant vertu a   590
de genz engingnier et sousprendre."
     Par les prestres vous vueil aprendre
que folie est de covoitier
autrui fame, ne acointier.
Ceste resons est bien aperte.   595
Cuidiez vous por nule poverte
que preude fame se descorge?
Nenil, ainz se leroit la gorge
soier a un trenchant rasoir
qu'ele feïst ja por avoir   600
chose dont ses sire eüst blasme.
Cil ne furent mie de basme
embaussemé a l'enfouir,
qui Yfame voudrent honir,
ainz furent paié a lor droit.   605
Cis fabliaus moustre en bon endroit,
qui enseigne a chascun provoire
que il se gardent bien de boire

Tonight, by the faith I owe Saint Amant.
Now you can indeed make your demands
On my body and on my property."
Estormi said, "I never heard of such a thing!   560
I don't care about money or goods.
But, dear Uncle, tell me truly
Whether the priest has come back."
"No, I really have been saved;
I will never be found out."   565
"Ha! Dear Uncle, I will tell you
A good piece of mischief.
When I had covered up the priest,
Now listen to what happened to me:
The priest came back in front of me   570
When I had to get back to town;
He intended to get away from me by trickery,
And I gave him one with the pick
So hard that I made
His brains flow out on the street.   575
Then I took him, and I went back
Down there by the back door.
And I threw him down;
I stuck him into a mud pit."
When John had heard   580
The account which his nephew gave him,
He said, "You are indeed avenged!"
Then he said (very low and quietly):
"In faith, now things are going worse,
Because this man hadn't done anything wrong here.   585
Someone is paying the penalty
Who has not deserved death for it.
Very unjustly did the priest
Whom Estormi killed lose his life.
The devil has a great talent   590
For tricking and trapping people."
    Through these priests, I would like to teach you
That it is folly to covet
Or woo somebody else's wife.
The reason for this is very clear.   595
Do you think that because of any poverty
A decent woman would forget her duties?
No! She would rather let her throat
Be cut with a sharp razor
Than ever to do for money   600
A thing that would bring shame to her lord.
Those men who tried to shame
Yfame were not embalmed
With balm at their burial,
But were paid as they deserved.   605
This fabliau teaches in the correct manner,
For it instructs every priest
To be careful not to drink

25

a tel hanap comme cil burent,
qui par lor fol sens ocis furent   610
et par lor grant maleürté:
vous avez molt bien escouté
comme il furent en terre mis.
    Au mengier s'assist Estormis;
assez but et assez menja.   615
Aprés mengier l'acompaingna
Jehans ses oncles a son bien;
mes je ne sai mie combien
il furent puissedi ensamble.
Mes on ne doit pas, ce me samble,   620
avoir, por nule povreté
son petit parent en viuté,
s'il n'est ou trahitres ou lerres;
que s'il est fols ou tremeleres,
il s'en retret au chief de foiz.   625
Vous avez oï mainte foiz
en cest fablel que Jehans fust,
se ses niez Estormis ne fust,
honiz entre lui et s'ancele.
Cest fablel fist Hues Piaucele.   630

From the same cup that these drank from,
Who were killed by their foolish wits   610
And by their great misfortune.
You have heard very well
How they were put into the ground.
    Estormi sat down to eat;
He ate and drank plenty.   615
After the meal, John, his uncle,
Kept him company for his own good;
I do not know how long
They were together after this day.
But one should not, it seems to me,   620
Because of any amount of poverty, leave
One's poor relation in misery
If he is not a traitor or a thief,
Because if he is given over to folly or dicing,
He gets it in the end.   625
You have heard many times
In this fabliau that,
If it had not been for his nephew Estormi,
John would have been shamed--he and his wife.
Hues Piaucele made this fabliau.   630

2.

Qui de biau dire s'entremet,
n'est pas merveille s'il i met
aucun biau mot selonc son sens.
   Il ot un jougleor a Sens
qui molt ert de povre riviere: 5
n'avoit pas sovent robe entiere,
mes molt sovent en la chemise
estoit au vent et a la bise.
De lui ne sai que je vous mente.
N'avoit pas sovent chaucemente   10
et quant a la foiz avenoit
que il uns solleres avoit
pertuisiez et deforetez,
molt i ert grande la clartez.
Sovent estoit sanz sa viele,   15
et sanz sorcot et sanz cotele;
ses chauces erent forment chieres.
De son col naissent les lanieres
et molt ert povres ses ators.
En la taverne ert ses retors,   20
et de la taverne au bordel;
a ces .II. porte le cembel.
Les dez et la taverne amoit,
tout son gaaing i despendoit,
toz jors voloit estre en la boule,   25
en la taverne ou en la houle.
Un vert chapelet en sa teste,
toz jors vousist que il fust feste:
molt desirroit le diemenche.
Onques n'ama noise ne tence,   30
en fole vie se maintint.
Or orrez ja com li avint.
    En fols pechiez mist son usage;
quant ot vescu tout son eage,
morir l'estut et trespasser.   35
Deables, qui ne puet cesser
des genz engingnier et sousprendre,
s'en vint au cors por l'ame prendre;
un mois ot fors d'enfer esté,
ainz n'avoit ame conquesté.   40

28

SAINT PETER AND THE JONGLEUR

2.

If anyone sets out to say something fine,
It is no wonder if he puts into it
Any fine word that suits his meaning.
    There was a jongleur at Sens
Who was in a very poor way: 5
He usually didn't have a whole garment,
But often in his shirt he stood
In the wind and in the breeze.
I'm not going to tell you any lies about him.
He rarely had any shoes,   10
And when it happened once
That he did have a pair of shoes,
Riddled with holes and with the fur worn off,
The light that came through was very great.
Often he was without his fiddle,   15
And without a coat or a tunic;
He considered his britches very dear.
His garments hung tattered from his neck,
And he was ill-clad.
The tavern was his refuge   20
And from the tavern to the brothel,
In both of these he led a merry life.
He loved dice and the tavern
And spent all his earnings there.
He always wanted to be gaming   25
In the tavern or in the whorehouse.
With a green cap on his head,
He always wished it were a holiday.
He always wanted it to be Sunday;
He never loved noise or quarreling;   30
He maintained a foolish life.
Now hear what happened to him.
      He invested his time in foolish sin;
When he lived out his life,
He had to die and pass away.   35
The devil, who cannot stop
From tricking and catching people,
Came to the body to take the soul.
He had been out of Hell for a month,
But he had not won over a soul.   40

Quant vit le jougleor morir,
si en corut l'ame sesir;
por ce que morut en pechié,
ne li a on pas chalengié.
A son col le geta errant,   45
vers enfer s'en vint acorant.
Si compaignon par le païs
avoient molt de gent conquis:
li uns aporte champions,
l'autre prestres, l'autre larrons,   50
moines, evesques et abez,
et chevaliers et genz assez,
qui en pechié mortel estoient,
et en la fin pris i estoient.
Puis s'en reperent a enfer,   55
lor mestre truevent Lucifer.
Quant les voit venir si chargiez,
"Par ma foi," fet il, "bien veigniez!
Vous n'avez pas toz jors festé.
Cist seront ja mal ostelé."   60
En la chaudiere furent mis.
"Seignor," fet it, "il m'est avis,
a ce que je en ai veü,
que vous n'estes pas tuit venu."
"Si sommes, sire, fors uns seus,   65
uns chetiz, uns maleüreus,
qui ne set ames gaaignier,
ne ne set les genz engignier."
    Atant voient celui venir
qui aportoit tout par loisir   70
desor son col le jougleor,
qui molt estoit de povre ator.
En enfer est entrez toz nus.
Le jougleor a gete jus.
Li mestres si l'aresona,   75
"Vassal," dist il, "entendez ça,
fus tu ribaus, trahitre ou lere?"
"Nenil," fet il, "ainz fui jouglere.
Avoec moi ai trestout l'avoir
que li cors seut au siecle avoir.   80
Li cors souffri mainte froidure,
s'oï mainte parole dure;
or sui ça dedenz ostelez,
si chanterai se vous volez."
"De chanter n'avons nous que fere,   85
d'autre mestier vous covient trere;
mes, por ce que tu es si nus
et si tres povrement vestus,
feras le feu souz la chaudiere."
"Volentiers," fet il, "par saint Piere.   90
Quar de chaufer ai grant mestier."
Atant s'assist lez le fouier,

When he saw the jongleur die,
He ran to seize the soul.
Since the man had died in sin,
Nobody challenged him.
The devil threw it over his back right away   45
And went running toward Hell.
Throughout the country, his comrades
Had conquered many people:
One was carrying famous warriors;
Another, priests; another, thieves,   50
Monks, bishops, and abbots,
And knights and plenty of people
Who lived in a state of mortal sin
And in the end had been taken.
The devils all went back to Hell   55
And found their master, Lucifer.
When he saw them coming so loaded down,
He said, "By my faith, welcome!
You have not been on holiday all this time.
Those people will soon be badly lodged."   60
They were put into an oven.
"Lords," said Lucifer, "it seems to me,
From what I've seen,
That you haven't all come back."
"Yes, we have, sir, except for one--   65
A laggard, a wretch,
Who doesn't know how to get souls
And doesn't know how to trick people."
        Soon they saw him coming
Bringing along, in his own good time,   70
Upon his back the jongleur
Who was wretchedly dressed.
He walked into Hell completely naked
And threw the jongleur down.
The master spoke with the corpse in this manner: 75
"Vassal," he said, "listen here:
Were you a rascal, a traitor, or a thief?"
"No," said he, "I was a jongleur.
I have all I own with me
That I was used to having on earth.   80
My body has suffered from much cold,
And I have heard many a harsh word;
Now I am here, lodged inside,
And I will sing if you like."
"We don't have anything to do with singing here.   85
You're going to take on another job.
Since you're so naked
And poorly dressed,
You will build the fire underneath the oven."
"Gladly," said he, "by Saint Peter,   90
Because I really need to warm up."
Then he sat by the fireplace

31

si fet le feu delivrement
et chaufe tout a son talent.
    Un jor avint que li maufé   95
furent leenz tuit assamblé;
d'enfer issirent por conquerre
les ames par toute la terre.
Li mestres vint au jougleor,
qui le feu fist et nuit et jor.   100
"Jouglere," fet il, "or escoute!
Je te commant ma gent trestoute,
garde ces ames sor tes iex
quar je tes creveroie an .II.
S'une en perdoies toute seule,   105
je te pendroie par la gueule!
"Sire," dist il, "alez vous ent!
Je les garderai leaument,
trestout au miex com je porrai,
toutes voz ames vous rendrai."   110
"Et je sor tant le te recroi,
mes ce saches tu bien en foi:
se une seule en desmanoies,
que trestoz vis mengiez seroies."
Atant s'en vont, et cil remaint,   115
qui du feu fere ne se faint.
    Or vous dirai comme il avint
au jougleor que enfer tint,
et com sainz Pieres esploita.
Droitement en enfer entra;   120
molt estoit bien appareilliez;
barbe ot noire, grenons trechiez.
En enfer est toz seus entrez;
un berlenc apporte et .III. dez,
delez le jougleor s'assist   125
tout coiement, et se li dist,
"Amis," fet il, "veus tu jouer?
Vois quel berlenc por haseter!
Et s'ai .III. dez qui sont plenier.
Tu pues bien a moi gaaingnier   130
bons esterlins priveement."
Lors li moustre delivrement
la borse ou li esterlin sont.
"Sire," li jougleres respont,
"Je vous jur Dieu, tout sanz faintise,   135
que n'ai el mont fors ma chemise.
Sire, por Dieu, alez vous ent!
Certes, je n'ai goute d'argent."
Dist sains Pieres: "Biauz dous amis,
met de ces ames .V. ou .VI."   140
"Sire," fet il, "je n'oseroie,
quar se une seule en perdoie,
mon mestre me ledengeroit
et trestout vif me mengeroit."

And quickly made the fire
And got as warm as he pleased.
    One day it happened that the devils   95
Had all gathered together outside.
They swarmed out of Hell to conquer
Souls all over the earth.
The master came to the jongleur,
Who tended the fire night and day.   100
"Jongleur," he said, "listen now:
I put all my people in your hands.
Keep these souls before your eyes,
Or I will gouge them both out.
If you lose a single soul,   105
I'll hang you by the gullet!"
"Sir," he said, "go on and leave!
I'll guard them faithfully,
To the very best of my ability.
I will return every one of your souls to you."   110
"I'm trusting you with all of them,
But know this in faith:
If you lose a single one,
You'll be completely eaten alive."
Then they went off, and he who didn't mind   115
Making a fire remained.
    Now I will tell you what happened
To the jongleur who was keeping Hell
And how Saint Peter managed.
He walked straight into Hell.   120
He was very well-dressed;
He had black hair and his mustache was groomed;
All alone he entered Hell;
He carried a gaming board and three dice,
Sat beside the jongleur   125
Very quietly and said to him:
"Friend," said he, "do you want to play?
Look at what a good board this is for dicing!
And I have three dice which are regular and even.
You can really win from me   130
Good pounds sterling for yourself."
Then he showed him at once
The purse where the pounds were.
"Sir," the jongleur replied,
"I swear to you by God, without lying,   135
That I don't have anything in the world besides my shirt.
Sir, for God's sake, go away!
Really, I don't have a bit of money."
Saint Peter said, "My dear friend,
Throw in some of these souls, five or six."   140
"Sir," said he, "I wouldn't dare,
For if I lost just one,
My master would abuse me
And eat me alive."

Dist sains Pieres: "Qui li dira?   145
Ja por .XX. ames n'i parra;
voiz ci l'argent qui toz est fins:
gaaigne a moi ces esterlins
qui tuit sont forgié de novel.
Je te doins .XX. sous de fardel: 150
si met des ames au vaillant."
Quant cil vit qu'il i en ot tant,
les esterlins molt couvoita,
les dez prist, si les manoia,
a saint Piere dist a droiture: 155
"Juons or, soit en aventure
une ame au cop tout a eschars."
"Mes .II.," dist il, "trop est coars!
Et qui bon l'a, si l'envit d'une,
ne m'en chaut quele, ou blanche ou brune!"   160
Dist le jougleres: "Je l'otri."
Et dist sains Pieres, "Je l'envi."
"Devant le cop?" fet il, "Deable!
Metez donc l'argent sus la table."
"Volentiers," fet il, "en non Dieu."   165
Lors met les esterlins au gieu;
assis se sont au tremerel
lui et sains Pieres au fornel.
"Gete, jougleres!" dist sains Pieres,
"Quar tu as molt les mains manieres."   170
Ci gete aval, "Si com je cuit,
par foi," dist sains Pieres, "j'ai .VIII.;
se tu getes aprés hasart,
j'avrai .III. ames a ma part."
Cil gete .III. et .II. et as,   175
et dist sains Pieres: "Perdu l'as."
"Voire," dist il, "par saint Denis!
Ces .III. avant si vaillent .VI."
Et dist sains Pieres: "Jel creant."
Lors a geté de maintenant   180
.XII. poins a icele voie:
"Tu me dois .IX., or croist ma joie."
"Droiz est," dist il, "je l'ai perdu,
se je l'envi, tendras le tu?"
"Oïl," dist sains Pieres, "par foi."   185
"Ces .IX. avant que je te doi,
et .XVII. vaille qui qui l'ait."
"Dehait," fet sains Pieres, "qui l'ait!"
Dist li jougleres: "Or getez!"
"Volentiers," fet il, "esgardez!   190
Je voi hasart, si com je cuit:
tu me dois .III. et .X. et .VIII."
"Vois," dist il, "por la teste Dieu,
ce n'avint onques mes a gieu.
Par la foi que vous me devez,   195
jouez me vous de .IIII. dez?

34

Saint Peter said, "Who will tell him?   145
Just twenty souls will never be missed.
Look at this silver here, which is very pure.
Win from me these pounds,
Which are all recently coined.
I'm putting in an initial stake of twenty sous   150
And you put some souls in the pot."
When he saw that there was so much there,
He greatly coveted the pounds.
He took the dice, grasped them,
And said straight to Saint Peter: 155
"Let's play now! Let one soul be wagered,
Only one, no more."
"No, two," said he; "you're too timid!
Whoever feels like it can raise it one--
I don't care which, white or brown!"   160
The jongleur said, "I agree."
And Saint Peter said, I raise it!"
"Before the throw?" asked the jongleur, "What the devil!
Then put the money on the table."
"Gladly," he said, "in the name of God."   165
Then he put the pounds into the game.
They sat down at the game of dice,
He and Saint Peter, by the furnace.
"Throw, jongleur!" said Saint Peter,
"For you have very clever hands."   170
The other rolled the dice. "I believe,
In faith," said Saint Peter, "I have eight;
If you throw six next,
I will have three souls for me."
The other threw three and two and one,   175
And Saint Peter said, "You've lost."
"That's true," said he, "by Saint Denis!
With those three gone, let's play for six."
And Saint Peter said, "That's fine with me."
Then he threw straightaway   180
Twelve points for that turn:
"You owe me nine; now my joy increases."
"That's fair," said the jongleur; "I lost them.
If I raise the bet, will you stay in?"
"Yes," said Saint Peter, "in faith."   185
"Include these nine that I owe you,
And whoever gets it wins twelve."
"Damn whoever gets it!" said Saint Peter.
The jongleur said, "Now throw!"
"Gladly," he said, "look!   190
I see *hasard*, it seems to me:
You owe me three and ten and eight."
"Look," he said, "by God's head,
This never happened in a game before.
By the faith you owe me,   195
Are you playing me with four dice?

35

Ou vous me jouez de mespoins.
Or vueil je jouer a plus poins."
"Amis, de par le saint Espir,
toz tes voloirs vueil acomplir: 200
or, soit ainsi comme tu veus!
Veus tu a un cop ou a .II.?"
"A un cop, soit," fet il, "adés:
ces .XX. avant et .XX. aprés."
Et dist sains Pieres: "Dieux m'aït!"   205
Lors a geté sanz contredit,
.XVII. poins (giete) et si se vante
qu'il le fera valoir .XL.
Dist li jougleres: "C'est a droit!
Je get aprés vous orendroit."   210
Lors gete deseur le berlenc.
"Cis cops ne vaut pas un mellenc,"
dist sains Pieres; "perdu l'avez,
quar je voi quisnes en .III. dez.
Huimés n'ere je trop destrois: 215
vous me devez .XL. et .III."
"Voire," fet il, "par le cuer bieu,
je ne vi onques mes tel gieu.
Par toz les sainz qui sont a Romme,
je ne croiroie vous ne homme   220
que ne m'asseïssiez toz cops."
"Getez aval! Estes vous fols?"
"Je cuit vous fustes uns fors lerres,
quant encore estes si guilerres
qu'encor ne vous poez tenir   225
des dez chengier et asseïr."
Sains Pieres l'ot, si en ot ire,
Par mautalent li prist a dire:
"Vous i mentez, se Diex me saut;
mes c'est coustume de ribaut   230
quant on ne fet sa volenté,
si dist c'on li change le dé.
Molt a en toi mauvés bricon
quant tu me tenis por larron;
molt s'en faut poi, par saint Marcel,   235
que je ne vous oing le musel!"
"Certes," fet cil, qui de duel art,
"Lerres estes, sire viellart,
qui mon geu me volez noier.
Ja voir n'en porterez denier!   240
Ba! Non! Quar vous les me toudrez,
venez avant, si les prenez!"
Cil saut sus por les deniers prendre,
et sains Pieres, sanz plus atendre,
le vous aert par les illiers,   245
et cil lest cheoir les deniers,
qui molt avoit le cuer mari;
si l'a par la barbe saisi,

Either that or you're playing with loaded dice.
Now I want to play at *plus poins*."
"Friend, by the Holy Spirit,
I want to do your every wish:
Any way you want it!   200
Do you want to play with one roll or two?"
"Let it always be one:
Those twenty which you won and twenty more."
Saint Peter said, "May God help me!"
Then, without further arguments,   205
He threw seventeen points, and he bragged
That this would make him win forty.
The jongleur said, "It's my right!
I get to throw immediately after you."
Then he threw on the gaming board.   210
"This throw isn't worth a whiting,"
Saint Peter said; "you've lost it,
Because I see fives on three dice.
I'm not having very bad luck today:
You owe me forty-three."   215
"Truly," said he, "by Gosh,
I never saw such a game.
By all the saints in Rome,
I wouldn't believe you or any man who said
You didn't load the dice for all the throws."   220
"Throw them down! Are you crazy?"
"I think you've been a big thief,
Since you're still so tricky
That you can't keep
From changing and loading the dice."   225
Saint Peter heard him and was very angry about it.
He spoke up angrily:
"You're lying about this, so help me God;
But that's how it is with a rascal
When people don't do what he wants,   230
To say that someone is changing the dice.
You're a wicked fool
When you take me for a thief;
For very little, by Saint Marcel,
I would grease your nose!"   235
"Surely," said the other, who was burning with grief,
"You are a thief, Sir Old Man,
Wanting to destroy my game.
Truly, you aren't going to get out with a denier!   240
Bah, no! You'll have to take them away from me.
Come on and take them!"
He jumped up to take the coins,
And Saint Peter, without waiting any longer,
Grabbed him by the flanks,
And the other, with a very   245
Bitter heart, dropped the deniers;
Then he seized him by the beard

molt forment a lui le tira,
et sains Pieres li deschira   250
toz ses dras jusques el braiel.
Or n'ot il onques mes tel duel
qu'il ot quant il vit sa char nue
paroir jusques a la çainture
molt se sont entrechapingnié,   255
batu et feru et sachié.
Or voit le jouglere molt bien
que sa force ne li vaut rien,
qu'il n'est ne si fors ne si granz
com sains Pieres, ne si poissanz;   260
et s'il maintient plus la meslee
sa robe ert ja si deschiree
qu'il n'en porra joïr jamés.
"Sire," dist il, "or fesons pes.
Bien nous sommes entressaié,   265
or rejons par amistié,
se il vous plest et atalente."
Dist sains Pieres: "Molt m'est a ente
que vous de mon geu me blasmastes
ne que vous larron m'apelastes."   270
"Sire," fet il, "je dis folie,
or m'en repent, n'en doutez mie.
Mes vous m'avez fet pis assez
qui mes dras m'avez deschirez,
dont je serai molt soufretous.   275
Or me clamez cuite, et je vous."
Et dist sains Pieres: "Je l'otroi."
Atant se besierent en foi.
    "Amis," dist sains Piere[s]," entendez,
.XL. et .III. ames devez."   280
"Voire," fet il, "par saint Cermain,
je commençai le geu trop main.
Or rejovons, si biau vous vient,
si soient ou .III. tans ou nient,
se no geu revient en tel mes."   285
"Par Dieu," fet cil, "j'en sui toz pres!
Mes escoutez, biaus amis chiers,
paierez me vous volentiers?"
"Oïl," dist cil, "molt bonement,
trestout a vo commandement: 290
chevaliers, dames et chanoines,
larrons ou champions ou moines,
volez frans hommes ou vilains,
volez prestres ou chapelains?"
"Amis," fet il, "tu dis reson!"   295
"Or gete aval sanz traïson."
Sains Pieres n'ot a cele voie
fors .V. et .IIII. et un seul troie.
Dist li jougleres: ".XII. i voi."
"Avoi!" dist sains Pieres, "Avoi!   300

38

And pulled him fiercely to him
And Saint Peter tore   250
All his clothes down to his shorts.
Never had he greater sorrow
Than when he saw his naked flesh
Appear down to his belt.
They tore at each other for a long time,   255
Beat and struck and yanked.
Now the jongleur saw very well
That his strength was not worth a thing,
For he was neither as strong nor as big
Nor as powerful as Saint Peter;   260
And if he kept up the fight
His robe would be so torn apart
That he would never be able to enjoy it.
"Sir," he said, "now let's make peace.
We have struggled enough.   265
Now let's play like friends,
If that pleases and satisfies you."
Saint Peter said, "It really disgusts me
That you slandered my playing
And called me a thief."   270
"Sir," he said, "I spoke foolishly.
Now I repent it, have no doubt.
But you have done much worse to me
By tearing my clothes,
And I'll greatly suffer for it.   275
Now call it even, and so will I."
Saint Peter said, "I agree."
Then they kissed each other as a sign of faith.
    "Friend," said Saint Peter, "listen:
You owe me forty-three souls."   280
"True," said he; "by Saint Germain,
I began playing too early.
Let's play again now, if that seems good to you,
And let it be triple or nothing,
If our game comes down to that."   285
"By God," the other said, "I'm all ready!
But listen, dear, good friend,
Will you willingly pay me?"
"Yes," said he, "very agreeably,
All at your command: 290
Knights, ladies, or canons,
Thieves or famous warriors or monks--
Do you want yeomen or peasants?
Do you want priests or chaplains?"
"Friend," he said, "you're speaking reasonably!"   295
"Then throw without any tricks."
This time Saint Peter didn't get anything
Except five and four and a single three.
The jongleur said, "I see twelve there."
"Aiee!" said Saint Peter, "Aiee!   300

Se Jhesus n'a de moi merci,
cis daarains cops m'a honi."
Cil gete aval molt durement
quisnes en un deus seulement.
"Diex," dist sains Pieres, "bon encontre!   305
Encor vendra a cest rencontre."
"Or soit .XII. .XX., fiere ou faille,"
dist li jougleres, "bien les vaille,
getez, .XII. .XX. i ait bien,"
"Je get, de par saint Julien."   310
Sains Pieres gete isnel le pas
sisnes et puis un tout seul as.
Dist sains Pieres: "J'ai bien geté,
quar je vous ai d'un point passé."
"Vois," fet cil, "comme il m'a pres point   315
qu'il m'a passé d'un tout seul point.
Je ne fui ainc aventureus,
mes toz jors un maleüreus,
uns chetis, et uns mescheans,
et ci et au siecle toz tans."   320
Quant les ames qui sont el fu
ont ce oï et entendu
que sains Pieres a gaaignié,
de toutes pars li ont huchié:
"Sire, por Dieu le glorious,   325
nous atendons du tout a vous."
Et dist sains Pieres: "Je l'otroi,
et je a vous et vous a moi.
Mes, se j'eüsse tout perdu,
n'i eüssiez pas atendu;   330
se Dieu plest, ainz la nuit serie,
serez tuit en ma compaignie."
Ne sai que plus vous en deïsse,
ne que lonc plet vous en feïsse.
Tant a sains Pieres tremelé   335
et tant le jougleor mené
que les ames gaaigna toutes;
d'enfer les en maine a granz routes,
si les mena en paradis.
Et cil remest toz esbahis,   340
qui est dolenz et irascuz.
     Ez vous les maufez revenuz.
Quant li mestres fu en meson,
garda entor et environ,
ne vit ame n'avant, n'arriere,   345
ne en fornel, ne en chaudiere.
Le jougleor a apelé.
"Di va," fet il, "ou sont alé
les ames que je te lessai?"
"Sire," fet il, "jel vous dirai.   350
Por Dieu, aiez de moi merci!
Uns viellars vint orains a mi

If Jesus doesn't have mercy on me,
This last throw has ruined me."
The other threw them hard on the ground:
Only a pair of fives and a two.
"God," said Saint Peter, "what luck!   305
Something will still come from this tie."
"Now let's play for twenty-two, win or lose,"
Said the jongleur; "let it really be for them.
Throw! Let's play for twenty dozen."
"I'm throwing, by Saint Julien."   310
Saint Peter immediately threw
Sixes and then a single one.
Saint Peter said: "I have thrown well,
For I've beaten you by one point."
"See," he said, "how he has harassed me,   315
For he has beaten me by a single point.
I was never lucky,
Always an unlucky man,
A wretch and a failure,
Both here and in the world, all the time."   320
When the souls who were in the fire
Heard this and understood
That Saint Peter had won,
They shouted to him from all sides:
"Sir, by God the glorious,   325
In all things we put our hope in you!"
And Saint Peter said, "I grant it,
Both I in all of you, and you in me.
But if I had lost everything,
You would not have had any hope;   330
God willing, before the quiet time of the night,
You will all be in my company."
I do not know what more to tell you,
Nor do I want to make a long speech about this.
Saint Peter played the game so well   335
And handled the jongleur so well
That he won all the souls;
He led them out of Hell in great crowds,
Guiding them into Paradise.
And the other remained all downcast,   340
Grieved and angry.
          And then the devils came back.
When the master was in the house,
He looked up and down and around,
And did not see one soul in front or in back,   345
Or in the furnace or in the oven.
He called to the jongleur:
"Speak up," he said; "where have the souls
That I left with you gone?"
"Sir," he said, "I will tell you.   350
For God's sake, have mercy on me!
An old man came to me a while ago

41

si m'aporta molt grant avoir;
bien le cuidai trestout avoir,
si jouasmes et moi et lui,   355
molt me torna a grant anui.
"Filz a putain," fet il, "lechiere,
vo jouglerie m'est trop chiere!
Dehait qui vous i aporta!
Par mon chief il le comparra!"   360
A celui sont venu tout droit,
qui leenz aporté l'avoit;
tant l'ont batu, tant l'ont bouté,
que cil lor a acreanté
que li jamés a nis un jor   365
n'i aportera jougleor.
Dist li mestres au menestrel:
"Biaus amis, vuidiez mon ostel!
Mal dehez ait vo jouglerie,
quant j'ai perdu ma mesnie!   370
Alez a Dieu, je n'en ai cure!"
Et cil s'en va grant aleüre
que d'enfer chacent li tirant:
vers paradiz s'en vint errant.
Quant sains Pieres le vit venir,   375
se li corut la porte ouvrir;
richement le fist osteler,
or facent joie li jougler,
feste et solaz a lor talent,
quar ja d'enfer n'avront torment: 380
cil les en a treztoz getez,
qui les ames perdi aus dez.

And brought me a whole lot of money;
I really thought I could get it all
If he and I gambled. 355
It turned out very badly for me."
"Son of a whore," he said, "you debauchee,
Your juggling costs too much for me!
Damn whoever brought you here!
By my head, he'll pay for it!" 360
They then went straight to the devil
Who had brought him there.
They beat him so much and pushed him so much
That he promised them
That he would never on any day 365
Bring another jongleur there.
The master said to the minstrel:
"Good friend, get out of my house!
May your tricks be damned,
Since I have lost my household! 370
Go to God! I don't care!"
And the other left quickly,
For the devils were chasing him from Hell.
He went running toward Paradise.
When Saint Peter saw him coming, 375
He ran to open the door;
He had him richly lodged.
Now let all jongleurs rejoice,
Feast, and have pleasure as much as they please,
For they will not suffer pains in Hell: 380
The one who lost the souls at dice
Has gotten them all out of it.

DE SIRE HAIN ET DE DAME ANIEUSE

by

Hues Piaucele

3.

Hues Piaucele, qui trova
cest fablel, par reson prova
que cil qui a fame rubeste
est garnis de mauvese beste:
si le prueve par cest reclaim   5
d'Anieuse et de sire Hain.
Sire Hains savoit bon mestier,
quar il savoit bien rafetier
les coteles et les mantiaus.
Toz jors erent a chavestriaus   10
entre lui et dame Anieuse,
qui n'estoit pas trop volenteuse
de lui servir a son voloir,
quar quant li preudom veut avoir
poree, se li fesoit pois,   15
et si estoit tout seur son pois;
et quant il voloit pois mengier,
se li fesoit por engaignier
un poi de poree mal cuite.
Anieuse ert de mal porçuite   20
vers son seignor quanqu'ele pot
quar quant il voloit char en pot
dont li fesoit ele rostir
et toute en la cendre honir,
por ce qu'il n'en peüst gouster.   25
Se vous me volez escouter,
je vous dirai bon helemot:
riens ne vaut se chascuns ne m'ot,
quar cil pert molt bien l'auleluye
qui par un noiseus le desluie,   30
c'est por noient; n'i faudrai mie!
       Sire Hains a dit: "Douce amie,
alez me achater du poisson."
"Vous en aurez a grant foison,"
dist Anieuse, "par saint Cire.   35
Mes or me dites, biauz douz sire,

SIR HATE AND LADY HATEFUL

by

Hues Piaucele

3.

Hues Piaucele, who composed
This fabliau, proved by logic
That whoever has a cantankerous wife
Is furnished with a wicked beast.
And he proves it by this lesson   5
Of Lady Hateful and Sir Hate.
Sir Hate had a good trade,
For he knew how to repair
Dresses and coats.
There was always quarreling   10
Between him and Lady Hateful,
Who was not very willing
To serve him the way he wanted;
For when the gentleman wanted to have
Stewed vegetables, she'd fix peas for him,   15
And she just couldn't help it;
And when he wanted to eat peas,
As a trick she would fix him
A few stewed vegetables, badly cooked.
Hateful was plotting   20
Against her lord whenever she could,
For when he wanted meat in a pot,
Then she roasted it for him
And got it all dirty in the ashes,
So that he couldn't taste it.   25
If you listen to me,
I will tell you a good saying:
Nothing is worthwhile if no one hears me,
For a person loses credit
When he spoils it by quarreling.   30
Quarreling's futile; I won't make that mistake!
    Sir Hate said, "My dear girl,
Go and buy me some fish."
"You'll get plenty of them,"
Said Hateful, "by Saint Cyril;   35
But now tell me, fine sir,

45

se vous le volez d'eve douce."
Et cil, qui volentiers l'adouce,
li a dit: "Mes de mer, amie!"
Anieuse ne tarda mie,   40
qui molt fu plaine de mal art.
Au pont vient si trueve Guillart,
qui estoit ses cousins germains:
"Guillart," dist ele, "c'est du mains,
je vueil avoir des epinoches.   45
Mon mari, qui de males broches
ait crevez les iex de la teste,
demande poisson a areste."
Et cil, qui fu de male part,
li a tornees d'une part,   50
se li a mis en son platel;
puis les cuevre de son mantel,
en sa meson en vint tout troit.
Sire Hains, quant venir la voit,
li a dit: "Bien veigniez vous, dame;   55
foi que vous devez Notre Dame,
est ce raie, ou chien de mer?"
"L'en faut molt bien a son esmer!"
Fet Anieuse, "Sire Hain,
Volez vous lier vostre estrain,   60
qui me demandez tel viande?
Molt est ore fols qui demande
chose que l'en ne puet avoir:
vous savez bien trestout de voir
qu'il a anuit toute nuit plut: 65
toz li poissons de la hors put."
"Put!" fet sire Hains; "Dieu merci,
j'en vi ore porter par ci
de si bons dedenz un panier."
"Vous en porrez ja tant pledier,"   70
fet cele, qui le het de cuer,
"que je geterai ja tout puer.
Dehait qui le dit s'il nel fet!"
Les espinoches tout a fet
a semees aval la cort.   75
"Diex!" fet Hains, "Com tu me tiens cort!
A paines os je dire mot!
Grant honte ai quant mon voisin m'ot,
que tu me maines si viument."
"Ba! Si en prenez vengement,"   80
fet ele, "se vous l'osez fere."
"Tais toi, fame de put afere!"
Fet sire Hains, "lai moi ester!
Ne fust por ma chose haster
por aler au marchié demain,   85
tu le compraisses aparmain."
"Comperaisse!" fet Anieuse,
"Par mon chief, je vous en di beuse;

If you want them fresh-water fish."
And he who willingly soothed her
Told her, "No, salt-water fish, dear."
Hateful, who was full of wicked tricks   40
Did not delay.
She went to the bridge and found Guillart,
Who was her first cousin;
"Guillart," she said, "good morning!
I want to have some stickleback.   45
My husband (may the eyes in his head
Be pierced by evil needles)
Would like a fish with bones."
And he, who had a bad nature,
Prepared some for her   50
And put some on her plate.
Then she covered them with her coat
And went straight back to her house.
Sir Hate, when he saw her coming,
Said, "Welcome, lady,   55
By the faith you owe Our Lady,
Is it ray or is it dog-fish?"
"It isn't even near that quality!"
Hateful said; "Sir Hate,
Why don't you go tie your straws,   60
Asking me for such a meat!
A man's a fool who asks
For a thing that he can't have:
Indeed, you know very well
It rained all last night.   65
All the fish out there at sea stink."
"Stink!" said Sir Hate; "God have mercy,
Just now I saw some very good ones
Carried by here in a basket."
"You will soon be able to argue enough,"   70
Said she, who hated him from her heart,
"When I throw them all outside.
Curses on whoever says this if he doesn't do it!"
At that she suddenly scattered
The stickleback out into the yard.   75
"God!" said Hate, "how little you respect me!
I hardly dare say a word!
I'm terribly ashamed when my neighbor hears this,
Because you treat me so vilely."
"Bah! Then take vengeance for it,"   80
She said, "if you dare."
"Quiet, filthy woman!"
Said Sir Hate, "leave me alone!
If my affairs weren't pressing me
To go to market tomorrow,   85
You would pay for this right now."
"I would pay?" said Hateful;
"By my head, I say *poo* to that.

quant vos volez, si commenciez!"
Sire Hains fu molt corouciez.　　　　　　　　　　　　90
Un petitelet se porpensse;
aprés a dit ce que il pensse,
quant fu apoiez sor son coute.
"Anieuse," fet il, "ç'acoute:
il m'est avis, et si me samble,　　　　　　　　　　　95
que ja ne serons bien ensamble
se nous ne tornons a un chief."
"Or dites donques derechief,"
fet ele, "se vous l'osez fere,
a quel chief vous en volez trere."　　　　　　　　　100
"Oïl," fet il, "bien l'ose dire:
le matinet, sanz contredire,
voudrai mes braies deschaucier,
et enmi nostre cort couchier;
et qui conquerre les porra,　　　　　　　　　　　105
par bone reson mousterra
qu'il ert sire et dame du nostre."
"Je l'otroi bien, par saint Apostre,"
fet Anieuse, "de bon cuer!
Et se je les braies conquer,　　　　　　　　　　110
cui en trerai a tesmoignage?"
"Nous prendrons en nostre visnage
un homme que nous miex amon."
"Je l'otroi bien; prenons Symon,
et ma commere dame Aupais.　　　　　　　　　　115
Que qu'il aviegne de la pais,
cil dui garderont bien au droit.
Hucherai les je orendroit?"
"Diex!" fet Hains, "Com tu es hastiue!
Or cuides bien que ja soit tiue　　　　　　　　　　120
la baillie de no meson;
ainz auras de molt fort poison
beü, foi que doi saint Climent.
Molt va pres que je ne comment."
"Commencier!" fet dame Anieuse,　　　　　　　　　125
"Je sui assez plus covoiteuse
que vous n'estes del commencier.
Or n'i a fors que del huchier
noz voisins." "Certes ce n'a mon!"
"Sire Symon, sire Symon!　　　　　　　　　　130
Quar venez avant, biaus compere!
Et si amenez ma commere
s'orrez ce que nous volons dire."
"Je l'otroi bien sanz contredire,"
fet Symons debonerement.　　　　　　　　　　135
Adonc s'en vindrent eraument,
si s'assiëent l'un delez l'autre.
Sire Hains, l'un mot aprés l'autre,
lor a contee la reson
et descouverte l'achoison　　　　　　　　　　140

48

Whenever you want, then, go ahead."
Sir Hate was very angry.   90
He thought it over a little;
Then he said what he was thinking
As he leaned on his elbow.
"Hateful," he said, "listen to this:
I believe and it seems to me   95
That we never will be good together
If we don't agree on a household leader."
"Well, tell me now, right away,"
She said, "if you dare to,
What leader you want to choose."   100
"Yes," he said, "I do dare;
This morning, without contradiction
I will take off my britches
And lay them out in your yard,
And whoever can get them   105
Will show by good logic
That he will be lord and lady of our household."
"I grant it well, by the holy apostle,"
Said Hateful, "with a true heart.
And if I get the britches,   110
Whom shall I call as a witness?"
"We will get from our neighborhood
A man whom we love well."
"I grant it then; let's get Simon
And my gossip, Lady Peacewell;   115
Whatever comes of this pact,
These two will stick to what is right.
Shall I call them now?"
"God!" said Hate, "what a hurry you're in!
You must think the management   120
Of our house is already yours.
You're going to drink some very strong poison
First, by the faith I owe Saint Clement.
I'm about to start right now."
"Begin!" said Lady Hateful;   125
"I'm a good bit more eager
Than you are to begin it.
Now there is nothing to do but call
Our neighbors." "Certainly, let's get going!"
"Sir Simon, Sir Simon!   130
Come here, old friend!
And bring my old gossip too,
And listen to what we want to say."
"I will indeed without contradiction,"
Said Simon pleasantly.   135
Then they came running
And sat down, one beside the other.
Sir Hate, word for word,
Told them the argument
And revealed the reason   140

por qoi la bataille doit estre.
"Ha!" fet Symons, "Ce ne puet estre
que vous ainsi vous combatez!"
Anieuse dist: "Escoutez!
Li plais est pris en tel maniere   145
que nus n'en puet aler arriere.
Foi que doi au baron saint Leu,
je vueil que soiez en no leu;
si ferons que fere devons."
Dont primes a parlé Symons: 150
"Je ne vos porroie achoisier,
ne acorder, ne apesier,
ainz aurez esprové voz forces.
Or garde bien que tu ne porces,
Anieuse, se ton poing non.   155
Sire Hain, je vous di par non,
gardez bien que vous ne porciez
nule chose dont vous faciez
vo fame mal, fors de voz mains."
"Sire, si m'aït sainz Germains,"   160
fet sire Hains, "non ferai gié!
Mes or nous donez le congié
de no meslee commencier,
il n'i a fors del deschaucier
les braies dont la noise monte."   165
      Que vous feroie plus lonc conte?
Les braies furent deschauciés
et enz en mi la cort lanciés.
Chascuns s'apresta de combatre;
ja lor verra lor os debatre,   170
sire Symons, qui le parc garde.
Ainz que Hains s'en fust donez garde
le fiert Anieuse a plains braz.
"Vilains," dist ele, "je te haz;
or me garde ceste alemite."   175
"Ha!" dist Hains, "Tres orde traïtre,
m'es tu ja venue ferir?
Je ne porroie plus souffrir,
puisque tu m'as avant requis;
mes, si m'aït Sainz Esperis,   180
je te ferai male nuit trere."
"Par bieu, je ne vous doute guere,"
fet cele, "por vostre manace.
Puisque nous sommes en la place,
face chascuns du pis qu'il puet."   185
A cest mot sire Hains s'esmuet,
d'ire et de mautalent espris;
la cors fu granz et li porpris,
bien s'i pooit l'en retorner.
Et, quant cele vit atorner   190
son baron por li domagier,
onques ne se vout esmaier,

Why the battle had to be.
"Ha!" said Simon. "It cannot be
That you fight with each other like that!"
Hateful said, "Listen!
This quarrel has gone so far   145
That no one can go back.
By the faith I owe brave Saint Leu,
I want you to be here with us;
And we will do what we have to do."
Then Simon spoke first: 150
"I couldn't get you to agree
Or come to any accord or make peace
Before you've put your strengths to the test.
Now take care you don't strike,
Hateful, except with your fist.   155
Sir Hate, I say to you by name,
Be careful not to strike
With anything which will do
Harm to your wife, except your hands."
"Sir, so help me Saint Germain,"   160
Said Sir Hate, "I will not!
But now give us permission
To begin our free-for-all.
There's nothing to do except take off
The britches which are the cause of the quarrel."   165
      Why should I make the story longer for you?
The britches were taken off
And hurled into the middle of the yard.
Each of them got ready for combat;
Now Sir Simon, who was guarding the yard,   170
Would see them beat each other's bones.
Before Hate had gotten ready for it,
Hateful hit him with her full arms:
"Clod," she said, "I hate you.
Now keep that blow for me."   175
"Ha!" said Hate, "you stinking traitress,
Have you already come to strike me?
I couldn't hold back any more,
Since you got me first.
But so help me Holy Spirit,   180
I'll make you have a bad night."
"By Gosh, I'm not a bit worried,"
Said she, "about your threat.
Since we are on the spot,
Let each one inflict the worst he can."   185
At this word, Sir Hate got going,
Seized with anger and wrath;
The yard and the enclosure were big;
They could move around in it well.
And when she saw her husband   190
Getting ready to hit her,
She wasn't a bit dismayed,

ainz li cort sus a plain eslais.
Huimés devendra li jeus lais,
quar sire Hains sa fame ataint   195
si grant cop que trestout li taint
le cuir, sor le sorcil, en pers.
"Anieuse," dist il, "tu pers!
Or t'ai ta colee rendue."
Cele ne fu mie esperdue,   200
ainz li cort sus isnelement,
se li done hastivement
un cop par deseur le sorcil
qu'a poi que delez un bercil
ne l'abati trestout envers.   205
"Trop vous estiiez descouvers,"
fet Anieuse, "ceste part!"
Puis a esgardé d'autre part
s'a veü les braies gesir;
hastivement les cort sesir   210
si les lieve par le braioel.
Et li vileus par le tuiel
les empoigne par molt grant ire:
li uns sache, li autres tire;
la toile desront et despiece;   215
par la cort en gist maint piece;
par vive force jus les metent,
a la meslee se remetent.
Hains fiert sa fame enmi les denz
tel cop que la bouche dedenz   220
li a toute emplie de sanc.
"Tien ore," dist sire Hains, "anc!"
"Je cuit que je t'ai bien atainte.
Or t'ai je de .II. colors tainte!
J'aurai les braies toutes voies."   225
Dist Anieuse: "Ainz que tu voies
le jor de demain au matin,
chanteras tu d'autre martin,
que je ne te pris .II. mellenz.
Filz a putain, vilains pullenz,   230
me cuides tu avoir sorprise?"
A cest mot, de grant ire esprise,
le fiert Anieuse esraument:
li cops vint par grant mautalent
que dame Anieuse geta;   235
delez l'oreille l'acosta
que toute sa force i emploie.
A sire Hain l'eschine ploie,
quar del grant cop molt se detort.
"Vilains," dist ele, "tu as tort,   240
qui ne me lais les braies prendre."
Fet sire Hains: "Or puis aprendre
que tu ne m'espargnes noient!
Mes se par tens ne le te rent

52

But ran full tilt upon him.
Now the game would get ugly,
For Sir Hate dealt his wife   195
Such a blow that he completely dyed
Her skin above the eye a persian blue:
"Hateful," he said, "you're losing!
Now I've returned your blow."
She wasn't at a loss,   200
But ran upon him at once
And quickly gave him
A blow above the eyebrow
Which almost knocked him completely
Over beside the sheep-pen.   205
"You were too much off your guard,"
Said Hateful, "on that side!"
Then she looked in the other direction
And saw the britches lying there;
She ran in a hurry to grab them   210
And lift them by the belt.
And the peasant very angrily grabbed
Them with his fist by the pant leg.
One snatched, the other pulled;
The cloth ripped and fell apart;   215
Many a piece lay all over the yard;
With great force they tossed them around,
Throwing themselves into the melee again.
Hate struck such a blow
At his wife's teeth that the inside   220
Of her mouth filled up with blood.
"Take that," said Sir Hate. "Pow!"
I think I've gotten to you now.
I've painted you two colors!
I'll have the britches anyway."   225
Hateful replied, "Before you see
Daylight tomorrow morning,
You'll sing another song,
For I value you very little;
You son of a bitch, you stinking clod,   230
Do you think you've got me beat?"
With those words, seized with great anger,
Hateful swiftly struck him:
The blow came from the great spite
Which Lady Hateful struck with;   235
She hit him beside the ear,
And she used all her strength in it.
Sir Hate's backbone bent,
Because he was much twisted by the great blow.
"Clod," she said, "you are wrong   240
Not to let me take the britches."
Sir Hate said, "Now I can see
You don't spare me at all!
But if Sir Hate doesn't give

sire Hains, dont li faille Diex;   245
or croist a double tes granz diex,
quar je te tuerai ancui."
Anieuse respondi: "Qui
tuerez vous, sire vilains?
Se je vous puis tenir aus mains,   250
Je vous ferai en mon Dieu croire!
Vous ne me verrez ja recroire,
ainz morras ainçois que m'eschapes."
"Tien or ainçois ces .II. soupapes,"
fet sire Hains, "ainz que je muire;   255
je le te metrai molt bien cuire
se j'en puis venir au desus."
A cest mot se recorent sus
si s'entredonent molt granz caus.
Sire Hains fu hastis et chaus,   260
qui del ferir molt se coitoit;
n'en pot mes, quar molt le hastoit
Anieuse, qui pas nel doute:
des .II. poins si forment le boute
que sire Hains va chancelant.   265
Que vous iroie je contant?
Tout furent sanglent lor drapel,
quar maint cop et maint hatiplel
se sont doné par grant aïr.
Anieuse le cort sesir,   270
qui n'ert pas petit ne manche;
sire Hains au tor de la hanche
l'abat si durement sus coste
qu'a poi ne li brise une coste.
Cele chose forment li grieve;   275
mes Anieuse se relieve,
un petit s'est arriere traite.
Aupais le voit, si se deshaite,
qui le parc garde o son baron.
"Ha! Por Dieu," fet ele, "Symon,   280
quar parlons ore de la pes!"
[Et] dist Symon, "Lai moi en pes,
[si] t'ait or sains Bertremiex
[que] s'Anieuse en fust au miex,
que tu m'en priaisses aussi;   285
non feïsses, par saint Forsi.
Tu ne m'en priaisses a piece.
Or atent encore une piece,
tant que li uns le pis en ait,
autrement n'auront il ja fait: 290
souffrir te covient se tu veus."
Cil refurent ja par cheveus,
qui erent en molt grant destrece:
Hains tient sa fame par la trece,
et cele, qui de duel esprent,   295
son baron par les chevex prent.

It back to you soon, then God is failing him.   245
You'd better believe doubly in your great gods,
For I shall kill you now."
Hateful replied, "Whom
Will you kill, Sir Clod?
If I can get you in my hands,   250
I'll make you believe in my God!
You'll never see me give up.
Instead, you'll die before you escape."
"Then take these two blows to the chin first,"
Said Hate, "before I die;   255
I'll fix you up all right
If I can come out on top with this."
At this word they ran together
And gave each other very big blows.
Sir Hate, who was spurring himself on   260
To strike, was hot and hasty;
He couldn't do much though, because Hateful,
Who didn't fear him, was pressing him.
With her two fists she pushed him so hard
That Sir Hate went tottering.   265
Why should I go on with the story?
Their clothes were full of blood,
For many a blow and a slap
They gave each other in great anger.
Hateful, who was neither small   270
Nor crippled, ran to seize him.
Sir Hate, with a twist of his hip,
Hit her so hard on the side
That he almost broke one of her ribs.
This hurt her greatly;   275
But Hateful got up again.
Then she drew back a little way.
Peacewell, who was guarding the yard with
Her husband, saw her and was grieved.
"Ha! by God," she said, "Simon,   280
Now let's talk about peace!"
And Simon said, "Leave me in peace.
May Saint Bartimaeus help you,
Because if Hateful were doing better
You wouldn't be begging for peace.   285
You wouldn't do it, by Saint Forsi.
You weren't begging me for it a while ago.
Now wait a little while longer
Until one has the worst of it.
Otherwise they will never have this settled.   290
You must bear it if you will."
The others, who were in very great distress,
Had each other by the hair:
Hate held his wife by the tresses,
And she, who was burning with pain,   295
Took her husband by the hair

Si le sache que tout l'embronche.
Aupais le voit, en haut s'esfronche
por enhardir dame Anieuse.
Quant Symons a choisi s'espeuse   300
et l'esme qu'ele li a fete.
"Aupais," dist il, "tu es mesfete
a poi que ferir ne te vois.
Se tu fez plus oïr ta vois
des que li uns en soit au miex,   305
tu le comperras, par mes iex."
Cele se tut, qui le cremi.
    Tant ont feru et escremi
cil qui se combatent ensamble
que li contes dit, ce me samble,   310
qu'Anieuse le pis en ot;
quar sire Hains a force l'ot
reculee encontre une treille.
En coste avoit une corbeille;
Anieuse i cheï arriere,   315
quar a ses talons par derriere
estoit, si ne s'en donoit garde.
Et quant sire Hains la regarde,
s'en a un poi ris de mal cuer.
"Anieuse," fet il, "ma suer,   320
tu es el paradis Bertran;
or pues tu chanter de Tristran,
ou de plus longue, se tu sez!
Se je fusse autressi versez,
tu me tenisses ja molt cort."   325
Atant vers les braies s'en cort
si les prist et si les chauça.
Vers sa fame se radreça,
qui en la corbeille ert versee.
Malement l'eüst confessee,   330
ne fust Symons qui li escrie:
"Fui toi, musart, n'en tue mie!
Bien voi que tu es au desus.
Anieuse, veus en tu plus?"
Fet Symons, qui la va gabant.   335
"Bien a abatu ton beubant
sire Hains par ceste meslee:
seras tu mes si emparlee
com tu as esté jusqu'a ore?"
"Sire, foi que doi saint Grigoire,"   340
fet cele, "ne fusse hui lassee,
se je ne fusse ci versee;
mes or vous proi par amistez,
biaus sire, que vous m'en getez."
Fet Symons: "Ainz qu'isses issi,   345
fianceras orendroit ci
que tu jamés ne mesferas
et que en la merci seras

And pulled him so that she toppled him over.
Peacewell saw it and snorted loudly
To encourage Lady Hateful.
When Simon spied his wife   300
And the attempt she had made for her,
He said, "Peacewell, you have done wrong.
I am just about to beat you.
If you make your voice heard any more
When one of them gets an advantage,   305
You'll pay for it, by my eyes!"
She kept quiet because she feared him.
    Those who were holding combat together
Beat and clashed so much
That the story says, it seems to me,   310
That Hateful got the worst of it,
For Sir Hate had powerfully
Thrown her back against a trellis.
There was a basket alongside;
Hateful fell back into it,   315
Because she was turned back on her heels
And she didn't watch out for it.
And when Sir Hate looked at her,
He laughed a little with a spiteful heart:
"Hateful," he said, "my sister,   320
You are in the Paradise of Bertram;
Now you may sing of Tristan
Or a longer song if you know how.
If I were turned over like that,
You would soon grab hold of me."   325
Then he ran to the britches,
Took them on, and put them on.
He came back to his wife,
Who was sitting up-ended in the basket.
He would have given her a tough penance   330
If it hadn't been for Simon, who cried out:
"Get out of there, you bum! Don't do any killing!
I can see very well you have the upper hand.
Hateful, do you want any more?"
Said Simon, who went on teasing her;   335
"Sir Hate has really beaten down
Your pride by this free-for-all.
Will you be as talkative from now on
As you've been up till now?"
"Sir, by the faith I owe Saint Gregory,"   340
She said, "I would not be overcome now
If I weren't overturned here;
But now I beg you for the sake of friendship,
Good Lord, to get me out of this."
Simon said, "Before you get out of there,   345
You must guarantee here and now
That you will never misbehave,
And that you will be under the control

57

```
    sire Hain, a toz les jors mes,
    et que tu ne feras jamés                             350
    chose nule qu'il te desfenge."
    "Ba! Deable, et s'il me ledenge,"
    fet Anieuse, "ne cort seure,
    et j'en puis venir au deseure,
    ne me desfenderai je mie?"                           355
    "Escoute de ceste anemie,"
    fet Symons, "qu'ele a respondu,
    Aupais! En as tu entendu?"
    "Oïl voir, sire, bien l'entent!
    Anieuse, je te blastent                              360
    que tu respons si fetement,
    quar tu vois bien apertement
    que tu ne pues plus maintenant.
    Si te covient d'ore en avant
    fere del tout a son plesir,                          365
    quar de ci ne pues tu issir
    se par son commandement non."
    Anieuse respondi: "Non!
    Conseilliez moi que je ferai."
    "Par foi," dit Aupais, "non ferai,                   370
    que tu ne m'en croiroies mie."
    "Si ferai, bele douce amie:
    je m'en tendrai a vostre esgart."
    "Or t'estuet il, se Diex me gart,
    orendroit fiancier ta foi.                           375
    Je ne sai se ce ert en foi,
    mes toutes voies le feras,
    que tu ton baron serviras
    si com preude fame doit fere,
    ne jamés por nul mal afere                           380
    ne te dreceras contre lui."
    Anieuse dist sanz delui:
    "Par foi, bien le vueil creanter,
    por que je m'en puisse garder.
    Ainsi en vueil fere l'otroi."                        385
    A cest mot en risent tuit troi,
    sire Hains, Symons et Aupais.
    Toutes voies firent la pais,
    de la corbeille la geterent,
    et en meson la ramenerent:                           390
    molt sovent s'est clamee lasse.
    Mais Diex i mist tant de sa grace,
    que puis cele nuit en avant
    onques ne s'ala percevant
    sire Hains qu'el ne li feïst                         395
    trestout ce qu'il li requeïst:
    de lui servir s'avolentoit,
    et, por ce que les cops doutoit,
    nel desdisoit de nule chose.
    Si vous di bien a la parclose,                       400
```

Of Sir Hate forevermore,
And that you will never do
Anything that he forbids."   350
"Bah, the devil! If he abused me,"
Said Hateful, "or attacked me
And I could get the upper hand,
Couldn't I defend myself at all?"
"Listen to that fiend,"   355
Said Simon, "and what she has answered.
Peacewell! Did you hear any of that?"
"Yes, indeed, sir, I do hear it!
Hateful, I blame you
For answering that way,   360
Because you clearly see
There's nothing left for you to do now.
From now on you have to act
According to his pleasure,
Because you can't get out of here   365
Unless by his order."
Hateful replied, "No!
Advise me what to do."
"By faith," said Peacewell, "I will not,   370
Because you won't believe me."
"Yes, I will, dear sweet friend.
I will hold to your judgment."
"Then, as God may keep me, you must
Pledge your faith right now.   375
I don't know whether it will be in faith,
But anyway, you will do it;
For you will serve your lord
Just as a decent woman ought to do,
And never for any evil business   380
Will you stand against him."
Hateful said, without deceit,
"By faith, I really will guarantee it
So that I can get out of this.
In this way I will make the pact."   385
At this word all three laughed about it,
Sir Hate, Simon, and Peacewell.
Anyway, they made peace.
They dumped her out of the basket
And led her back into the house;   390
She kept crying out in misery.
But God put so much of His grace into this business
That from that night on
Sir Hate never did notice
That she would fail to do   395
Anything that he required:
She was very willing to serve him,
And since she feared the blows,
She never contradicted him in anything.
And I tell you at the end: 400

en fu a sire Hain molt bel.
    Ainz que je aie cest fablel
finé, vous di je bien en foi,
se voz fames mainent bufoi
deseur vous nul jor par male art,   405
que ne soiez pas si musart
que vous le souffrez longuement,
mes fetes aussi fetement
comme Hains fist de sa moillier   410
qui ainc ne le vout adaingnier,
fors tout le mains que ele pot,
dusques a tant que il li ot
batu et les os et l'eschine.
Tout issi cis fabliaus define.

Sir Hate liked it very much.
    Before I finish this
Fabliau, I tell you in good faith:
If your wives lord it proudly
Over you at any time in an evil way,   405
You should not be so lazy
As to endure it long,
But do exactly as
Hate did with his wife,
Who would not respect him before,   410
Except in the smallest way she could,
Until the time that he
Had beaten her on her bones and back.
Right here this fabliau ends.

4.

Molt bons lechierres fu Boivins.
Porpenssa soi que a Prouvins
a la foire voudra aler,
et si fera de lui parler.
Ainsi le fet com l'a empris: 5
Vestuz se fu d'un burel gris,
cote, et sorcot, et chape ensamble,
qui tout fu d'un, si com moi samble,
et si ot coiffe de borras.
Ses sollers ne sont mie a las,   10
ainz sont de vache dur et fort;
et cil, qui molt de barat sot,
un mois et plus estoit remese
sa barbe qu'ele ne fu rese,
un aguillon prist en sa main,   15
por ce que miex samblast vilain.
Une borse grant acheta,
.XII. deniers dedenz mis a,
que il n'avoit ne plus ne mains;
et vint en la rue aus putains   20
tout droit devant l'ostel Mabile,
qui plus savoit barat et guile
que fame nule qui i fust.
Iluec s'assist desus un fust
qui estoit delez sa meson.   25
Delez lui mist son aguillon,
un poi torna son dos vers l'uis.
Huimés orrez que il fist puis:
"Par foi," fet il, "ce est la voire,
puisque je sui hors de la foire   30
et en bon leu et loing de gent,
deüsse bien de mon argent
tout seul par moi savoir la somme.
Ainsi le font tuit li sage homme.
J'oi de Rouget .XXXIX. saus;   35
.XII. deniers en ot Giraus
qui mes .II. bues m'aida a vendre.
A males forches puist il pendre,
por ce qu'il retint mes deniers!
.XII. en retint li pautoniers,   40

BOIVIN FROM PROVINS

4.

Boivin was a jolly good fellow.
He decided he would go
To the fair at Provins
And there he would make a name for himself.
He did just as he had planned: 5
He was dressed in gray homespun,
Jacket and overcoat and cape together,
All in one piece, it seems to me,
And also he had a rough linen hood,
And his shoes were not shabby,   10
But were made of hard, strong cowhide;
And he, who knew much about trickery,
Left his beard alone for over
A month so that it was unshaven.
He carried a sharp stick in his hand   15
To seem more like a peasant.
He bought a large purse
And put twelve deniers inside it,
So that he had no more and no less;
And he came to the street of whores   20
Right in front of the house that belonged to Mabel,
Who knew more about trickery and guile
Than any woman who ever was.
There he sat down on a log
Which lay in front of her house.   25
He laid his stick beside him
And turned his back a little toward the door.
Now you will hear what he did next:
"By Gosh," he said, "this is the truth:
Since I'm out of the fair   30
And in a good place and far from people,
I ought to find out the sum
Of my money all by myself.
That's what all wise men do.
I had thirty-nine sous from Rouget;   35
Giraut, who helped me sell my
Two oxen, got twelve deniers from it.
May he hang from cursed branches,
Because he kept my deniers!
The good-for-nothing kept twelve of them,   40

63

et se li ai je fet maint bien!
Or est ainsi: ce ne vaut rien!
Il me vendra mes bues requerre
quant il voudra arer sa terre
et il devra semer son orge. 45
Mal dehez ait toute ma gorge,
s'il a jamés de moi nul preu!
Je lui cuit molt bien metre en leu,
honiz soit il et toute s'aire!
Or parlerai de mon afaire. 50
J'oi de Sorin .XIX. saus;
de ceus ne fui je mie faus,
quar mon compere dans Gautiers
ne m'en donast pas tant deniers
com j'ai eü, de tout le mendre. 55
Por ce fet bon au marchié vendre!
Il vousist ja creance avoir,
et j'ai assamblé mon avoir:
.XIX. saus et .XXXIX.,
itant furent vendu mi buef. 60
Diex! C'or ne sai que tout ce monte!
Si meïsse tout en un conte,
je ne le savroie sommer.
Qui me devroit tout assommer,
ne le savroie je des mois, 65
se n'avoie feves ou pois,
que chascuns pois feïst un sout:
ainsi le savroie je tout.
Et neporquant me dist Sirous
que j'oi des bues .L. sous, 70
qui les conta, si les reçut,
mes je ne sai s'il m'en deçut
ne s'il m'en a neant emblé,
qu'entre .II. sestiere de blé
et ma jument et mes porciaus 75
et la laine de mes aigniaus
me rendirent tout autrestant.
.II. fois .L., ce sont .C.,
ce dist uns gars qui fist mon conte;
.V. livres dist que tout ce monte. 80
Or ne lerai por nule paine
que ma borse qu'est toute plaine
ne soit vuidie en mon giron."
    Et li houlier de la meson
dient: "Ça vien, Mabile, escoute! 85
Cil denier sont nostre, sanz doute,
se tu mes ceenz ce vilain.
Il ne sont mie a son oés sain!"
Dist Mabile: "Lessiez le en pes!
Lessiez le conter tout adés. 90
Lessiez le conter tout en pes
qu'il ne me puet eschaper mes.

And here I have done him many a good deed!
That's the way it is. No use fretting!
He'll come asking for my oxen
When he wants to plow his land
And has to sow his barley.   45
Damnation take my throat
If he ever gets any profit out of me.
I know very well how to get even with him.
Shame on him and all his progeny!
Now I'll speak about my business.   50
I had nineteen sous from Sorin;
I didn't go wrong there,
Because my neighbor, Mr. Walter,
Would not have given me so many deniers
As I got, not in the least.   55
That's why it's best to sell at the market!
He would have even wanted credit,
But I've got all my money together:
Nineteen sous and thirty-nine.
My oxen were sold for that.   60
Lord! I don't know what that comes to!
If I put them all into one account,
I couldn't add it up.
If someone was about to knock me in the head,
I couldn't do it if I had months to do it in,   65
Unless I had beans or peas
So that each one could stand for a sou:
That way I would know the whole.
And yet Sirous, who counted them
And took them in, told me that   70
I had fifty sous for the oxen.
But I don't know whether he tricked me
Or whether he stole some of it from me,
For what with sixteen measures of wheat
And my mare and my pigs   75
And the wool of my lambs,
They gave me exactly as much.
Two times fifty--that makes a hundred.
That's what the boy who did my counting said;
He said all that adds up to five pounds.   80
Now I'm not going to let my purse,
Which is very full in my front pouch,
Be emptied for any touble whatever."
      The pimps of the house inside
Said, "Come here, Mabel, listen!   85
This man's money is no doubt ours
If you can get that clod in here.
It's not much use to him!"
Mabel said: "Leave him in peace!
Let him keep counting.   90
Let him count in peace,
Because he can't get away from me.

Toz les deniers je les vous doi.
Les iex me crevez, je l'otroi,
se il en est a dire uns seus." 95
Mes autrement ira li geus
qu'ele ne cuide, ce me samble,
quar li vilains conte et assamble
.XII. deniers, sanz plus, qu'il a.
Tant va contant et ça et la 100
qu'il dist: "Or est .XX. sols .V. foiz.
Des ore mes est il bien droiz
que je les gart; ce sera sens.
Mes d'une chose me porpens:
S'or eüsse ma douce niece, 105
qui fu fille de ma suer Tiece,
dame fust or de mon avoir.
El s'en ala par fol savoir
hors du païs en autre terre,
et je l'ai fete maint jor querre 110
en maint païs, en mainte vile.
Ahi! Douce niece Mabile,
tant estiiez de bon lingnage!
Dont vous vint ore tel corage?
Or sont tuit troi mort mi enfant, 115
et ma fame dame Siersant!
Jamés en mon cuer n'avrai joie
devant cele eure que je voie
ma douce niece en aucun tans.
Lors me rendisse moines blans; 120
dame fust or de mon avoir,
riche mari peüst avoir."
Ainsi la plaint, ainsi la pleure.
Et Mabile saut en cele eure,
lez lui s'assist et dist: "Preudon, 125
dont estes vous et vostre non?"
"Je ai non Fouchier de la Brouce;
mes vous samblez ma niece douce
plus que nule fame qui fust."
Cele se pasme sor le fust. 130
Quant se redrece, si dist tant:
"Or ai je ce que je demant!"
Puis si l'acole et si l'embrace,
et puis li bese bouche et face,
que ja n'en samble estre saoule. 135
Et celui qui molt sot de boule
estraint les denz et puis souspire:
"Bele niece, ne vous puis dire
la grant joie que j'ai au cuer.
Estes vous fille de ma suer?" 140
"Oïl, sire, de dame Tiece."
"Molt ai esté por vous grant piece,"
fet li vilains, "sanz avoir aise."
Estroitement l'acole et baise.

I promise you all the money.
Gouge my eyes out--I give you permission--
If there will be one sou left for him to count."   95
But the game will turn out differently
From what she thinks, it seems to me,
For the peasant was counting and collecting
His twelve deniers--no more.
He kept on counting, this way and that,   100
Until he said, "Now it's twenty sous five times.
From now on it's best
For me to hold onto them. That will be sensible.
But I'm bothered about one thing:
If I had my dear niece now,   105
Who's the daughter of my sister, Tess,
She would now be the mistress of all my money.
And yet she foolishly left
This country to go into another land;
For many a day I had people looking for her   110
In many countries, in many towns.
O dear! Sweet niece, my Mabel,
You were from such a good family!
Where did you get such an idea?
Now all three of my children are dead   115
Along with my wife, Lady Siersant!
I will never ever have joy
In my heart until that hour
When I see my sweet niece.
Then I'll become a white monk.   120
She'll be the mistress of my money.
She could have a rich husband then."
And so he mourned her; and so he wept for her.
Mabel jumped up at that moment
And sat beside him and said, "Good sir,   125
Where are you from, and what is your name?"
"My name is Fouchier de la Brouce;
But you look like my dear niece
More than any woman who ever was."
She fainted upon the log.   130
When she got up, she said:
"Now I have what I've been asking for!"
Then she kissed him and embraced him,
And kissed him on the mouth and face
So that she seemed never to get enough,   135
And he, who was very tricky,
Gritted his teeth and sighed:
"Lovely niece, I can't tell you
The great joy I feel in my heart.
Are you the daughter of my sister?"   140
"Yes, sir, of Lady Tess!"
"For a long time," said the peasant,
"I've been very worried about you."
He kissed and hugged her tightly.

ainsi aus .II. mainent grant joie.   145
Et .II. houliers en mi la voie
issirent fors de la meson.
Font li houlier: "Icist preudon
est il or nez de vostre vile?"
"Voir, c'est mon oncle," dist Mabile,   150
"dont vous avoie tant bien dit."
Vers aus se retorne un petit,
et tret la langue et tuert la joe,
et li houlier refont la moe:
"Est il donc vostre oncle? "Oïl voir."   155
"Grant honor i poez avoir,
et il en vous, sanz nul redout.
Et vous, preudom, du tout en tout,"
font li houlier, "sommes tuit vostre.
Par saint Pierre le bon apostre,   160
l'ostel avrez saint Julien.
Il n'a homme jusqu'a Gien
que plus de vous eüssons chier."
Par les braz prenent dant Fouchier,
si l'ont dedenz lor ostel mis.   165
"Or tost," ce dist Mabile, "amis,
achatez öés et chapons."
"Dame," font il, "venez ça dons.
Ja n'avons nous goute d'argent."
"Tesiez," fet el, "mauvese gent!   170
Metez houces, metez sorcos,
sor le vilain ert li escos.
Cis escos vous sera bien saus:
sempres avrez plus de .C. saus."
       Que vous iroie je contant?   175
Li dui houlier de maintenant
comment qu'il aient fet chevance,
.II. cras chapons sanz demorance
ont aporté avoec .II. oés.
Et Boivin lor a fet les moés   180
en tant comme il se sont tornez.
Mabile lor dist: "Or soiez
preus et vistes d'appareillier!"
Qui donc veïst com li houlier
plument chapons et plument oies!   185
Et Ysane fist toutes voies
le feu et ce qu'ele ot a fere.
Et Mabile ne se pot tere
qu'el ne parlast a son vilain:
"Biaus oncles, sont ore tuit sain   190
vostre fame, et mi dui neveu?
Je cuit qu'il sont ore molt preu."
Et li vilains si li respont:
"Bele niece, tuit troi mort sont,
par pou de duel n'ai esté mors.   195
Or serez vous toz mes confors

And so the two of them were very joyful.   145
Then two pimps came out
Into the road from the house.
The pimps said: "This gentleman--
Is he a native of your town?"
"Yes! It's my uncle!" said Mabel,   150
"The one I've told you so much about."
She turned toward them a little
And stuck out her tongue and twisted it in her cheek,
And the pimps made a face back at her:
"Is he really your uncle?" "Yes, indeed."   155
"You can take great pride in that,
And he in you, no doubt.
And you, sir, we are at your disposal
In absolutely everything," said the pimps;
"By Saint Peter, the good apostle,   160
You will have the Saint Julien Hotel.
There is no man from here to Gien
Whom we would hold more dear."
They took Mr. Fouchier by the arm
And led him into their house.   165
"Now quickly, friends," said Mabel,
"Buy some geese and capons."
"Lady," they said, "come off it!
We don't have a bit of money now."
"Quiet," said she, "you wicked people!   170
Pawn some blankets. Pawn your coats.
The ticket will be charged to the peasant.
This ticket will be very good for you:
You will soon have more than one hundred sous."
    What more shall I say?   175
At that, the two pimps
Somehow furnished the supplies;
In no time, they brought
Two fat capons with two geese.
And Boivin made a face at them   180
As soon as they turned away.
Mabel told them: "Now be
Wise and quick in the preparations!"
Then you should have seen how the pimps
Plucked the capons and plucked the geese!   185
And meanwhile, Ysane made
The fire and did what she had to do.
And Mabel couldn't keep quiet,
What with talking to the peasant:
"Dear uncle, are they all still in good health,   190
Your wife and my two cousins?
I guess they're very wise by now."
And the peasant answered her:
"Dear niece, they are all three dead.
I almost died myself of grief.   195
Now you will be all my comfort

en mon païs, en nostre vile,
"Ahi! Lasse!" ce dist Mabile,
"Bien deüsse or vive enragier;
lasse! S'il fust aprés mengier,   200
il n'alast pas si malement.
Lasse! Je vi en mon dormant
ceste aventure en ceste nuit."
"Dame, li chapon sont tout cuit
et les .II. oies en un haste,"   205
ce dist Ysane qui les haste.
"Ma douce dame, alez laver,
et si lessiez vostre plorer."
Adonc font au vilain le lorgne,
et [voit] li vilains, qui n'ert (pas) borgne,   210
qu'il le moquent en la meson.
Font li houlier: "Sire preudon,
n'estes pas sages, ce m'est vis:
lessons les mors, prenons les vis."
    Adonc sont assis a la table,   215
mes du mengier ne fu pas fable,
assez en orent a plenté.
De bons vins n'orent pas chierté,
assez en font au vilain boivre
por enyvrer et por deçoivre.   220
Mes il ne les crient ne ne doute.
Desouz sa chape sa main boute
et fet samblant de trere argent.
Dist Mabile: "Qu'alez querant,
biaus douz oncles, dites le moi?"   225
"Bele niece, bien sai et voi
que molt vous couste cis mengiers:
je metrai ci .XII. deniers."
Mabile jure, et li houlier,
que il ja n'i metra denier.   230
La table ostent quant ont mengié;
et Mabile a doné congié
aus .II. houliers d'aler la hors:
"Si vous sera bons li essors,
que bien avez eü disner.   235
Or prenez garde du souper!"
Li dui houlier s'en sont torné;
aprés aus sont li huis fermé.
    Mabile prist a demander:
"Biaus douz oncles, ne me celer   240
s'eüstes pieça compaignie
a fame, nel me celez mie,
puis que vostre fame fu morte.
Il est molt fols qui trop sorporte
talent de fame, c'est folie,   245
autressi comme de famie."
"Niece, il a bien .VII. ans toz plains."
"Tant a il bien?" "A tout le mains!

In my country, in our town."
"Oh! Alas!" said Mabel,
"I must go mad now;
Alas! If it were after dinner,   200
It wouldn't be so bad.
Alas! I saw this thing happening
In my sleep last night."
"Lady, the capons are all cooked
And the two geese on a spit,"   205
Said Ysane, telling them to hurry.
"My dear lady, go wash up,
And leave your weeping."
Then they winked at the peasant,
And the peasant, who was not one-eyed,   210
Saw they were making fun of him in their house.
And the pimps said, "Good sir,
This is not wise, in my opinion:
Let the dead go. Cling to the living."
        Then they sat at the table,   215
And the food was not make-believe--
They had more than enough.
There was no lack of good wines.
They made the peasant drink enough
To get him drunk and to deceive him.   220
But he was not afraid of them or worried.
He stuck his hand beneath his cloak
And made a show of pulling some money out.
Mabel said, "What are you looking for,
Dear sweet uncle, tell me?"   225
"Dear niece, I know very well, and can tell
That this meal is costing you a lot.
I will put in these twelve deniers."
Mabel swore and declared to him
That he would not put in a penny.   230
When they had eaten, they cleared off the table,
And Mabel gave permission
To the two pimps to go outside:
"The fresh air will be good for you,
For you have had a good dinner.   235
Now get ready for supper."
The two pimps turned around;
The doors were shut behind them.
        Mabel started out by asking,
"Dear, sweet uncle, don't keep it from me   240
If you have ever been
With a woman (don't keep it from me)
Since your wife died.
A man is a fool who endures for too long
A yearning for a woman--that's crazy;   245
It's like with hunger."
"Niece, it has been a full seven years, all in all."
"That long, really?" "At the very least!

Ne de ce n'ai je nul talant."
"Tesiez, oncles, Diex vous avant!   250
Mes regardez ceste meschine!"
Adonc bat .III. fois sa poitrine:
"Oncles, je ai molt fort pechié,
qu'a ses parenz l'ai fort trechié.
Por seul son pucelage avoir,   255
eüsse je molt grant avoir.
Mes vous l'avrez, que je le vueil."
A Ysane cluingne de l'ueil,
que la borse li soit copee.
Li vilains ot bien en penssee   260
de coper la avant qu'Isane.
La borse prent et si la trenche
dans Fouchiers, et puis si l'estuie:
en son sain, pres de sa char nue,
la mist, et puis si s'en retorne.   265
Vers Ysane sa chiere torne,
et s'en vindrent li uns vers l'autre:
andui se vont couchier el piautre.
Ysane va avant couchier,
et molt pria a dant Fouchier   270
por Dieu que il ne la bleçast.
Adonc covint que il ostast
la coiffe au cul por fere l'uevre.
De sa chemise la descuevre,
puis si commence a arecier,   275
et cele la borse a cerchier:
que qu'ele cerche, et cil l'estraint,
de la pointe du vit la point;
el con li met jusqu'a la coille,
dont li bat le cul, et rooille   280
tant, ce m'est vis, qu'il ot foutu.
Ses braies monte, s'a veü
de sa borse les deux pendanz.
"Hai las!" fet il, "Chetiz dolanz,
Tant ai hui fet male jornee!   285
Niece, ma borse m'est copee.
Ceste fame le m'a trenchie."
Mabile l'ot; s'en fut molt lie,
que bien cuide que ce soit voir,
qu'ele covoitoit molt l'avoir.   290
Maintenant a son huis desclos:
"Dant vilain," fet ele, "alez hors!"
"Dont me fetes ma borse rendre."
"Je vous baudrai la hart a pendre!
Alez tost hors de ma meson,   295
ainçois que je praingne un baston."
Cele un tison prent a .II. mains.
Adonc s'en va hors li vilains
qui n'ot cure d'avoir des cops.
    Aprés lui fu tost li huis clos.   300

72

And I don't have any desire for it."
"Quiet, uncle. God protect you!
But look at that girl!"   250
Then she beat her breast three times:
"Uncle, I have committed a great sin
Because I took her away from her parents.
Just for keeping her a virgin,
I would get a great deal of money.   255
But you can have her, because I want you to."
She winked at Ysane
To let her know that the purse should be cut.
The peasant very much intended
To cut it before Ysane did.   260
Mr. Fouchier took the purse
And cut and then hid it:
He put it at his breast,
Next to his bare skin, and then turned back.   265
He turned his face toward Ysane,
And they approached each other.
Both went to lie down on the straw.
Ysane went and lay down first
And earnestly begged Mr. Fouchier,   270
For God's sake, not to hurt her.
First he had to take off
His loin-covering to do the job.
Then he took off her shirt.
Then he began to get hard,   275
And she, to search for the purse.
While she was searching and he was embracing her,
With the point of his penis he pricked her.
He put it into her cunt all the way up to his balls,
With which he beat her ass and banged   280
So much that, in my opinion, he screwed her.
He pulled up his britches, and he saw
The two straps hanging from his purse:
"Alas!" said he, "miserable wretch!
I have made a bad day of today.   285
Niece! My purse has been cut!
That woman clipped it from me!"
Mabel heard it. She was very happy about it,
Thinking that it was true,
For she very much coveted the money.   290
Now she opened the door:
"Sir Peasant," she said, "get out!"
"Then give me back my purse."
"I'll give you the rope to hang yourself!
Get out of my house right now,   295
Before I get a stick."
She took a cane in her two hands.
Then the peasant, who did not care
To receive any blows, went out.
    The door was closed quickly after him.   300

Tout entor lui chascuns assamble
et il lor moustre a toz ensamble
que sa borse li ont copee.
Et Mabile l'a demandee
a Ysane: "Baille ça tost,   305
que li vilains va au provost."
"Foi que je doi saint Nicholas,"
dist Ysane, "je ne l'ai pas;
si l'ai je molt cerchie et quise."
"Par un poi que je ne te brise,   310
pute orde viex, toutes les danz!
Enne vi je les .II. pendanz
que tu copas? Jel sai de voir!
Cuides les tu par toi avoir?
Se tu m'en fez plus dire mot--   315
pute vielle, baille ça tost!"
"Dame, comment vous baillerai,"
dist Ysane, "ce que je n'ai?"
Et Mabile aus cheveus li cort,
qui n'estoient mie trop cort,   320
que jusqu'a la terre l'abat:
aus piez et aus poins la debat,
qu'ele le fet poirre et chier:
"Par Dieu, pute, ce n'a mestier!"
"Dame, or lessiez; je les querrai   325
tant, se puis, que les troverai,
se de ci me lessiez torner."
"Va," fet ele, "sanz demorer."
Mes Mabile l'estrain reborse,
qu'ele cuide trover la borse.   330
"Dame, or entent," ce dist Ysane,
"perdre puisse je cors et ame,
s'onques la borse soi ne vi:
or me poez tuer ici!"
"Par Dieu, pute, tu i morras!"   335
Par les cheveus et par les dras
l'a tiree jusqu'a ses piez;
et ele crie: "Aidiez! Aidiez!"
Quant son houlier dehors l'entent,
cele part cort isnelement;   340
l'uis fiert du pié sanz demorer,
si qu'il le fet des gons voler.
Mabile prist par la chevece,
si qu'il la deront par destrece.
Tant est la robe derompue   345
que dusqu'au cul en remest nue.
Puis l'a prise par les chevols,
du poing li done de granz cops
par mi le vis, en mi les joes,
si qu'eles sont perses et bloes.   350
Mes ele avra par tens secors
que son ami i vient le cors,

74

Everyone gathered around him,
And he showed everyone gathered there
That his purse had been snipped from him.
Mabel then asked for it
From Ysane: "Hand it over quickly,   305
For the peasant is going to the magistrate."
"By the faith I owe Saint Nicholas,"
Said Ysane, "I don't have it;
And I really looked and searched for it."
"I ought to break   310
All your teeth, you stinking old whore!
Didn't I see the two straps hanging down,
Which you cut? I know it for certain!
Do you expect to have them for yourself?
If you say another word to me about it--   315
You old whore, hand it over now!"
"Lady, how can I give you,"
Said Ysane, "something I don't have?"
Then Mabel ran and grabbed her hair,
Which was not at all too short.   320
She threw her down to the floor
And beat her with her feet and her fists,
So that she made her fart and shit:
"By God, whore, there's no need for this!"
"Lady, stop! I'll look for them   325
So hard, maybe, that I'll find them,
If you let go of me here."
"Go," she said, "without delay!"
Then Mabel turned the straw bed over,
Because she intended to find the purse.   330
"Lady, listen now," said Ysane,
"May I lose body and soul,
If ever I saw this purse at all:
Now you can kill me here!"
"By God, you whore, you'll die here!"   335
By the hair and by the clothes
She pulled her to her feet;
And Ysane cried: "Help! Help!"
When her pimp heard her from outside,
He ran there immediately;   340
Without delay he kicked the door,
So that he made it fly from the hinges.
He grabbed Mabel by the collar,
Tearing it violently.
The dress was so torn   345
That she was left naked all the way down to her ass.
Then he took her by the hair.
He struck great blows with his fist
On her face, on her cheeks,
Until they were gray-green and blue.   350
But soon she would have help,
Because her lover, who heard

qui au crier l'a entendue.
Tout maintenant, sanz atendue,
s'entreprennent li dui glouton.   355
Lors veïssiez emplir meson
et de houliers et de putains!
Chascuns i mist adonc les mains.
Lors veïssiez cheveus tirer,
tisons voler, draps deschirer,   360
et l'un desouz l'autre cheïr!
Li marcheant corent veïr
ceus qui orent rouge testee,
que molt i ot dure meslee,
et se s'i mistrent de tel gent   365
qui ne s'en partirent pas gent:
teus i entra a robe vaire
qui la trest rouge et a refaire.
    Boivin s'en vint droit au provost,
se li a conté mot a mot   370
de chief en chief la verité.
Et li provos l'a escouté,
qui molt ama la lecherie.
Sovent li fist conter sa vie
a ses parens, a ses amis,   375
qui molt s'en sont joué et ris.
Boivin remest .III. jors entiers;
se li dona de ses deniers
li provos .X. saus a Boivins,
qui cest fablel fist a Provins.   380

NOTE: Lines 312-380 differ so much in P that we give below that
       manuscript's version.

Tant par ores de maupens!
Tu la copas, jel se de voir;
la cuides tu par toi avoir?
Par la sainte digne char Dé,
mar te vint onques en pensé!"   5
Lors l'a Mabille si combree
que contre terre l'a getee;
si l'a tant frapee et batue,
par un petit qu'el(le) ne la tue.
Et son houlier i est venus,   10
qui molt en par fu iracus.
Quant il voit sa meschine batre,
entr'eulz .II. se vout entrebatre.
Et li autres houlier (i) survient,
qui a molt grant merveille vient.   15
Quant il voit Mabile en tel point,
lors fiert et frape et empoint
et se prent au houlier Ysanne.
Sa robe qui ert de couleur fanne

Her crying out, came running.
Right away, without waiting,
The two gluttons went for each other.
Then you should have seen the pimps   355
And whores fill up the house!
Everyone got his hands into it then.
Then you should have seen the hair pulled,
The sticks fly, clothes torn,
And people falling on top of each other!   360
The merchants ran to see
The people with their bloody heads,
For this was a very rough brawl,
And if they got mixed up with those people,
They themselves did not leave in good shape.   365
Some came in with green clothes
Who took them out red and needing mending.
    Boivin went straight to the magistrate
And told him the truth, word
For word from beginning to end.   370
And the magistrate, who greatly loved
A bawdy story, listened to him.
He kept making him tell the whole experience
To his relatives and to his friends,
Who enjoyed it very much and laughed about it.   375
Boivin stayed there three whole days;
And the magistrate gave ten sous
Of his own money to Boivin,
Who made this fabliau in Provins.
                                                        380

You are such an evil person!
You cut it, I know you did!
Do you expect to have it for yourself?
By God's holy worthy flesh,
That thought should have never occurred to you!"   5
Then Mabel got such a hold on her
That she threw her to the ground
And struck her and beat her so much
That she came close to killing her.
And her pimp came,   10
Who was very hot-tempered.
When he saw his wench beaten,
He wanted to get in on the fight between them.
And along came the other pimp,
Who arrived very much amazed.   15
When he saw Mabel in such a fix,
He struck and hit and punched
And had it out with Ysane's pimp.
He ripped and tore her dress

li despiece toute et chapigne; 20
n'i remest coiffe de Compigne
a descirer ne chaperon.
Tant s'entrebatent li glouton
et tant ont hurté et bouté
que tuit se sont ensanglanté; 25
il se derompent les pointrines.
Et ausi firent les meschines.
Il s'entrerompirent les piaus.
Sachiez, s'il i eüst coustiaus,
(Ja) se fussent entredommagiez; 30
mes il les orent engagiez
pour le vin qu'orent au disner.
Chier leur couvandra acheter,
ce vous dis je bien, cest escot,
si en seront tenuz pour sot, 35
si comme vous pourrez oïr,
mes que voeilliez un pou tesir.
Li vilains tout droit s'en ala
ou le prevost trouver cuida,
car il savoit bien ou il ere; 40
li vilains ne se tret arriere,
ainz va la ou le prevost fu.
Quant dant Fouchiers l'ot conneü,
tretout li conta mot a mot,
c'onques n'en failli d'un seul mot, 45
la lecherie qu'il ot faite.
Et li prevolz vers lui s'esploite,
si le fist .III. jours sejorner
pour la moquerie conter;
et quant dant Boivin s'en ala, 50
le prevost .XX. soulz li donna.
Et Mabile si fu moustree
et par Prouvins de tous moquee,
qui miex amast estre a Coloigne
qu'avenu(e) li fust tel(le) besoigne, 55
pour ce qu'el(le) cuidoit plus savoir
d'omme trichier et decevoir
par barat et par traïson
que nulle fame ne nulz hon.
Pour ce di a touz, ce me semble, 60
bon larron est qui autre emble.

Which was beech-colored; 20
There wasn't a Compiegne hairpiece
Or a cap left to tear.
The gluttons beat each other so much
And hit and pushed so much
That they were all bloody; 25
They broke each other's chests.
And the wenches did likewise.
They tore each other's skin.
Believe me, if there had been any knives,
They would have done great harm to each other by now; 30
But they had all been pawned
For the wine which they had at dinner.
I tell you, they had to pay
Dearly for that meal,
And they would be accounted fools, 35
Just as you will be able to hear,
If you would only keep quiet for a while.
The peasant went straight
To where he thought he could find the magistrate,
Because he knew well where he was; 40
The peasant did not hold back,
But came straight to where the magistrate was.
After Sir Fouchier met him,
He told him all, word for word,
(So that he didn't leave out a single word) 45
The trick that he had played.
And the magistrate took care of him
And made him stay three days
To tell about the fun;
And when Sir Boivin left, 50
The magistrate gave him twenty sous.
And Mabel was shown up so badly
And made fun of throughout Provins,
So that she would have preferred to be at Cologne
Than have had such a business happen to her, 55
Because she thought she knew more
About cheating and deceiving men
Through trickery and betrayal
Than any woman or any man.
For this reason I tell you all, it seems to me, 60
A good thief is one who steals from another one.

DES .III. AVUGLES DE COMPIEGNE

par

Cortebarbe

5.

Une matere ci dirai
d'un fablel que vous conterai.
On tient le menestrel a sage
qui met en trover son usage
de fere biaus dis et biaus contes   5
c'on dit devant dus, devant contes.
Fablel sont bon a escouter,
maint duel, maint mal font mescont[er]
et maint anui et maint meffet.
Cortebarbe a cest fablel fet,   10
si croi bien qu'encor l'en soviegne.
      Il avint ja defors Compiegne
Troi[s] avugle un chemin aloient.
Entr'eus nis un garcon n'avoient
qui les menast ne conduisist   15
ne le chemin lor apresist.
Chascuns avoit son hanepel;
molt povre estoient lor drapel,
quar vestu furent povrement.
Tout le chemin si fetement   20
s'en aloient devers Senlis.
Uns clers qui venoit de Paris,
qui bien et mal assez savoit,
escuier et sommier avoit,
et bel palefroi chevauchant,   25
les avugles vint aprochant,
quar grant ambleüre venoit.
Si vit que nus ne les menoit,
si pensse que aucuns (n')en voie:
comment alaissent il la voie?   30
Puis dist: "El cors me fiere goute
se je ne sai s'il voient goute."
Li avugle venir l'oïrent,
erraument d'une part se tindrent,
si s'escrient: "Fetes nous bien,   35
povre sommes sor toute rien,

80

THE THREE BLIND MEN FROM COMPIEGNE

by

Cortebarbe

5.

I will tell you the plot
Of a fabliau which I will narrate for you.
Any minstrel is said to be wise
Who puts his time into composing
And making fine poems and fine tales   5
Which are told before dukes and before counts.
Fabliaux are good to listen to:
They make people forget many sorrows and many evils
And many worries and many wrongs.
Cortebarbe made up this fabliau.   10
Indeed, I believe people still remember it.
　　　It once happened that outside Compiegne
Three blind men were going along the road.
They did not even have one boy among them
To lead them or guide them   15
Or show them the way.
Each one had his little cup;
Their clothing was very poor,
For they were dressed very poorly.
They were merrily going   20
Along the road to Senlis.
A clerk, who knew plenty of good and evil,
Was coming from Paris.
With a servant and a pack horse
And a beautiful palfrey,   25
He was riding toward the blind men,
And he was coming very fast.
He saw that no one was leading them,
And he thought one of them must be able to see.
Otherwise how could they be going along the road?   30
Then he said, "May the gout strike me
If I know whether they see anything or not."
The blind men heard him coming.
They quickly stood aside,
And they cried out: "Do us a good turn.   35
We are poorer than anything.

cil est molt povres qui ne voit."
Li clers esraument se porvoit,
qui les veut aler falordant;
"Vez ici," fet il, "un besant   40
que je vous done entre vous .III."
"Diex le vous mire et sainte Croiz,"
fet chascuns, "ci n'a pas don lait."
Chascuns cuide ses compains l'ait.
Li clers maintenant s'en depart,   45
puis dist qu'il veut vir lor depart.
Esraument a pié descendi;
si escouta et entendi
comment li avugle disoient,
et comment entr'eus devisoient.   50
Li plus mestres de .III. a dit:
"Ne nous a or mie escondit
qui a nous cest besant dona;
en un besant molt biau don a.
Je vous dirai que nous ferons: 55
vers Compiegne retornerons;
grant tens a ne fumes aaise;
or est bien droiz que chascuns s'aise.
Compiegne est de toz biens plentive."
"Com ci a parole soutive!"   60
Chascuns des autres li respont:
"C'or eüssons passé le pont!"
Vers Compiegne sont retorné,
ainsi comme il sont atorné,
molt furent lié, baut et joiant.   65
Li clers les va adés sivant,
et dist que adés les siurra
de si adont que il saura
lor fin. Dedenz la vile entrerent,
si oïrent et escouterent   70
c'on crioit par mi le chastel:
"Ci a bon vin fres et novel,
ça d'Auçoire, ça de Soissons,
pain et char, pastez et poissons;
ceenz fet bon despendre argent,   75
ostel i a a toute gent;
ceenz fet molt bon herbregier."
Cele part vont tout sanz dangier,
si s'en entrent en la meson,
le borgois ont mis a reson,   80
"Entendez ça a nous," font il,
"ne nous tenez mie por vil
se nous sommes si povrement;
estre volons priveement
en une loge bele et painte: 85
miex vous paierons que plus cointe,
quar nous volons assez avoir."
L'ostes pensse qu'il dient voir;

He who cannot see is very poor."
Right away the clerk decided
That he would play a trick on them:
"See this bezant here," he said,   40
"Which I am giving the three of you?"
"God and the Holy Cross reward you!"
Said each one; "this is no stingy gift."
Each one of them thought that his fellow had it.
Then the clerk left them;   45
Then he decided that he wanted to see them leaving.
Quickly he dismounted
And listened and heard
What the blind men were saying
And how they deliberated among themselves.   50
The one of the three who had most authority said:
"The man who gave us this bezant
Did not hold back from us;
A bezant makes a very good gift.
I'll tell you what we'll do: 55
We'll go back to Compiegne;
It has been a long time since we have been comfortable;
Now it is certainly right for everyone to take comfort.
Compiegne is full of all good things."
"What a wise speech this is!"   60
Each of the others answered:
"If only we were back over the bridge now!"
Back toward Compiegne they returned,
Just as they had planned.
They were very happy, merry, and festive.   65
The clerk went along, following them continually,
And he said to himself that he would keep following them
From here until he knew
The outcome. They came into the town
And heard and listened to   70
Somebody shouting in the middle of the walled town:
"Here there's fresh and new wine,
Auxerre wine, Soisson wine,
Bread and meat, paté and fish;
In here it is good to spend money.   75
There's room for everybody;
It's very good to lodge in here."
Without any trouble, they all went over there
And entered the house.
They spoke to the tavernkeeper: 80
"Listen to us," they said;
"Don't take us to be low-class
Just because we are so poorly clothed;
We want to be by ourselves
In a beautifully painted room: 85
The prettier the room, the more we will pay,
Because we want to have a lot."
The host thought they were telling the truth;

si fete gent ont deniers granz.
D'aus aaisier fu molt engranz;   90
en la haute loge les maine.
"Seignor," fet il, "une semaine
porriez ci estre bien et bel.
En la vile n'a bon morsel
que vous n'aiez, se vos volez."   95
"Sire," font il, "or tost alez;
si nous fets assez venir."
"Or m'en lessiez dont convenir,"
fet li borgois, puis si s'en torne.
De .V. mes pleniers lor atorne   100
pain, et char, pastez et poissons,
et vins, mes que ce fu des bons;
puis si lor fist la sus trametre,
et fist du charbon el feu metre.
Assis se sont a haute table.   105
Li vallés au clerc en l'estable
tret ses chevaus, l'ostel a pris.
Li clers, qui molt ert bien apris
et bien vestuz et cointement,
avoec l'oste molt hautement   110
sist au mengier la matinee,
et puis au souper la vespree.
Et li avugle du solier
furent servi com chevalier.
Chascuns grant paticle menoit,   115
l'uns a l'autre le vin donoit:
"Tien, je t'en doing, aprés m'en done,
cis crut sor une vingne bone!"
Ne cuidiez pas qu'il lor anuit.
Ainsi jusqu'a la mienuit   120
furent en solaz sanz dangier.
Li lit sont fet, si vont couchier
jusqu'au demain qu'il fu bele eure.
Et li clers tout adés demeure,
por ce qu'il veut savoir lor fin.   125
Et l'ostes fu levez matin
et son vallet, puis si conterent
combien char et poisson cousterent.
Dist li vallés: "En verité,
li pains, li vins et li pasté   130
ont bien cousté plus de .X. saus,
tant ont il bien eü entre aus.
Li clers en a .V. saus par lui."
"De lui ne puis avoir anui.
Va la sus, si me fai paier."   135
Et li vallés sanz delaier
vint aus avugles, si lor dist
que chascuns errant se vestit:
ses sires veut estre paiez.
Font il: "Or ne vous esmaiez,   140

84

Such happy people do have a lot of money.
He was very eager to make them comfortable;   90
He led them to an upstairs private room:
"Lords," he said, "for a week
You can be well and comfortable here.
There is not a good bite to eat in town
Which you will not have, if you want."   95
"Sir," they said, "now go quickly
And have a lot brought up to us."
"Then let me take care of it,"
Said the tavernkeeper. Then he left.
He prepared five full dishes for them,   100
Bread and meat, paté and fish
And wines, but only the good ones;
Then he had it all sent up to them
And had coals thrown on the fire.
They sat at a high table.   105
Into the stable the clerk's servant
Brought his horses, and he engaged a room.
The clerk, who was very alert
And well and nicely dressed,
Sat down very elegantly   110
With the host to eat during the morning,
And then for supper during the evening.
And the blind men in the upstairs room
Were served like knights.
They all made a lot of noise.   115
They served one another the wine:
"Well, let me give you some; then you give me some.
This grew on a good vine!"
Don't think that all this displeased them.
And so up until midnight   120
They were happy and carefree.
Their beds were made up, and they went to sleep
Until early the next day.
And the clerk was staying there all the time,
Because he wanted to know how it would turn out.   125
The host and his servant were
Up very early, and they counted
How much the meat and fish cost.
The servant said, "Indeed,
The bread, the wines, and the paté   130
Cost well more than ten sous--
That's how much they had all together!
The clerk had five sous on him."
"I'm not going to have any trouble from him.
Go up there. Make sure I get paid."   135
And the servant, with no delay,
Went to the blind men and told them
That each one should dress in a hurry:
His master wanted to be paid.
They said, "Now don't worry,   140

quar molt tres bien li paierons.
Savez," font il, "que nous devons?"
"Oïl," dist il, ".X. saus devez."
"Bien le vaut." Chascuns s'est levez.
Tuit troi sont aval descendu.   145
Li clers a tout ce entendu,
qui se chauçoit devant son lit.
Li troi avugle a l'oste ont dit:
"Sire, nous avons un besant,
je croi qu'il est molt bien pesant.   150
Quar nous en rendez le sorplus,
ainçois que du vostre aions plus."
"Volentiers," li ostes respont.
Fait li uns: "Quar li baille dont."
"Liquels l'a?" "Bé, je n'en ai mie."   155
"Dont l'a Robers Barbeflorie."
"Non ai, mes vous l'avez, bien sai."
"Par le cuer bieu, mie n'en ai!"
"Liquels l'a dont?" "Tu l'as." "Mes tu."
"Fetes, ou vous serez batu,"   160
dist li ostes, "seignor truant,
et mis en longaingne puant,
ainçois que vous partez de ci."
Il li crient: "Por Dieu merci,
sire, molt bien vous paierons."   165
Dont recommence lor tençons,
"Robers," fet l'uns, "quar li donez
le besant! Devant nous menez:
vous le reçustes premerains."
"Mes vous, qui venez daarains,   170
li bailliez, quar je n'en ai point."
"Or sui je bien venuz a point,"
fet li ostes, "quant on me truffe."
L'un va donner une grant buffe,
puis fait aporter .II. lingnas.   175
Li clers, qui fu a biaus harnas,
qui le conte forment amoit,
de ris en aise se pasmoit.
Quant il vit le ledengement,
a l'oste vint isnelement,   180
se li demande qu'il avoit,
quel chose ces genz demandoit.
Fet l'ostes: "Du mien ont eü
.X. saus, c'ont mengié et beü,
si ne m'en font fors escharnir.   185
Mes de ce les vueil bien garnir:
chascuns aura de son cors honte."
"Ainçois le metez sor mon conte,"
fet li clers, ".XV. saus vous doi;
mal fet povre gent fere anoi."   190
L'oste respont: "Molt volentiers.
Vaillanz clers estes et entiers."

Because we will pay him very well.
Do you know," they said, "how much we owe him?"
"Yes," he said; "you owe ten sous."
"It's well worth it." Each one got up,
And then all three went downstairs.   145
The clerk, who was putting on his shoes
In front of the bed, heard all this.
The three blind men said to the host:
"Sir, we have a bezant.
I think it is very heavy,   150
So give us the change
Before we have anything else of yours."
"Certainly," answered the host.
One of them said, "Well, give it to him."
"Who has it?" "Heck, I don't have it."   155
Then Robert Flower-beard has it."
"I don't have it; you do. I know that very well."
"By Gar's heart, I don't have it!"
"Then who does have it?" "*You* have it!" "No, *you!*"
"Be done with it! Or you'll be beaten,   160
Sir Tramps," said the host,
"And be thrown into the stinking cesspool
Before you leave here."
They shouted at him, "By the grace of God,
Sir, we'll pay you very well."   165
Then they began their quarreling again:
"Robert," said one, "give him
The bezant! You always lead us:
You received it first."
"No, you who come last,   170
Hand it over to him; I don't have it at all."
"Now I've come to a sorry state,"
Said the host, "when people trifle with me."
He gave one a big shove;
Then he had two sticks brought.   175
The clerk, who had very nice-looking gear,
And who was really enjoying these events,
Was fainting from laughter.
When he saw the abuse,
He quickly came up to the host   180
And asked him what the matter was with him,
And what he was asking from these people.
The host said, "They've eaten up
Ten sous' worth from me,
And all they do is poke fun at me.   185
But I intend to reward them well for that:
Each will have his flesh tormented."
"Put it on my account instead,"
Said the clerk; "I owe you fifteen sous;
It's bad business to give poor people a hard time."   190
The host replied, "Very well.
You are a valiant and honest clerk."

Li avugle s'en vont tout cuite.
    Or oiez comfete refuite
li clers porpenssa maintenant.   195
On aloit la messe sonant;
a l'oste vint, si l'aresone.
"Ostes," fet il, "vostre persone
du moustier dont ne connissiez?
Ces .XV. saus bien li croiriez,   200
se por moi les vos voloit rendre?"
"De .ce ne sui mie a aprendre,"
fet li borgois, "par saint Silvestre,
que je croiroie nostre prestre,
s'il voloit, plus de .XXX. livres."   205
"Dont dites j'en soie delivres
esraument com je reviendrai:
au moustier paier vous ferai."
L'ostes le commande esraument,
et li clers ainsi fetement   210
dist son garcon qu'il atornast
son palefroi, et qu'il troussast,
que tout soit prest quant il reviegne.
A l'oste a dit que il s'en viegne.
Ambedui el moustier en vont,   215
dedenz le chancel entré sont.
Li clers qui les .XV. saus doit
a pris son oste par le doit,
si l'a fet delez lui assir,
puis dist: "Je n'ai mie loisir   220
de demorer dusqu'aprés messe.
Avoir vos ferai vo promesse,
je l'irai dire qu'il vous pait
.XV. saus trestout entresait
tantost que il aura chanté."   225
"Fetes en vostre volenté,"
fet li borgois, qui bien le croit.
Li prestres revestuz estoit,
qui maintenant devoit chanter.
Li clers vint devant lui ester,   230
qui bien sot dire sa reson.
Bien sambloit estre gentiz hom,
n'avoit pas la chiere reborse.
.XII. deniers tret de sa borse,
le prestre les met en la main.   235
"Sire," fet il, "por saint Germain,
entendez ça un poi a mi.
Tuit li clerc doivent estre ami,
por ce vieng je pres de l'autel.
Je giuc anuit a un ostel   240
chiés a un borgois qui molt vaut:
li douz Jhesucriz le consaut,
quar preudom est et sanz boisdie.
Mes une cruel maladie

And the blind men got off scot-free.
   Now hear what a skillful trick
The clerk thought of next.   195
They were ringing the bell for mass;
He came to the host and made a proposal.
"Host," said he, "don't you know
The parson of your church?
Would you credit those fifteen sous to him,   200
If he's willing to give them back to you for me?"
"About this I don't need to be instructed,"
Said the tavernkeeper, "by Saint Sylvester,
For I would credit our priest,
If he wanted, with more than thirty pounds."   205
"Say, then, that I'll be paid up
As soon as I come back:
I'll see that you are paid at the church."
The host quickly told him to do it,
And so the clerk   210
Told the boy to prepare
His horse and to pack,
So that everything would be ready when he got back.
He told the host to come along.
Both of them went on to the church.   215
They went into the chancel.
The clerk, who owed the fifteen sous,
Took the host by the finger
And had him sit by him.
Then he said: "I don't have time   220
To wait until mass is over.
I will see that you get what I promised you;
I will go tell you
Fifteen sous right away
As soon as he has finished singing."   225
"Do as you like,"
Said the tavernkeeper, who really believed him.
The priest had changed his clothes
Because he had to sing now.
The clerk, who knew very well how   230
To say his part, went up to him.
He really seemed to be a decent man.
He didn't look disagreeable.
He pulled out twelve deniers from his purse
And put them into the priest's hand.   235
"Sir," he said, "by Saint Germain,
Listen to me a little here.
All clerks should be friends.
That's why I come close to the altar here.
Last night I stayed at the inn   240
Of a very worthy bourgeois:
May sweet Jesus Christ save him,
For he is a gentleman without deceit,
But a cruel sickness

li prist ersoir dedenz sa teste,   245
entruesque nous demeniens feste,
si qu'il fu trestoz marvoiez.
Dieu merci, or est ravoiez,
mes encore li deut li chiez.
Si vous pri que vous li lisiez,   250
aprés chanter, une evangille
desus son chief." "Et par saint Gille,
fet li prestres, "je li lirai."
Au borgois dist: "Je le ferai
tantost com j'aurai messe dite."   255
"Dont en claime je le clerc cuite,"
fet li borgois, "miex ne demant."
"Sire prestre, a Dieu vous commant,"
fet li clers. "Adieu, biaus douz mestre."
Li prestres a l'autel va estre,   260
hautement grant messe commence.
Par un jor fu de diemenche,
au moustier vindrent molt de genz.
Li clers, qui fu et biaus et genz,
vint a son oste congié prendre;   265
et li borgois sanz plus atendre
dusqu'a son ostel le convoie.
Li clers monte, si va sa voie.
    Et li borgois tantost aprés
vint au moustier: molt fu engrés   270
de ses .XV. saus recevoir:
avoir les cuide tout por voir.
Enz el chancel tant atendi
que li prestres se desvesti.
Et que la messe fu chantee.   275
Et li prestres, sanz demoree,
a pris le livre et puis l'estole,
si a huchié: "Sire Nichole,
venez avant, agenoilliez!"
De ces paroles n'est pas liez   280
li borgois, ainz li respondi:
"Je ne ving mie por ceci,
mes mes .XV. saus me paiez."
"Voirement est il marvoiez,"
dist li prestres, "*Nomini* Dame,   285
aidiez a cest preudome a l'ame!
Je sai de voir qu'il est dervez."
"Oëz," dist li borgois, "öez
com cis prestres or m'escharnist!
Por poi que mes cuers du sens n'ist,   290
quant son livre m'a ci tramis."
"Je vous dirai, biaus douz amis,"
fet li prestres, "comment qu'il praingne,
tout adés de Dieu vous soviegne,
si ne pöez avoir meschief."   295
Le livre li mist sor le chief,

Took hold of him inside his head   245
While we were feasting together,
So that he completely lost his wits.
Thank God, he's returned to his senses,
But his head still hurts him.
So after your singing,   250
I beg you to read him a gospel
Over his head." "By St. Giles,"
Said the priest, "I will read it to him."
To the bourgeois, he said, "I'll do it
As soon as I've said mass."   255
"Then I'll consider the clerk paid up,"
The bourgeois said: "I ask no more than that."
"Sir Priest, I commend you to God,"
Said the clerk. "Goodbye, my dear, good sir."
The priest went to stand before the altar.   260
He began to say high mass out loud.
It was a Sunday,
And many people were coming to church.
The clerk, who was both handsome and elegant,
Came to say goodbye to his host;   265
And the tavernkeeper, without waiting any longer,
Accompanied him back to his inn.
The clerk mounted and went on his way.
     And the tavernkeeper, immediately after,
Came to the church: he was very eager   270
To receive his fifteen sous:
He really thought he would get them.
He waited in the chancel
Until the priest changed his clothes
And the mass was sung.   275
And the priest, without waiting,
Took the book and then the stole
And called out, "Sir Nicholas,
Come forward, kneel down!"
The tavernkeeper was not pleased   280
With these words. Rather, he replied:
"I didn't come here for that;
Pay me my fifteen sous."
"Truly, he has lost his wits,"
Said the priest; "in the name of the Lord,   285
Help this good man's soul!
I know for sure that he is mad."
"Listen," said the tavernkeeper, "listen
To how this priest is making fun of me!
My heart almost leaves its senses   290
When he puts his book over me like this."
"I'll tell you, dear good friend,"
Said the priest, "whatever happens,
To always keep your mind on God.
That way you can't be hurt."   295
He put the book over his head

l'evangille li voloit lire.
Et li borgois commence a dire:
"J'ai en meson besoingne a fere.
Je n'ai cure de tel afere,   300
mais paiez moi tost ma monnoie."
Au prestre durement anoie,
toz ses paroschïens apele,
chascuns entor lui s'atropele.
Puis dist: "Cest homme me tenez!   305
Bien sai de voir qu'il est dervez."
"Non sui," fet il, "par saint Cornille,
ne, par la foi que doi ma fille,
mes .XV. saus me paierez.
Ja ainsi ne me gaberez!"   310
"Prenez le tost," le prestre a dit.
Li paroschien sanz contredit
le vont tantost molt fort prenant;
les mains li vont trestuit tenant.
Chascuns molt bel le reconforte,   315
et li prestres le livre aporte,
se li a mis deseur son chief,
l'evangille de chief en chief
Li lut, l'estole entor le col,
mes a tort le tenoit por fol,   320
puis l'esproha d'eve benoite.
Et li borgois forment covoite
qu'a son ostel fust revenuz.
Lessiez fu, ne fu plus tenuz.
Li prestres de sa main le saine,   325
puis dist: "Esté avez en paine,"
Et li borgois s'est toz cois teus.
Corouciez est et molt honteus
de ce qu'il fu si atrapez.
Liez fu quant il fu eschapez.   330
A son ostel en vint tout droit.
    Cortebarbe dist orendroit
c'on fet a tort maint homme honte.
A tant definerai mon conte.

And wanted to read him the gospel.
And the tavernkeeper started saying:
"I have work at the house to do.
I don't care for such business;
Just pay me my money."   300
This really worried the priest.
He called to all his parishioners,
Who all flocked around him.
Then he said, "Take hold of this man for me!
I know for a fact that he's crazy."   305
"I am not," he said, "by St. Cornelius,
Not by the faith I owe my daughter!
You pay me my fifteen sous.
And don't keep making fun of me like that!"
"Get him quickly," the priest said.   310
Without arguing, the parishioners
Went and took a strong grip on him
And got hold of both his hands.
They all comforted him very well,
And the priest brought the book   315
And put it over his head.
With the stole around his neck, he read
The gospel to him from start to finish.
But they were wrong in considering him crazy.
Then he sprinkled him with holy water,   320
And the tavernkeeper really wished
That he was back home again,
Left alone, and no longer held.
The priest made the sign of the cross with his hand
And then said, "You have been in pain."   325
And the tavernkeeper kept very quiet;
He was angry and very much ashamed
Of having been tricked this way.
He was happy to get away;
And so he went straight home.   330
      Cortebarbe says now
That many a man is wrongfully shamed.
And here I will finish my tale.

LI LAIS D'ARISTOTE

par

Henri d'Andeli

6.

De biaus mos conter et retrere
ne se doit on mie retrere,
ainz doit on volentiers entendre
biaus mos, quar on i puet aprendre   5
sens et cortoisie en l'oïr,
de bien se doit on esjoïr
li bons, quar c'est droiz et coustume;
et li mauvés en font la frume
esraument que il dire l'öent,   10
ausi com li un le bien loent,
et vont la bone gent loant,
le[s] despisent li mesdisant
quant il pis ne lor pueent fere.
Quar envie est de lor afere   15
qu'ele maint tout adés el cuer
a ceus qui sont mis en tel fuer
[qu'il n'öent de nului bien dire
qu'il ne le vueillent contredire.]
Si me merveil por qoi il poise   20
Gent felonesse et peu cortoise,
por qoi metez vous sor autrui
vostre mesfet et vostre anui?
Ci a trop fel escusement;
vous pechiez .II. fois mortelment: 25
l'une est de mesdire entremetre,
et li autre s'est desus metre
vostre mesdit, vo vilonie.
Certes c'est cuers de felonie,
[mais envie point ne s'estanche.   30
Je ne vorrai faire arrestance
ne demorer ici endroit:
ge croi que petit me vaudroit]
de blasmer les crueus felons
c'on puet apeler Guenelons,   35
qui retenir ne se porroient
de mesdire, s'il ne moroient,

THE LAY OF ARISTOTLE

by

Henri d'Andeli

6.

One should not hesitate
To fashion and relate fine speech,
Because people should willingly listen
To fine speech, for they can learn
Wisdom and courtliness by hearing it.   5
Good people must take pleasure in good,
For that is right and fitting;
But evil people pout
As soon as they hear it said,
For just as some praise the good,   10
And praise people who are good,
Slanderers despise them
When they can do no worse to them.
For envy is their business
Because it always remains in the heart   15
Of those that are fashioned in such a way,
Because they never hear any good said of anyone
Without wanting to contradict it.
Why it bothers them amazes me.
Wicked and graceless people,   20
Why do you put your misdeeds
And distress on other people?
There is very little excuse for this;
You commit a mortal sin twice:
One is by going around slandering,   25
And the other is by putting your own wickedness
Into your slander.
It certainly is a wicked heart,
[but envy does not stop flowing.
I wouldn't want to halt   30
Or delay at this subject:
I think it would do me little good]
To be blaming cruel villains,
Who should be called Ganelons
And who could not keep   35
From slandering if they died,

tant i sont mis et afetié.
  Or revendrai a mon ditié
d'une aventure qu'emprise ai,
dont la matere molt prisai   40
quant je oi la novele oïe,
qui bien doit estre desploïe
et dite par rime et retraite
sanz vilonie et sanz retraite,
quar oevre ou vilonie cort   45
ne doit estre noncie a cort;
ne jor que vive en mon rimer
ne quier de vilonie ouvrer.
Ne ne l'empris, ne n'emprendrai
ja vilain mot n'entreprendrai   50
en dit n'en oevre que je face;
quar vilonie se desface
toute riens et tolt sa savor.
Ne ja ne me ferai trovor
de rien que voie en mon vivant   55
quar vilain mot vont anuiant.
Ainz dirai de droit examplere
chose qui doit valoir et plere;
s'ert en leu de fruit et d'espece.
  Nous trovons que li rois de Gresse   60
Alixandres, qui si fu sire,
que a tant prince moustra s'ire
por aus abessier et donter
et por lui croistre et amonter,
ce li fist larguece sa mere   65
qui a toz avers est amere
et douce a toute large gent
que tant comme avers aime argent,
le het larguece a soustenir,
por ce que biens n'en puet venir   70
[por tant qu'il soit mis en estui.
Onques n'ot pooir sor cestui
riens qui venist d'argent ne d'or,
ainz fist de chevaliers tresor.
Ce ne font pas li autre prince;   75
quar chascuns recoppe et rechince
et muce et repont si le sien,
hennor n'en a ne autre bien.
Cil que on apele Alixandre
Recuilli por par tot espandre,   80
tot ot, tot prist et tot dona,
quar a largece abandona
le franc por mielz son pooir faire.
Repairer vueil a mon affaire.]
  Li bons rois de Gresse et d'Egite   85
avoit desouz ses piez sougite
de novel Ynde la major
ou ert demorez a sejor.

Because they are so dedicated and used to it.
    Now I will return to my telling
Of the adventure which I have undertaken,
Whose matter I valued very highly   40
When I heard the story;
It should be developed well
And told in rhyme and delivered
Without crudeness and without hedging,
Because a work that has crudeness running through it   45
Should not be spoken at court.
Never in my life do I seek
To relate crudeness in my work.
I never dealt with it and never will.
I will never use crude language   50
In my speech or in any work I undertake.
For crudeness deforms everything
And takes away its flavor.
I will never let myself make up
Such things that I see, as long as I live,   55
For crude words cause trouble.
But I will tell in an upright, moral tale
Something which must be worthwhile and pleasing;
This will be in the place of fruit and spice.
    We find that the king of Greece,   60
Alexander, who was such a great lord,
Demonstrated his wrath to so many princes
In order to bring them down and subject them
And to grow and lift himself up--
Largesse, his mother, who seems harsh   65
Against all misers and sweet to all
Generous people, made this possible:
For as long as a miser loves money,
So long does Largesse hate to uphold him,
So that wealth cannot come   70
[As long as it is kept in hiding.
Nothing that came from silver or gold
Ever had power over Alexander.
Rather, he made his knights his treasure.
Other princes don't do this,   75
For each one cuts corners and exchanges
And hides and puts his money back so much
That he has no other honor or good.
The one they call Alexander
Gathered it in order to distribute it everywhere.   80
He had all, took all, and gave all,
Because the generous man gave himself up
To Largesse to make his power greater.
Now I will return to my theme.]
    The good king of Greece and Egypt   85
Had once again laid
Greater India beneath his feet,
And he was detained there a long time.

Se vous me voliiez enquerre
por qoi demoroit en la terre   90
si volentiers, et tenoit qoi,
bien vos dirai reson por qoi.
Amors, qui tout prent et embrace
et tout aert et tout enlace,
l'avoit ja si en buies mis   95
qu'il ert devenuz fins amis,
dont il ne se repentoit mie,
quar il avoit trové amie
si bele c'on pot souhaidier.
N'avoit cure d'aillors plaidier   100
fors qu'avoec li manoir et estre.
Bien est amors poissanz et mestre
quant du monde le plus poissant
fet si humble et obeissant
qu'il ne prent nul conroi de lui,   105
ainz s'oublie tout por autrui.
C'est droiz, qu'amors est de tel pris
que, puis qu'ele a un homme empris,
n'i doit avoir nul desroi,
qu'autant a amors sor un roi   110
de droit pooir, ce est la somme,
comme sor tout le plus povre homme
qui soit en Champaigne n'en France,
tant est sa seignorie franche.
    Li rois avoec s'amie maint,   115
s'en parolent maintes et maint,
de ce que en tel point s'afole
et qu'il maine vie si fole,
onques d'avoec li ne se muet
com cil qui refuser nel puet.   120
[Ainsi le velt amors et cele
qui l'a point d'ardant estancele;
d'ardant estancele l'a point
cele qui si l'a mis a point.
Por quant ele n'en est pas quite,   125
ainz est si partie la luite
que je n'en sai le meillor prandre,
car de quanque cuers puet esprandre,
rest la pucele enamoree.
Et si fait iluec demoree,   130
ce n'est mie molt grant merveille,
puis que volentez li conseille;
il li covient, ce n'est pas doute,
parfornir sa volenté tote,
ou il desferoit le commant   135
qu'amors commande a fin amant.]
Molt de sa gent parler n'en osent,
mes par derriere molt n'en chosent.
Quant son mestre Aristote[s] l'ot
si est bien droiz qu'il li deslot.   140

And if you wish to ask me
Why he remained in the land
So willingly and stayed there still,   90
I will tell you the reason why.
Love, which takes and embraces all things
And seizes all and ties all things,
Had done such a good job of putting him in chains   95
That he became a noble lover,
Which he did not repent at all,
For he had found a friend
As beautiful as could be wished.
He didn't care for any other business   100
Except to remain and stay with her.
Love is really powerful and masterful
When it makes the most powerful man
In the world so humble and obedient
That he takes no care of himself,   105
But forgets himself completely for someone else.
This is right, for love has such force
That when it has taken a man,
There should be no conflict,
For love has as much true power   110
Over a king (this is the whole truth)
As over the very poorest man
In Champagne or the Ile de France;
That is how absolute its rule is.
    The king spent his time with his friend,   115
And many people had much to say about it--
That he was making a fool of himself
And that he was leading his life so foolishly
That he could not move from her side--
Like a man who couldn't help himself.   120
[That is what love wanted, and so did she
Who had pricked him with a burning spark;
She who settled his account
Had pricked him with a burning spark.
Nevertheless, she didn't get off scot-free;   125
Rather, the struggle was so equal
That I don't know how to choose the winner,
For however much she could kindle a heart,
The maiden was still in love.
And if he stayed on there,   130
It was no great wonder,
Since his will advised him;
He had to (there is no doubt)
Accomplish all her will,
Or he would break the command   135
Which love gives to a courtly lover.]
Many of his people did not dare speak of it,
But they gossiped about it behind his back.
When his master professor, Aristotle, heard it,
It was quite right for him to chide him.   140

Belement a conseil l'a mis;
si dist: "Mar avez deguerpis
toz les barons de vo roiame
por l'amor d'une estrange fame."
Alixandres li respondi   145
tantost com dire li oï:
"Quantes en i covient il donques?
Je cuit que cil n'amerent onques
qui por fol m'en voudrent clamer,
c'on n'en puet c'une seule amer   150
ne n'en doit par droit plere c'une,
et qui de ce homme rancune,
e'il maint la ou ses cuers li rueve
petit d'amor[s] dedenz li trueve."
Aristote[s], qui tout savoit   155
quanques droite clergie avoit,
respont au roi, et si li conte
que li atornoit a grant honte
de ce qu'en tel point se demaine
que toute entiere la semaine   160
est avoec s'amie et arreste,
qu'il ne fet ne solaz ne feste
a sa chevalerie toute.
"Je cuit que vous ne veez goute,
rois," dist Aristote[s] son mestre;   165
"Or vous puet on bien mener pestre
tout issi comme beste en pré.
Trop avez le sens destempré,
quant por une meschine estrange
voz cuers si durement se change   170
c'on n'i puet mesure trover.
Je vous vueil proier et rouver
a departir de tel usage,
quar trop i paiez le musage."
[Ainsi chastoie son seignor   175
maistre Aristote(s) por s'amor,
et li rois debonnairement
li repondi honteusement
qu'il s'en garderoit volentiers
comme cil qui ert siens entiers.]   180
        Alixandres ainsi demeure,
et atent maint jor et mainte eure
qu'a s'amie ne va n'aproche
por le dit et por le reproche
qu'il oï son mestre reprendre,   185
mes sa volentez n'est pas mendre;
encor n'i voist il comme il seut,
mes miex l'en aime et miex l'en veut
que il ne feïst onques mes.
[Paor de mesprendre et esmais   190
l'en font estre son gré tenir;
mais il n'a pas le souvenir

Graciously he made him listen to advice
And said: "You have disgracefully abandoned
All the barons of your kingdom
For the love of a foreign woman."
Alexander answered him
As soon as he heard it and said to him: 145
"What must be done about it then?
I think that these people, who would like
To call me a fool for it, never did love,
For one can love only one woman
And should rightly please only one,   150
And anyone who resents this man
For staying where his heart orders
Finds little love within himself."
Aristotle, who knew all
That there ever was of true knowledge,   155
Answered the king and told him
That people were attributing great shame to him
For behaving in such a way
That for the entire week
He was with and remained with his beloved   160
And neither comforted nor honored with feasting
All of his company of knights.
"I think that you don't see a thing,
King," said Aristotle, his professor;
"Now they could easily lead you out to graze   165
Right here like a beast in the meadow.
Your wits are too deranged,
Since for a foreign wench
Your heart changes so drastically
That no moderation can be found in it.   170
I want to beg you and order you
To cease from such behavior,
For you are paying too much for your dissipation."
[Thus Master Aristotle chided
His lord for his love,   175
And the king, who was ashamed,
Answered him graciously
That he would willingly guard against it
Like one who was entirely his.]
      And so Alexander stayed   180
And waited many a day and many an hour,
And he didn't go to or come near his friend
Because of the speech and the reproach
That he heard his professor repeating,
But his will was no less;   185
He didn't go there again the way he used to,
But he loved her better now and wanted her more
Than he ever had before.
[Fear of acting wrongly and worry
Made him stay and hold his desire in check.   190
But he hadn't lost the memory

laissié ensanble avec la voie,
qu'amors li ramenbre et ravoie
son cler vis, sa bele façon   195
ou il n'a nule retraçon
de vilenie ne de mal,
front poli plus cler de cristal,
beau cors, bele bouche, blont chief.
"Ha!" fait il, "Com a grant meschief   200
vuelent tote gent que ge vive!
Mes maistres velt que ge estrive
vers ce qui enz el cuer me gist.
Tant me destraint, tant me sogist
autrui grez que m'en tieg por fol.   205
Quant por autrui voloir m'afol,
ce est folie, ce me sanble.
Mes maistres et mi home ensanble
ne sentent pas ce que ge sent,
et se ge plus a ax m'asent,   210
tot ai perdu, ce m'est avis.
Vielt amors vivre par devis?
Nenil, mais a sa volenté."
Ainsi s'est li rois dementé,
puis s'en torna veoir celui   215
qui molt li plot et abeli.]
Et la dame est en piez saillie
qui molt estoit desconseillie
por la demoree le roi.
Lors dist: "Por vostre grant desroi   220
sui bien aperceüe, sire!
Finz amans comment se consire
d'aler veoir ce que li plest?"
A cest mot pleure, si se test.
Et li rois li respont: "Amie,   225
ne vous en esmerveilliez mie
qu'el demorer ot achoison.
Mi chevalier et mi baron
me blasmoient trop malement
de ce que trop escharsement   230
aloie et venoie avoec aus;
et mon mestre dist que c'ert maus,
qui laidement m'en a repris.
Ne porquant bien sai qu'ai mespris
[qu'onques por lui defis en mi   235
la volenté de fin ami;]
mes je doutai despit et honte."
"Sire, je sai bien que ce monte,"
dist la dame, "se Diex me saut!
Mes, s'engins et sens ne me faut,   240
par tens m'en voudrai bien vengier.
Et miex le porrez ledengier
et prendre de honte plus male,
vostre mestre chanu et pale,

Of the road to her door.
For love recalled for him and reminded him
Of her bright face, her lovely shape,   195
Where there was no reproach
Of ugliness or evil,
Polished forehead, clearer than crystal,
Beautiful body, beautiful mouth, blond hair.
"Ah!" he said, "with what great distress   200
Everybody wants me to live!
My professor wants me to fight
Against what lies in my heart.
Other people's wishes oppress me and
Subdue me so much that I am going crazy.   205
When I go crazy for other people's will,
That's crazy, it seems to me.
My professor and my men together
Don't feel what I feel,
And if I give in any more to them,   210
All is lost--that's what I think.
Will love live by rules?
Not at all, but according to its own will."
And so the king reflected.
Then he left to see the person   215
Who pleased him greatly and brightened his life.]
The lady, who was very downhearted
Because of the absence of the king,
Leaped to her feet.
Then she said, "I am very much aware   220
Of your great distress, Lord!
How does a noble lover refrain
From going to see what pleases him so much?"
With that word, she wept and said nothing.
The king replied, "Beloved,   225
Don't be amazed,
For there was reason for the absence.
My knights and my barons
Were blaming me too severely
Because too rarely   230
I came and went with them;
And my master professor said it was wrong
And harshly took me to task for it.
Nevertheless, I know I have done wrong
[In suppressing for his sake   235
The will of a noble lover,]
But I was afraid of scorn and shame."
"Sir, I know well what this amounts to,"
The lady said; "may God save me!
But unless I lack strategy and wit,   240
In time I'll soon get vengeance.
And you'll be able to abuse your pale,
Whiteheaded master better
And catch him in worse shame,

se je vif demain jusqu'a nonne 245
et amors sa force m'en donne
qui ja poissance ne faudra;
ne ja vers moi ne li vaudra
dialetique ne gramaire.
[Se par moi nature nel maire, 250
puis que je me sui aramie]
donc saura il trop d'escremie,
et sel perceverez demain.
Sire rois, or vous levez main,
[si verroiz Nature apointer 255
au maistre por lui despointer
de son sens et de sa clergie.
Ainz de si tranchant escorgie
ne fu feruz, ne de si cointe
com il avra demain acointe, 260
se ge puis ne aler ne estre
le matin devant sa fenestre.
Mar nos a laidi ne gabé!
Or soiez demain en abé]
aus fenestres de cele tor, 265
et je porverrai mon ator."
Alixandres molt s'esjoï
de ce que dire li oï!
[Puis l'acola estroitement.
Si le dist debonnairement:] 270
"Molt estes vaillanz, biaus cuers dous,
et, se je aim autrui que vous,
si me doinst Diex mauvés acueil.
Amors ai teles com je veuil,
si que nule autre ne claim part." 275
A tant de s'amie se part,
si s'en va, et cele demeure.
    Au matin, quant fu tens et eure,
sans esveillier autrui se lieve,
quar li levers pas ne li grieve. 280
Si s'est en pure sa chemise
enz el vergier souz la tor mise,
en un bliaut ynde gouté,
en la matinee ert d'esté
[et li vergiers plains de verdure. 285
Si ne doutoit pas la froidure,
qu'il faisoit chalt et dolz oré.]
Bien l'avoit Nature enfloré
son cler vis de lis et de rose,
n'en toute sa taille n'ot chose 290
qui par droit estre n'i deüst,
et si ne cuidiez qu'ele eüst
loïe ne guimple ne bende;
si l'embelist molt et amende
sa bele treche longue et blonde. 295
N'a pas deservi qu'on la tonde

If I live till mid-afternoon tomorrow   245
And if love, whose power will never fail,
Gives me its strength for it;
Neither logic nor science
Will be of any use to him against me.
[If nature doesn't master him through me,   250
Since I've committed myself to it,]
Then he will experience a lot of combat.
And if you will observe him tomorrow,
Sir King, then get up early,
[And you will see Nature take charge   255
Of the professor in order to deprive
Him of his senses and his learning.
Never has he been struck with such
A cutting or such a beautiful whip
As he will experience tomorrow,   260
If I can go and stand
In front of his window in the morning.
Woe to him for abusing or insulting us!
Now tomorrow be on the watch]
At the window of that tower,   265
And I will see to my preparations."
Alexander rejoiced greatly
In what he heard her tell him!
[Then he embraced her tightly
And told her graciously:]   270
"You are valiant, my dear sweetheart,
And if I love anyone else but you,
May God give me an evil reception.
I have love, just as I want,
So that I want no claim on any other."   275
Finally he left his friend:
He went away and she stayed.
        In the morning, when it was the right time and hour,
Without awakening anyone else, she arose,
Because getting up was not a chore for her.   280
Naked under her shirt, she placed
Herself in the orchard underneath the tower
In an india-blue dotted dress.
It was a summer morning,
[And the orchard was full of greenery,   285
And she wasn't afraid of the cold,
For it was warm, with a sweet breeze.]
Nature had blossomed
In her bright face with the colors of lilies and roses.
In her whole figure there was nothing   290
Which shouldn't rightly have been there,
And don't think that she had
Tied on a wimple or a headband.
She made herself beautiful, arranging
Her lovely, long blond tresses.   295
The lady who had such a charming head of hair

la dame qui si biau chief porte;
par mi le vergier se deporte
[cele, qui nature avoit painte,
nuz piez, desloiee, deschainte,]   300
si va escorçant son bliaut,
et va chantant, non mie haut:
     C'est la jus desoz l'olive.
     or la voi venir m'amie!
     La fontaine i sort serie,   305
     el glaioloi, desoz l'aunoi.
     Or la voi, la voi, la voi,
     la bele blonde! A li m'otroi!
Quant li rois la chançon entent,
qui l'oreille et le cuer i tent   310
a la fenestre por oïr.
Molt l'a fait s'amie esjoïr
de son dit et de son chanter.
Anqui se porra bien vanter
son mestre Aristote[s] d'Ataines   315
qu'amors bone[s] leaus lontaine[s]
se desirent a aprochier.
Ne mes n'en ira reprochier
le roi, ne n'en rendra anui,
quar il trovera tant en lui   320
et ert de volenté si yvres.
Levez est, si siet a ses livres,
voit la dame aler et venir,
el cuer li met un souvenir
tel que son livre li fet clore.   325
"He, Diex!" fet il, "Quar venist ore
cil mireoirs plus pres de ci,
si me metroie en sa merci.
Comment! Se m'i metroie donques?
Non feroie, ce n'avint onques   330
que je, qui tant sai et tant puis,
tant de folie en mon cuer truis
c'un[s] seul[s] veoirs tout mon cuer oste.
Amors veut que le tiengne a oste,
mes honors le tient a hontage   335
tel sovenir et tel hommage.
Avoi! Qu'est mon cuers devenuz?
Que je sui toz viex et chenuz,
lais et pales et noirs et maigres,
et plus en sui aspres et aigres   340
que nus c'on sache ne ne cuide.
Mal ai emploié mon estuide,
qui onques ne finai d'aprendre.
Or me desaprent por miex prendre
amors, qui maint preudomme a pris.   345
S'ai en apren(d)ant desapris;
desapris ai en aprenant.
Puis qu'amors me va si prenant

Did not deserve to have it cut.
Walking through the orchard,
[She whom nature had painted
Came barefoot, loosely arrayed, without a belt,]   300
And she went about tucking up her dress,
And she went about singing, not very loudly:
    There, under the olive tree.
    I see my beloved coming near!
    The fountain springs serene there,   305
    In the gladioli underneath the alder grove.
    I see her, see her, see her,
    The beautiful blonde--I give myself to her!
When the king heard the little tune,
He stretched out his heart and his ear   310
At the window to hear.
His loved one made him rejoice greatly
In her words and in her song.
In this his master, Professor Aristotle
Of Athens, will be able to boast   315
That good, loyal loves, far from each other,
Want to come close to each other.
He will never again reproach
The king or cause trouble
Because he will find the same thing in himself   320
And will be very drunk in his lust.
He rose and sat at his books.
He saw the lady coming and going.
She excited a memory in his heart
That made him close his book: 325
"Oh God!" he said, "let this wonder
Come a bit closer now,
And I will put myself at her mercy.
What then! If I do put myself there?
I will not do it! It has never happened   330
That I, who know and am capable of so much,
Could find so much folly in my heart
That one single sight could take all my heart away.
Love wants me to keep it as a guest.
My honor considers such a thought   335
And such homage to be a shame.
Ah! What has become of my heart?
I am completely old and gray,
Ugly and pale and black and thin,
And more bitter and sour   340
Than anyone who is either known or thought of.
I, who never stopped studying,
Have badly used my studies.
Now love, which has taken many a good man,
Unlearns me, the better to take me.   345
And in learning I have become unlearned;
I have lost my love in learning.
Since love is taking such a hold on me,

[et des que ne m'en puis resqueurre,
au convenir soit et droiz queure,   350
ne ja por moi droiz ne remaigne.
Viegne amors herbegier, or viegne
en moi, ge n'en sai el que dire,
puis que je nel puis contredire."
     Si com li maistres se demente,]   355
la dame en un rainssel de mente
fist un chapel de maintes flors.
Au fere li sovint d'amors;
si chante en cueillant les floretes:
    Ci me tienent amoretes;   360
    dras i gaoit meschinete.
    Bele, trop vous aim!
    Ci me tienent amoretes
    Ou je tieng ma main.
Ainsi chante, ainsi s'esbanoie.   365
Mestre Aristote molt anoie
de ce qu'ele plus pres ne vient.
Ele set bien quanqu'il covient
a lui eschaufer et retrere.
De tel saiete le veut trere   370
qui cointement soit empenee.
Molt s'est traveillie et penee
que sa volenté l'a atret.
Tout belement et tout a tret
son chapel en son biau chef pose;   375
ne fet samblant de nule chose
que le voie ne aperçoive.
Et por ce que miex le deçoive
et plus bel le voist enchantant,
vers la fenestre va chantant   380
les vers d'une chançon de toile,
quar ne veut pas que cil se çoile
qui tout a mis en la querele:
    En un vergier, lez une fontenele,
    dont clere est l'onde et blanche la gravele,   385
    siet fille a roi, sa main a sa maissele;
    En soupirant son douz ami apele:
      Haï, cuens Guis amis!
    La vostre amors me tolt solaz et ris.
    Quant ele ot ce dit, si s'en passe   390
lez la large fenestre basse.
Et cil par le bliaut l'aert
qui trop cuidoit avoir souffert,
tant a desirré la pucele.
A cest cop parchiet la chandeille   395
toute jus a terre au viel chat
qui pris est sanz point de rachat.
Et la damoisele s'escrie:
"Qu'est ce?" fet ele, "Dieus aïe!
A foi! Qui m'a ci retenue?"   400

[And since I cannot rescue myself,
Let it be as it must, and let Law go.   350
Do not let Law remain on my account.
Come here to dwell, Love, now come
To me--I don't know what else to say,
Since I can't contradict it."
  While the master was going out of his head,]   355
The lady was making a garland
Of many flowers on a sprig of mint.
While making it, she remembered love;
And she sang while gathering the little flowers:
  These loves have gotten hold of me.   360
  The girl was washing sheets there.
  Sweetheart, I love you too much!
  These loves have gotten hold of me
  Where I hold out my hand.
And so she sang, and so she strolled.   365
Master Aristotle was much annoyed
Because she didn't come any closer.
She knew very well what was necessary
To warm him up and lure him.
She wanted to strike him with a very   370
Beautifully feathered arrow.
She worked and took much effort
So that she drew him to her will.
Very nicely and leisurely
She put her garland on her lovely head;   375
She pretended not to see
Or notice anything at all.
And in order to deceive him better
And go on bewitching him more successfully,
She went toward the window singing   380
Verses from a weaving song,
For she, who had put her all into the affair,
Did not want him to hide:
  In an orchard, by a fountain,
  Whose water is clear and the pebbles are white,   385
  Sits the daughter of the king, her hand on her cheek;
  Sighing, she calls her sweet friend:
  "Oh! Count Guy, my friend!
  Your love deprives me of laughter and joy.
  As she sang this, she passed so close   390
To the large low window
That he, who thought he had suffered too much
Because he desired the young girl so marvelously,
Seized her by her dress.
At this blow the candle of the old cat   395
Fell to the ground.
He was unredeemably caught.
The young lady cried out:
"What is this?" and said; "Lord, help!
In faith! Who grabbed me here?"   400

"Dame, bien soiez vous venue,"
fet cil qui provos est et maire
de la folie qui le maire.
"Sire," ce dist la dame, "avoi!
Estes vous ce que je ci voi?" 405
"Oïl," dist il, "ma douce dame,
por vous metrai et cors et ame,
vie et honor en aventure.
Tant m'a fet amors et nature
que de vous partir ne me puis." 410
"Ha! Sire," fet ele, "despuis
qu'ainsi est que vous tant m'amez,
ja par moi n'en serez blasmez.
Mes la chose est molt mal alee.
Ne sai qui m'a au roi meslee 415
et molt blasmé de ce que tant
s'aloit o moi esbanoiant."
"Dame," dist il, "or vous tesiez
que par moi sera rapesiez
et li mautalenz et li cris 420
et li blasmes et li estris!
[Quar li rois m'aime et crient et doute
plus que s'autre maisnie tote.]
Mes, por Dieu! Ceenz vous traiez,
et mon desir me rapaiez 425
de vostre cors gent et poli!"
"Mestres, ainçois qu'a vous foli,"
dist la dame, "vous covient fere
avant un molt divers afere,
se tant estes d'amors souspris; 430
quar une molt un granz talenz m'est pris
de vous un petit chevauchier
desus ceste herbe en cest vergier.
Et si vueil," dist la damoisele,
"qu'il ait sor vo doz une sele, 435
si serai plus honestement."
Li mestres li respont briefment
que ce fera il volentiers
com cil qui est siens toz entiers.
Bien l'a mis amors a desroi 440
quant la sele d'un palefroi
li fet comporter a son col.
[Or, croi qu'il sanblera bien fol
quant desor le col il est mise!
Et cele s'en est entremise 445
tant qu'ele li met sor le dos.]
Bien fait amors de sage fol
puis que Nature le semont,
que tout le meillor clerc du mont
fet comme roncin enseler, 450
et puis a .IIII. piez aler
a chatonant par desus l'erbe.

"Lady, may you be welcome,"
Said he who was the magistrate and master
Of the folly which mastered him.
"Sir!" said the lady. "What!
Are you the one I see here?"   405
"Yes," said he, "my sweet lady,
For you I will put both body and soul,
Life and honor at stake.
Love and nature have done so much to me
That I cannot leave you."   410
"Ah, Sir!" said she, "since
That's the way it is, since you love me so much,
You won't be blamed for it by me.
But the thing has gone very badly.
I don't know who has interfered with the king   415
And blamed him so much for spending
So much time with me."
"Lady," he said, "now be quiet,
For it will be fixed up by me,
Both the scandal and the outcry   420
And the blame and the squabbling!
[For the king loves and fears and respects me
More than all the rest of his court.]
But for God's sake, come in,
And repay my desire   425
With your smooth and noble body!"
"Master, before I give myself over to folly
With you," said the lady, "you must do
A very different thing for me
If you are so love-struck,   430
For I am seized with a great yearning
To ride you horsey-back a little
On the grass in this orchard.
Also," said the young lady, "I want
You to have a saddle on your back.   435
That way I will go more honorably."
The professor replied briefly
That he would do it willingly,
Like one who wanted to be hers entirely.
Love had really subdued him   440
When it made him bear a
Horse's saddle on his back.
[Now I think he will seem really foolish
When this is put on his back!
Then she got busy   445
Until she put it on his back.]
After Nature summons him,
Love makes a fool of a wise man,
For it made the best scholar in the world
Get saddled like a packhorse   450
And then go on four feet
Scampering across the grass.

Ci vous di example et proverbe,
sel saurai bien a point conter.
La damoisele fet monter   455
sor son dos, et puis si la porte;
par mi le le vergier se deporte
[en veoir et en esgarder
celui qui sens ne pot garder
qu'amors ne l'ait mis a folie.   460
Et la damoisele trop lie
aval le vergier le conduit;
en lui chevauchier se deduit,]
si chante cler et a vois plaine:
    Ainsi va qui amors maine,   465
    bele Doe i ghee laine;
    mestre musars me soustient!
    Ainsi va qui amors maine
    et ainsi qui les maintient!
Alixandres ert en la tor,   470
bien ot veü trestout l'ator.
Qui lui donast trestout l'empire
ne se tenist il pas de rire.
"Mestre," dist il, "por Dieu! Que vaut ce?
Je voi molt bien c'on vous chevauche.   475
Comment! Estes vous forsenez
qui en tel point estes menez?
Vous me feïstes l'autre fois
de li veoir si grant defoiz,
et or vous a mis en tel point   480
qu'il n'a en vous de reson point,
ainz vous metez a loi de beste."
Aristote[s] drece la teste,
et la damoisele descent.
Lors respondi honestement: 485
["Sire," fait il, "vos dites voir;
mais or poez apercevoir.]
J'oi droit se je doutai de vous
qui en droit jovent ardez vous
et an feu de droite jonece,   490
quant je, qui sui plains de viellece,
ne poi contre amor rendre estal
qu'ele ne m'ait torné a mal
si grant com vous avez veü.
Quanques j'ai apris et leü   495
me desfet nature en une eure
qui toute rien taut et deveure.
Et bien sachiez certainement
puis qu'il m'estuet apertement
fere folie si aperte,   500
vous n'en poez partir sans perte
ne sanz blasme de vostre gent."
Molt s'est rescous et bel et gent
Aristote[s] de son meschief,

Here I am telling you a lesson and a proverb,
And I know how to tell it just right.
He had the young lady mount   455
On his back, and then he carried her;
All through the orchard she was enjoying herself
[Seeing and looking at
The man who couldn't hold on to his senses enough
To keep love from making him foolish.   460
And the very happy young lady
Drove him down the orchard,
Delighting in riding him.]
And she sang brightly in a clear voice:
    This is how the one whom love leads goes.   465
    (Beautiful Doe is washing wool.)
    Doctor Donkey is bearing me!
    This is how one whom love leads goes
    And also the one who supports them!
Alexander was in the tower.   470
He had seen the whole trick very well.
Not even if someone had given him the whole empire
Could he have kept from laughing.
"Master," he said, "for God's sake, what's this?
I see very well that someone is riding you.   475
What? Are you crazy,
Letting yourself be brought to such a low point?
The other day you made
Such a great prohibition against my seeing her,
And now she's put you in a position   480
Where there's no reason in you at all;
Instead, you act according to the law of beasts."
Aristotle raised his head,
And the young lady got down.
Then he replied, sincerely: 485
["Sire," he said, "you are telling the truth;
But now you can perceive]
That I was right in fearing for you,
Who are all burning in exquisite youth
And in the fire of young manhood,   490
Since I, who am full of old age,
Can't put up a fight against love,
For she has misled me into an evil
As great as you have seen.
In one hour, Love, which taxes   495
And devours all, has undone
Everything I ever learned and read.
And know for certain,
Since it is obviously necessary for me
To commit such obvious folly,   500
You cannot get away without loss
Or without being blamed by your people."
Aristotle got out of his trouble
Very well and elegantly,

et la dame est venue a chief 505
de trestout quanques empris a.
Et li rois forment l'en prisa
quant de son mestre l'a vengié
qui l'ot blasmé et laidengié.
Mes tant s'en fu bien escusez 510
de ce qu'ainsi fu amusez
qu'en riant li rois li pardone,
et ses mestres li abandone
sa volenté a parfurnir,
quar n'a reson au retenir. 515
    Or vueil une demande fere,
en cest dit et en ceste afere
dont je trai Chaton a garant
qui fet l'auctorité parant,
qui bons clers fu et sages hom: 520
"Turpe est doctori, cum culpa redarguit ipsum."
    Chatons dist en cest vers la glose
que, quant on est repris de chose
c'on a blasmé a fere autrui,
puis c'on en a blasme et anui, 525
c'est grant folie qui ce fet;
son sens amenuise et desfet.
Voirs fu qu'Aristote[s] blasma
Alixandre et mesaesma,
qui tant s'estoit mis en amer, 530
et puis se lessa entamer
si en amor a une foiz
qu'il n'ot en lui point de defoiz.
Et s'il l'ot par force entrepris,
en doit il estre en mal repris? 535
Nenil, quar amors l'esforça
qui sa volenté li dona
sor toz et sor toutes ensamble,
dont n'a li mestres, ce me samble,
nule coupe en sa mespresure, 540
ne l'a pas fait par apresure,
mes par nature droite et fine.
    Henris cest aventure fine
qui dist et si moustre en la fin
c'on ne peut decevoir cuer fin 545
ne oster de sa volenté,
puis qu'amors l'a en volenté
por emprisoner et destraindre;
et cil qui de ce se veut faindre
n'est mie trop loiaus amere, 550
puis que s'amors li samble amere,
quar miex ne peut on endurer
amor que par dessavorer.
Por celui mal bien plere doivent
qu'aprés les maus les biens reçoivent 555
par maintes foiz li maltraiant

114

And the lady succeeded   505
In everything she had undertaken.
And the king greatly prized her for it
When she avenged herself on his professor,
Who had blamed and insulted her.
But he excused himself so well   510
For having been tricked that way
That, laughing, the King pardoned him,
And his professor conceded to let
Him fulfill his will,
For there was no reason in holding back.   515
    Now in this tale and in this affair,
I want to pose a question
Which I take from Cato as my source,
Who expresses himself with an authority,
Who was a good scholar and a wise man: 520
"The teacher is shamed when his guilt contradicts him."
    Cato glosses this line
Thus: when someone is caught in something
That he has blamed someone else for doing,
Since he gets blame and trouble out of it,   525
It is great folly, no matter who does it;
He diminishes and undoes his mind.
It is true that Aristotle
Blamed and scorned Alexander,
Who was so dedicated to love,   530
And then he let himself be affected
So much by love one time
That he did not have any defense within him.
And if he was forced to try it out,
Should he be condemned for it?   535
No, because love forced him,
Which imposes its will
Over all, both male and female.
Therefore, the professor has, I believe,
No guilt on account of his mistake.   540
He did not do it out of learning,
But out of Nature, direct and fine.
    Henri finishes this tale,
Saying and showing in the end
That a true heart cannot be disappointed   545
Or deprived of its will,
Since love has it in its power
To imprison or to torture;
And he who wants to hesitate over this
Is not a very loyal lover   550
Since his love seems bitter to him,
For one cannot better endure love
Than by tasting bitterness.
They should be pleased on account of this pain,
For after pains, miserable sufferers receive   555
Good things many times over,

qu'aussi amors vont essaiant.
Si set ele rasseürer
qui puet en leauté durer
s'atende et sueffre en son martire,   560
quar a joie li revient s'ire.
Si puet on par cest dist aprendre
c'on ne doit blasmer ne reprendre
les amies ne les amanz,
qu'amors a pooir et commanz   565
par deseur toz et deseur toutes,
et d'euls fet ses volentez toutes,
et tret a honor toz ses fez.
Despuis que cil en soustient fez
qui fu mestre en toute science,   570
bien devons prendre sapience
selonc ce que nous mains savons
les maus que por amor[s] avons;
quar qui por amor[s] sueffre maus
bien li set merir ses travaus   575
que li amant sueffrent por li.
Veritez est, et je le di,
qu'amors vaint tout et tout vaincra
tant com cis siecles durera.

For they keep testing love affairs.
And love knows how to encourage
Whoever can remain steadfast in loyalty
To wait and suffer in its martyrdom,   560
Because its pain will return to him as joy.
And one can learn from this lesson
That one should not blame or chide
Lovers or their loved ones,
For love has power and command   565
Over all, both male and female,
And love works all its will with them
And turns all its burdens to honor.
Since he who was a master of all knowledge
Bore his burden,   570
We ought to learn wisdom
In proportion as we have less knowledge
Of the pain which we have for love;
For whoever suffers pain for love
Really knows how to deserve the woes   575
That lovers suffer for it.
That is the truth. I say this:
That love conquers all and will conquer all
As long as this world will last.

7.

Jadis avoit en Carembant
une riche vielle manant
a une vilete champestre.
Un fil avoit qui menoit pestre
toute jor en champ ses brebis;   5
molt estoit fols et entombis
de fol sens et de fole chiere.
Sa mere n'avoit rien tant chiere
qui veve estoit, n'ot plus enfant.
Li vallés crut et devint grant.   10
S'il fust sages, assez fust genz,
mes il croissoit devant son sens:
ausi font encor, tels i a.
La vielle, sa mere, espia
un vavassor molt endeté;   15
une fille ot de grant biauté
qui bien et mal assez savoit,
et por ce que la vielle avoit
bons cortiz et bon heritage,
voloit fere le mariage   20
du vallet et de la meschine.
Un jor, por veoir le couvine,
a pris la vielle un sien mantel,
de .II. qu'ele en ot le plus bel,
l'un de taissons, l'autre de chas: 25
a son col le pent par le las.
Bien s'apareille gentement,
au mez s'en vint isnelement
la ou li vavassors manoit.
Venue i fu or: "Diex i soit!   30
Bien viegniez vous, dame Ermengart."
"Diex soit o vous, sire Girart!
Comment vous baretez vous ore?"
"Par foi, je doi assez encore
qui vaut plus de .LX. livres."   35
"En volez vous estre delivres?"
"Oïl, mes je ne sai comment."
"Bien vous dirai comfetement
ne devrez vaillant une bille."
"Comment?" "Donez Meheut vo fille   40

118

7.

Once there was an old woman
Living in Carembant
In a little country town.
She had a son who took her sheep
Every day into the field to graze;   5
He was very foolish and simple,
With a foolish mind and a foolish face.
His mother, who was a widow, held nothing so
Dear as him. (She had no other children.)
The boy got bigger and grew up.   10
If he had been wise, he would have been attractive,
But he was getting big before he was wise.
(They still do that--there are some people like that.)
The old lady, his mother, found out about
A gentleman who was very much in debt;   15
He had a very beautiful daughter
Who knew plenty about good and evil,
And since the old woman had
Good gardens and a good inheritance,
She wanted to arrange a marriage   20
Between the young man and the girl.
One day, in order to see to the arrangement,
The old woman took one of her coats,
The finer of the two she had
(One of badger, the other of cat),   25
And hung it from her neck by a strap.
She got dressed up very nicely
And went quickly to the house
Where the nobleman lived.
She arrived there in good time: "God be with us!   30
Welcome, Lady Ermengart."
"God be with you, Sir Girard!
How are you managing now?"
By faith, I still owe plenty,
More than sixty pounds worth."   35
"Do you want to get out of it?"
"Yes, but I don't know how."
"I'll tell you exactly how.
You won't owe as much as a marble."
"How?" "Give your daughter Mahaud   40

119

a fame mon fil Robinet:
trop bele branche de vallet
a en lui et trop bien seant,
et si ne set ne tant ne quant
ne de taverne ne de jus."   45
Tant parlerent ha sus bon jus
qu'il en firent le mariage:
si les dut tenir en mesnage
li vavassors .V. anz entiers.
Ainsi l'otrient volentiers   50
et pristrent jor des noces fere.
La vielle s'est mise el repere,
qui plus ne vaut iluec muser.
Quant vint au jor de l'espouser,
la vielle charga Robinet   55
son fil un menestrel Jouglet
que il au moustier le menast
et apreïst et enseignast,
qu'il estoit sages et soutiex,
et ses filz estoit enfantiex.   60
Jouglés molt volentiers le fist,
mes onques bien ne li aprist
ne riens que li eüst mestier,
quar, ainz c'on alast au moustier,
le mena en un plaisseïs   65
a un perier d'estrangleïs.
Si le fist deseure monter.
Robins commença a brouster
de ces poires a grant esploit,
et Jouglés, qui fol le veoit,   70
metoit les keues en [un] gant.
Puis li dist que il menjast tant
de ces poires a tout le mains
que son gant fust de keues plains,
quar ce li covenoit il fere.   75
Robins n'ot soing de tel afere,
ainz li dist que il ne porroit
et qu'il a le ventre si roit
et s'est si plains et si enflez,
qui li donroit .IIII. citez,   80
ne feroit il ce qu'il li rueve.
Et Jouglés, qui la borde trueve,
li dist que fere li covient:
puis que li hom a fame vient,
c'est droiz, a fere li estuet.   85
Robins dist bien que il ne puet,
mes il ne l'osoit coroucier;
s'il peüst son ventre vuidier,
il ne fust mie si mal mis:
"En non Dieu," fet Jouglés, "amis,   90
sachiez que l'en ne chie mie
le jor c'on espeuse s'amie,

As a wife to my son Robby.
He's a fine sprig of a youth,
And quite well established,
And he doesn't know a thing
About taverns or gambling."   45
They discussed it up and down
Until they arranged the marriage.
The nobleman was to put them up
For five whole years.
So they agreed to it willingly   50
And fixed a day to have the wedding.
Since there was no point in dawdling there,
The old woman went back home.
When the day of the wedding came,
The old woman made a minstrel,   55
Jouglet, responsible for bringing
Her son Robby to church
And for teaching and instructing him,
Because he was wise and clever,
And her son was childish.   60
Jouglet very willingly did it,
But he never taught him anything good
Or anything that he would need,
Because before they went to church,
He took him to an orchard,   65
To a chokepear tree,
And he made him climb up into it.
Robin began to fill himself
At a great speed with these pears,
And Jouglet, who saw that he was foolish,   70
Was putting the stems in a glove.
Then he told him that he should
Eat at least enough
For his glove to be full of stems,
Because that's what he was supposed to do.   75
Robin didn't care for such a scheme;
Instead, he told him that he couldn't do it
And that his belly was so taut
And was so full and so swollen,
That, even if someone had given him four cities,   80
He couldn't have done what he was asking.
Jouglet, who was making up the joke,
Told him that he had to do it.
When a man goes to a woman,
It is right; he has to do it.   85
Robin said that he really couldn't do it,
But he didn't dare make him angry;
If he could empty his bowels,
He wouldn't be so bad off.
"In the name of God," said Jouglet, "my friend,   90
Know that one doesn't shit
On the day he weds his beloved,

quar ce seroit trop grant ledure."
Robins au miex qu'il pot l'endure.
Son ventre molt forment li bruit.   95
    Ja estoient au moustier tuit
li parent a la damoisele.
Jouglés atempre sa viele,
si l'en maine tout vielant.
Que vous iroie je contant?   100
Au moustier vienent sanz atendre.
Robin fist on sa fame prendre,
et, quant ele espousee fu,
puis sont arriere revenu.
Cel jor furent bien conreé   105
c'on avoit assez atorné,
qui qu'en eüst ire ne duel,
bons flaons et bon morteruel
et bon lait bien boilli et cuit.
Robers en menjast bien, je cuit,   110
s'il n'eüst si mal en son ventre,
et Jouglés li sivoit soventre
quant on devoit mengier aler.
Ainc ne sot tant Robers parler
a Jouglet ne si bel proier   115
que il li vousist otroier
qu'il le lessast chier un peu,
et s'est plus dolereus d'un cleu
toz ses ventres, si granz qu'il est.
    Au vespre furent li lit prest,   120
la dame se coucha premiers.
Robers n'ert mie coustumiers
de couchier au vespre si fars.
"Biaus filz," ce dist dame Ermengars,
"com vous fetes or mate chiere."   125
"Dame," dist Jouglés li trichiere,
"quar il est honteus et sorpris
de ce que il n'est mie apris
ne de fame ne de tele oevre."
Robers se couche et on le cuevre;   130
si fet on la chambre vuidier,
mes ele ne fet que cuidier
de ce que Robers ne l'adoise.
"Lasse," fet ele, "com me poise
de ce nice, de ce musart!   135
Molt li deüst ore estre tart
qu'il m'acolast et me besast,
et q'o tel fame s'aaisast
com je sui et de tel afere.
Mes il ne set que l'en doit fere: 140
il ne me taste ne manie.
Por la char Dieu, com sui honie
quant cis vilains gist delez mi!
Se j'eüsse ore mon ami,

Because that would be too great an insult."
Robin endured it as best he could.
His stomach was making a lot of noise.
    All the young lady's relatives   95
Were already at the church.
Jouglet tuned his fiddle
And led him along playing upon it.
Why should I stretch this out?   100
Without delay they came to the church.
They made Robert take his wife,
And when she had been wed,
They went back home again.
They were well treated that day,   105
Because there was plenty prepared,
No matter who might not have like it:
Good custards and good soup
And good milk, well boiled and cooked.
Robert would have eaten plenty, I think,   110
If his stomach hadn't hurt him so much,
And Jouglet followed after him
When they were supposed to eat.
Robert couldn't speak enough
Or beg Jouglet hard enough   115
For him to agree
To let him shit a little bit.
And his whole stomach was so big that it
Was in worse pain than if it had been nailed.
    At evening the beds were ready.   120
The lady got in first.
Robert was not at all used
To going to bed so stuffed in the evening.
"Dear son," said Lady Ermengard,
"How discouraged you look!"   125
"Lady," said Jouglet, the trickster,
"It's because he is embarrassed and ashamed
Of not knowing very much
About women or this kind of business."
Robert went to bed and they covered him up   130
And cleared the room,
But all she did was worry
That Robert was not coming to her.
"Alas," she said, "how grieved I am
Because of this simpleton, this idiot!   135
It really must be about time
For him to hold and kiss me
And give solace to a woman
Such as I am, and in this situation.
But he doesn't know what's supposed to be done.   140
He doesn't touch or handle me.
By God's flesh, how disgraced I am
With this clod lying beside me!
If I had my lover now,

qui m'acolast et me besast   145
entre ses braz et m'aaisast,
molt me venist or miex assez
que cis vilains muse enpastez!
Honi soient tuit li parent
et trestuit li mien ensement   150
qui m'ont doné a ceste beste!"
Robers n'avoit cure de feste:
par le lit se va detordant,
son linçuel d'angoisse mordant,
et dist: "Las! Que porrai je fere?"   155
Cele escoute tout son afere,
qui n'ot cure de sommeillier;
forment se prent a merveillier
quel chose Robers puet avoir,
mes ele le voudra savoir   160
par biau parler et par biau faindre.
Et cil se commence a replaindre.
"Robert," dist ele, "qu'avez vous?
Dont n'est ce tout un entre nous?
A moi devez vous bien parler,   165
ne me devez mie celer
nule chose, laide ne bele."
"Par mon chief," fet il, "damoisele,
je nel vos oseroie dire."
"Por qoi? Dont n'estes vous me sire?   170
A cui, sire, direz vous don
vostre mesaise s'a moi non?
Qu'avez vous et quels maus vous tient?
Certes vous me direz dont vient
cis maus, que je le vueil savoir.   175
Vous le direz!" "Non ferai voir,
por tout l'avoir de ceste vile."
Cele qui molt savoit de guile
li dist, ausi comme en plorant:
"Robert, sire, por saint Amant   180
et por Dieu et por saint Espir,
ne vous lessiez mie morir!
Se vous morez, et je sui vive,
que devandra ceste chetive
qui tant vous aime durement?   185
Se vous morez sifetement
que ne me vueilliez descouvrir
vostre mal, il m'estuet morir."
Tant li commenca a proier
qu'il li dist: "Je muir de chier;   190
ainsi m'a Jouglés malbailli."
"Qui, por celui et por celi,
se vous a ainsi atorné,
or tost n'i ait plus demoré!
Il gist delez ceste paroit: 195
chiez a son chevés tout droit;

To kiss me and hold me   145
In his arms and give me solace,
I would be getting a whole lot more
Than from this stuffed idiotic clod!
May all his relatives be shamed
And all mine as well,   150
Who gave me to this beast!"
Robert did not care to celebrate.
He was twisting in the bed,
Biting his sheet in anguish.
"Alas!" he said, "What can I do?"   155
She, who did not care to sleep,
Listened to all his goings on;
She began to wonder very much
What could be the matter with Robert,
And tried to find out   160
By fair speech and by fair looks.
Then he began to moan again.
"Robert," she said, "what's the matter with you?
Isn't it all one between us?
You really should speak to me,   165
And you should never hide anything
From me, ugly or beautiful."
"By my head, young lady," said he,
"I wouldn't dare tell you."
"Why?" Aren't you my lord?   170
To whom, then, my lord, will you tell
Your trouble if not to me?
What's the matter, what evil has hold of you?
Certainly, you'll tell me where this evil
Comes from, because I want to know.   175
You must tell it!" "No, I will not,
Not for all the money in this town."
She, who knew a lot of trickery,
Said to him, just as if she were crying:
"Robert, lord, by Saint Amand   180
And by God and by the Holy Spirit,
Don't let yourself die!
If you die and I'm still alive,
What will become of this wretched woman
Who loves you so much?   185
If you die like this
Because you won't reveal
Your trouble to me, I will have to die."
She began begging so hard
That he told her: "I'm dying to shit.   190
That's how Jouglet misled me."
"Whoever that may be
Who put you in that fix--
Well, quick! No more delay!
He's lying by that wall.   195
Shit right at the head of his bed

si getez sa chemise puer."
"Or dites vous bien, bele suer,"
fet Robers qui mestier en a.
Et il maintenant se leva,   200
au lit s'en vint ou Jouglés gist;
tout droit a son chevés s'assist,
iluec desempli sa ventree:
Jouglés ot beü la vespree,
por ce ne s'esveilla il mie.   205
     Cil s'en revint delez s'amie;
si se coucha delez li droit,
mes or fu il plus a destroit
que il n'estoit devant assez.
"Robert, estes vous respassez,"   210
fet la damoisele, "et garis?"
"Damoisele, ainz sui plus maris
que je ne fui assez devant."
"Vous avez pou alé avant:
ralez chier droiz a l'esponde.   215
Dame Diex a foi me confonde,
s'il n'est bien droiz c'on le deçoive:
qui merde brasse, merde boive,
quar ce est bien resons et droiz."
Robers, qui molt estoit destroiz,   220
s'est levez sanz plus arester.
Au lit Jouglet en vint ester:
si pres de l'esponde chia
que toz les linceus cunchia,
puis se recouche isnel le pas.   225
Mes je vous di bien qu'il n'ot pas
en son lit geü longuement,
autant c'on eüst seulement
alé et venu de la fors,
quant ses ventres li reprent lors,   230
quar les poires si avaloient
qui de son cors issir voloient,
et il en souffroit grant torment.
"Robert, que est ce ne comment?
Cis ventres vous deut il or mes?"   235
"Oïl, dame, plus c'onques mes!
Je n'oi huimés si mal comme ore."
"Il vous covient chier encore,"
fet ele, "il n'i a autre tor!
Ralez a son lit tout entor,   240
tout droit a l'esponde de la."
Et cil maintenant s'en ala
au lit Jouglet tout a droiture.
Jouglés par sa male aventure
avoit la ses braies getees   245
et la les avoit oubliees
a l'esponde devers le fu,
et Robers, qui angoisseus fu,

And throw his shirt outside."
"Well said, sweet sister,"
Said Robert, who needed to do it.
And then he got up   200
And went to the bed where Jouglet lay;
He sat down right at his bedhead,
And there he unloaded his stomach.
Jouglet had been drinking that evening,
So he did not wake up at all.   205
       The other man went back to his beloved
And lay down beside her.
But now he was in even
Worse pain than before.
"Robert, are you better off,"   210
Said the young lady, "and cured?"
"No, Miss, I'm even worse off
Than I was before."
"You got a little ahead of yourself.
Go back and shit right on the edge of the bed.   215
By faith, may the Lord God confound me
If it isn't right to play a trick on him.
Whoever prepares shit should drink shit,
Because that's only right and fair."
Robert, who was in great pain,   220
Got up without waiting any longer
And went and stood by Jouglet's bed
And shat so close to the edge
That he shat all over the sheets.
Then he went straight back to bed.   225
But I tell you that he had not
Lain on his bed long enough
For a person simply to have gone
And come back from outside,
When his stomach took hold of him again,   230
Because the pears, which were trying to get
Out of his body, were going down in that direction,
And he was suffering great torment because of them.
"Robert, what is it now?
Is that stomach still hurting you?"   235
"Yes, lady. More than ever!
I never had such a bad one as now."
"You're going to have to shit again,"
She said; "there's no other way!
Go back all the way around his bed,   240
Straight to the other side."
And now he went straight
Over to Jouglet's bed.
Jouglet, unluckily for him,
Had thrown his britches off   245
And had forgotten them there
On the side next to the fire,
And Robert, who was in torment,

127

n'i atendi ne mains ne plus,
ainz a chié ausi droit sus   250
comme s'il i eüst gagié,
si en a son ventre alegié
un poi, si se recouche atant.
Et lors li va reborbetant
ses ventres, que il fu couchiez.   255
Sachiez, molt en fu corouciez!
Tout adés le covint veillier,
il ne finoit de ventreillier.
Robers menoit molt male fin.
"Or estes vous garis enfin,"   260
dist sa fame, "Robert, biaus frere?"
"Non sui, par l'ame de mon pere:
je n'oi hui si grant mal com j'ai,"
fet Robers, "je cuit, je morrai."
"Or tost, il vous covient chier   265
et vostre ventre bien vuidier.
Diex confonde le cors Jouglet!
Vous avez mauvés gibelet
eü anuit ceste vespree.
Honie soit or tel ventree   270
que il covient netoier tant!"
Que vous iroie je contant?
Le feu li a fet descouvrir
et chier enz, et puis couvrir
c'on n'i peüst merde cuidier.   275
Puis li fist le seel vuidier,
espandre l'eve et chiier enz.
Mes encore fu ce neenz
envers ce qu'ele li fist fere,
quar la viele li fist trere   280
qui estoit pendue au postel;
se li fist chier el forrel,
puis li fist remetre et fermer.
"Dame," dist il, "par saint Omer,
or sui je toz enfin garis   285
du mal dont g'ere si maris."
"Robert," dist ele, "ce vueil gié."
     Maintenant s'est lez li couchié,
si l'acole et le vaut besier.
Ele se prent a merveillier,   290
se li dist: "Que volez vous fere?"
"Par mon chief, je ne sai que fere,"
dist Robers, qui molt fu buisnars,
"Mes ma mere dame Ermengars,
avant que je fame preïsse,   295
me commanda qu'ainsi feïsse,
quant je reving de fiancier.
Mes je ne sai ou commencier
se vous ne m'enseigniez a fere."
Cele s'en rist, ne se pot tere,   300

128

Didn't wait a little or a lot,
But shat right down, just   250
As if he had contracted to do it,
And he relieved his belly
Somewhat and lay down at last.
Then his stomach started gurgling again
As soon as he had lain down.   255
Believe me, he was very angry!
He still had to stay awake;
His stomach wouldn't stop rumbling;
Robert was having a very bad time.
"Now, are you cured at last,   260
Robert, dear brother?" said his wife.
"No, I'm not, by my father's soul.
I never had such a bad pain as I have now,"
Said Robert; "I think I'm going to die."
"Then quick, you need to shit   265
And empty out your stomach.
God confound Jouglet's body!
You've had a very bad sport
All night long this evening!
Cursed be such a stomach   270
Which calls for so much cleaning out!"
Why should I keep on with this story?
She had him uncover the fire
And shit in it and then cover it up
So that nobody would think that shit was there.   275
Then she had him empty the bucket,
Throw out the water and shit in it.
But even that was nothing
To what she would have him do,
Because she had him take the fiddle   280
Which was hung on the post,
And she had him shit in the case.
Then she had him put it back and close it up.
"Lady," he said, "by Saint Omer,
Now I'm all cured at last   285
Of the sickness which so afflicted me."
"Robert," she said, "that's what I want."
    Then he lay down beside her.
He held her and tried to kiss her.
She became amazed   290
And said to him, "What are you trying to do?"
"By my head, I don't know what to do,"
Said Robert, who was very simple;
"But my mother, Lady Ermengard,
Before I took a wife,   295
Commanded me to act like this
When I came back from getting married,
And I don't know where to begin
If you don't teach me what to do."
She laughed at this. She couldn't have kept quiet   300

qui li donast .LX. livres.
"Robert," fet ele, "estes vous yvres?
Dont ne savez vous grant pieça
c'on requiert la fame de ça
par devers l'oreille senestre?"   305
"Dame," dist Robers, "bien puet estre!"
Que vous feroie plus lonc conte?
De l'uevre plus a moi ne monte
ne m'en chaut comment il aviegne,
mes a son talent l'en coviegne,   310
ou se ce non, s'en ait disete,
n'est droiz que plus m'en entremete.
    Ne demora pas longuement
qu'il ajorna isnelement.
La dame se drece en son lit,   315
encor paroit li jors petit.
Jouglet apele: "Or tost levez!
Levez vous sus, si vielez,
ne soiez pereceus ne lenz,
quar il m'est pris molt grant talenz   320
d'oïr un petit vieler."
Quant Jouglés s'oï apeler,
li cuers de joie li souslieve.
"Ha, dame," fet il, "je me lieve
se je avoie ma chemise."   325
Il taste au chevés, si a mise
tout droit en la merde sa main.
"Vois, por les plaies saint Germain,"
fet il, "qui m'a si cunchiié,
qui a a mon chevés chiié?   330
Ja ne sui je mie ribaut."
"Jouglet," ce dist dame Mehaut,
"Comment vous est? Esploitiez vous!
Ja estes vous mes amis dous."
Et cil gete sa main avant,   335
puis taste a l'esponde devant,
qu'il cuidoit ses braies aerdre.
Ses mains a bouté en la merde;
ne les pot metre en autre lieu.
"Voiz," fet il, "por la teste Dieu,   340
qui a ci ceste merde mise?
Puis que j'ai perdu ma chemise,
je tasterai viaus a mes braies."
Il se lieve, jurant les plaies.
Ses braies a pris por chaucier,   345
mes en lui n'ot que coroucier
quant il i sent la merde et flaire.
Il les regeta en mi l'aire
et jure comme uns renoiez:
"Qu'a males eves soit noiez,"   350
fet il, "qui m'a basti tel plet!"
"Qu'est ce, Jouglet? Que t'a on fet?

Even if someone had given her forty pounds.
"Robert," she said, "are you drunk?
Haven't you known for a long time
That you're supposed to ask a woman for that
Through the left ear?"   305
"Lady," said Robert, "I can do that very well."
Why should I make the story longer for you?
I am not concerned with this business anymore.
I don't care how it turns out.
But let him manage as he pleases.   310
If not, let him go without.
It's not right for me to meddle in this any longer.
   It wasn't long before
The day broke suddenly.
The lady sat up in her bed.   315
Early dawn was still appearing.
She called Jouglet: "Get up quickly!
Get up and play the fiddle.
Don't be lazy or slow,
For I have a great urge   320
To hear a little fiddling."
When Jouglet heard himself called for,
His heart swelled with joy.
"Ha, lady," he said, "I'm getting up--
if I just had my shirt."   325
He felt about at the head of the bed, and he put
His hand straight into the shit.
"Look, by Saint Germain's wounds,"
He asked, "who shat on me?
Who shat at the head of my bed?   330
I'm never a slob."
"Jouglet," said Lady Mahaud,
"How are you doing? Get moving.
You're still my dear friend."
And he thrust his hand forward   335
And felt around on the near side of the bed,
Expecting to find his pants.
He shoved his hands into the shit;
He couldn't put them anywhere else.
"Look," said he, "by God's head,   340
Who put this shit here?
Since I've lost my shirt,
At least I'll look for my pants."
He got up, swearing by the wounds.
He got his pants to put them on,   345
But there was nothing for him to do but get angry
When he felt and smelled the shit.
He threw them into the air
And he swore like an apostate:
"May whoever it was who put me in this fix,"   350
He said, "drown in foul water!"
"What is it, Jouglet? What has somebody done to you?

Qui vous a ainsi eschaufé?"
"Qui, dame?" fet il, "Li maufé,
qui ont esté entor mon lit   355
qu'il n'i a lieu grant ne petit
ou n'aie merde manoiee:
s'est ma chemise cunchiee
et mes braies sont paluees;
ce sont or les beles soudees   360
que j'avrai de voz noces fere!"
"Quel coupe ai je en cest afere,"
fet ele, "Jouglet, biaus amis?
Je ne sai qui merde i a mis,
ne que ce est ne que ce fu.   365
Mes alez alumer le fu:
qui n'i voit, il est malbaillis."
Tantost est cil du lit saillis,
sa cotele vest toute pure,
au feu en vint grant aleüre.   370
Ainsi comme il ert atornez,
au feu s'en vint toz bestornez,
mes n'ot rouable ne baston,
ne il n'i a feu ne charbon
fors merde qui dedenz estoit: 375
ses mains et ses dois i boutoit
dedenz la merde toz ensamble.
De mautalent fremist et tramble,
et maudist l'eure qu'il fu nez
quant il est ainsi atornez   380
ne quant il onques fu jouglere.
Dist la dame: "Jouglet, biaus frere,
qu'est ce? Est li feus estains dont?"
"Oïl, dame, il est un estront!
Il n'i a feu ne autre chose   385
fors merde qui enz est enclose."
"Jouglet," fet ele, "biaus amis,
puis que vous estes si honis,
alez vous laver au seel
qui pent encoste le reel,   390
tout droit a l'uis devers la cort."
Jouglés tantost cele part cort
qui molt se desirre a moillier:
ses mains commence a tooillier
enz el seel et a froter.   395
La merde sent esclaboter
qui molt li put au nez et flaire.
Il s'escrie, ne se pot taire:
"Li deable sont en cest estre,
et li deable i puissent estre   400
trestuit cil d'enfer a un mot!
Quar, se j'eüsse mon sorcot
et ma viele seulement,
je m'en alaisse isnelement."

Who's gotten you all riled up?"
"Who, lady?" he said: "Devils,
Who were all around my bed,   355
Because there's no place, large or small,
Where they haven't spread shit:
My shirt's been shat on
And my pants are soiled.
These are the excellent wages   360
I get for performing at your wedding!"
"Is this business any of my fault,"
She asked, "Jouglet, dear friend?
I don't know who put shit there,
Or what it is or what it was.   365
But go light the fire!
Anyone who can't see is in trouble."
Then he jumped out of bed,
Put his clean robe on, over nothing else,
And went quickly to the fire.   370
When he was all dressed,
He went to the fire all upset,
But there wasn't any poker or stick,
And there wasn't any fire or coal,
Except the shit that was in there.   375
His hand and fingers were sticking
All together in the shit.
He shook and shivered with rage
And cursed the hour when he was born,
When he was fixed like this,   380
And when he was ever a jongleur.
The lady said, "Jouglet, dear brother,
What is it? Has the fire gone out?"
"Yes, lady, it's shit!
There is no fire or anything else   385
Except the shit that's shut in there."
"Jouglet," she said, "dear friend,
Since you're in such a mess,
Go wash up in the bucket
That's hanging near the towel,   390
Right by the door to the yard."
At once, Jouglet, who wanted very much
To rinse off, ran over there
And started shaking and rubbing
His hands in the bucket.   395
He felt the shit spattering,
Smelling and stinking badly in his nose.
He cried out--he could not keep still:
"Devils are in this place,
And may the devils stay here--   400
All of them from Hell, at once!
But if I just had my overcoat
And my fiddle,
I'd get out of here at once."

133

Au lit s'en vint, plus n'i atent,   405
et sa viele a son col pent,
mes il i a fet mauvés change,
qu'il s'en va sanz chemise en lange,
n'a mie ore toz ses aviaus,
et bien sachiez que ses forriaus   410
ne flere pas clous de girofle.
     Cel jor fu feste saint Cristofle,
mien escïent un mercredi,
et Jouglés, si com je vous di,
par mi cele vile passa.   415
Entor lui grant gent amassa
droit a l'entree du moustier.
"Amis," font il, "de vo mestier
vous covient paier le travers."
Cil torne la teste en travers   420
et dist que il est deshaitiez,
"Ne vous chaut, vous estes gaitiez,"
font li vilain en lor françois
"Il vous covient chanter ainçois
que vous vous departez de ci."   425
Cil voit n'i a nule merci,
quar li vilain sont trop engrés.
"Tenez," fet il, "si desnoez
cest forrel ci, li uns de vous."
Li uns le prent sor ses genous   430
et uns autres l'a desnoué.
Andui se sont tuit emboué
de ce qu'est dedenz la viele.
La jornee ne fu pas bele
envers Jouglet, quar li vilain   435
le mistrent en molt lait pelain,
quar encontre terre l'abatent
et tant le fierent et debatent
par mi le dos, par mi le ventre,
c'on li peüst, mien escïentre,   440
toz les os en la pel hocier:
en tout l'an ne se pot aidier.
Ainsi fu cunchiez Jouglés
et ainsi gariz Robinés:
teus cuide cunchier autrui,   445
qui tout avant cunchie lui.

He went to the bed. He waited no longer,   405
And he hung his fiddle about his neck,
But he had struck a bad deal,
Because he was going off without his wool shirt.
He didn't have everything he wished,
And know indeed that his violin case   410
Did not smell like a clove.
    That day was the feast of Saint Christopher,
A Wednesday, I think,
And Jouglet, as I told you,
Went through that town.   415
Around him a great crowd was gathering
Right at the entrance of the church:
"Friend," they said, "you must pay
To get through by plying your trade."
He turned his head sideways   420
And said that he was indisposed.
"That doesn't make any difference. You're caught,"
Said the peasants in their own French;
"You must sing before
You leave here."   425
He saw that there was no mercy,
Because the peasants were too insistent.
"Here," he said, "one of you
Untie my case."
One of them took it on his knees   430
And another untied it.
Both got all smeared
From what was in the fiddle.
It was not a good day
For Jouglet, because the peasants   435
Put him in a very ugly state,
For they knocked him to the ground
And struck and beat him so much
In the back and in the stomach
That I think you could have   440
Rattled all the bones in his skin.
He was not able to heal for a whole year.
That's how Jouglet was shat on
And how Robby was relieved.
He who plans to shit on someone else   445
Gets shat on first.

135

8.

Oiez, seignor, un bon fablel.
Uns clers le fist por un anel
que .III. dames un main trouverent.
Entre eles .III. Jhesu jurerent
que icele l'anel auroit   5
qui son mari miex guileroit
por fere a son ami son buen,
l'anel auroit et seroit sien.
  La premiere se porpenssa
en quel guise l'anel aura.   10
Son ami a tantost mandé.
Quant il sot qu'el l'a commandé,
si vint a li delivrement,
quar il l'amoit molt durement,
et ele lui, si n'ot pas tort.   15
Del meillor vin et del plus fort
c'on pot trover en cele terre
fist la dame maintenant querre,
et si ot quis dras moniaus
qui assez furent bons et biaus;   20
del vin donna a son mari;
il en but tant, je le vous di,
qu'il ne savoit ou il estoit;
acoustumé pas ne l'avoit.
Quant li preudom fu endormi,   25
entre la dame et son ami
l'ont pris et rez et l'ont tondu
et coroné: tant ot beü
que l'en le peüst escorcier.
La dame et son douz ami chier   30
le prenent, et si l'ont porté
droit devant la porte a l'abé,
dont il erent assez prochain.
Iluec jut jusqu'a lendemain
que Dame Diex dona le jor.   35
Il s'esveilla, si ot paor,
quant il se vit si atorné,
"Diex!" dist il, "Qui m'a coroné?
Est ce donc par vostre voloir?
Oïl, ce puet on bien savoir,   40

136

THE THREE LADIES WHO FOUND A RING

8.

Listen, my lords, to a good fabliau.
A clerk composed it about a ring
Which three ladies found one morning.
They swore by Jesus between the three of them
That the one who best tricked her husband   5
In order to do her pleasure with her lover
Would get the ring;
She would have the ring and it would be hers.
    The first thought deeply
To find a trick to get the ring.   10
She immediately sent for her lover.
When he learned that she had called him,
He came quickly,
Because he loved her very much,
And she him (in this she was not wrong).   15
The lady now got some
Of the best and strongest wine
That could be found in the land,
And she also got some monastery robes
Which were very good and beautiful.   20
She gave some wine to her husband;
And he drank so much, I tell you,
That he didn't know where he was;
He wasn't used to it.
When the good man was asleep,   25
The lady and her friend together
Took him and shaved him and tonsured
And crowned him. He had drunk so much
That they could have skinned him.
The lady and her dear lover   30
Took him and carried him
Right to the door of the abbot,
Whom they lived fairly close to.
There he lay until the next day
When the Lord God gave the sunrise.   35
He awoke and was afraid
When he saw that he was made up the way he was.
"God," he said, "who crowned me?
Is it Your will, then?
Yes. Anyone can tell   40

137

que nus fors vous ne le m'a fait.
Or n'i a donc point de deshait;
vous volez que je soie moine,
et jel serai sanz nule essoine."
Maintenant sor ses piez se drece;   45
grant oirre, que ne s'aperece,
vient a la porte, si apele.
Li abés ert a la chapele,
qui maintenant l'a entendu.
La porte ouvri: quant l'a veü   50
a pié, et sanz ame, toz sous,
"Frere," fet il, "qui estes vous?"
"Sire," dist il, "je suis uns hom;
estre vueil de relegion.
De ci pres sui vostre voisin.   55
Sachiez que encore ier matin
ne savoie ceste aventure!
Mes Dame Diex, qui tout figure,
m'en a doné si bon talent
et moustré si cortoisement,   60
Sire, com vous m'oez conter;
quar il m'a fet ci aporter
tout coroné et tout tondu,
comme autre moine revestu.
Fetes moi mander ma moillier,   65
et se l'i ferai otroier:
de ma terre et de mon avoir
vous ferai tant ceenz avoir,
que toute en aurez ma partie
por estre de vostre abeie."   70
Li abés covoita la terre,
si envoia la dame querre,
et ele i vint delivrement,
quar bien savoit a escient
por qoi li abés l'ot mandee.   75
Et. quant el fu leenz entree
et ele a veü son seignor:
"Sire, por Dieu le creator,
volez vous moines devenir?
Je nel porroie pas soufrir!"   80
A la terre cheï pasmee.
Par faint samblant s'est demoree
une grande piece a la terre;
samblant fet que le cuer li serre.
Li abés li dist franchement: 85
"Dame, cest duel est por neent!
Vous deüssiez mener grant joie:
vostre sire est en bone voie;
Diex l'aime, ce pöez savoir,
qui a son oes le veut avoir."   90
El l'otria a quelque paine.
Uns gars a son ostel l'enmaine,

138

That no one but You has done this to me.
Therefore, there's nothing to be sad about;
You want me to be a monk,
And I will be, without trying to get out of it."
Then he got to his feet;   45
Quickly, so as not to waste time,
He came to the door and called.
The abbot, who heard him now,
Was in the chapel.
He opened the door: when he saw him   50
Standing there, not a soul with him, all alone,
He said, "Brother, who are you?"
"Lord," he replied, "I am a man.
I want to join a religious order.
I am a neighbor of yours from close by.   55
Know that even yesterday morning I still
Didn't know about this turn of events!
But the Lord God, who works everything out,
Has given me a worthy desire
And guided me very courteously,   60
Sir, as you hear me tell;
For He has had me brought here
All crowned and all tonsured,
Dressed like another monk.
Send for my wife,   65
And I'll make her agree to this:
I will let you people have so much
Of my land and of my money
That you will have my whole share
For letting me join your abbey."   70
The abbot coveted the land,
So he sent someone to get the lady,
And she came right away,
Because she knew for sure
Why the abbot had sent for her.   75
And when she had gone inside
And she saw her husband, she said,
"Lord, by God the Creator,
Do you want to become a monk?
I could not endure it!"   80
She fell to the ground in a faint.
Guilefully pretending, she stayed
A long time on the ground;
She made believe that her heart was breaking.
The abbot told her frankly: 85
"Lady, this grieving is useless!
You ought to be rejoicing greatly:
Your lord is on the right track;
God, who wants to have him
For His own use, loves him. You know that."   90
She agreed to it with some difficulty.
A boy brought her home,

ou ele trova son ami.
Maint preudome a esté trahi
par fame et par sa puterie. 95
Cil fu moines en l'abeïe,
ou il i fu molt longuement.
Por ce chasti je toute gent
qui cest fablel oient conter,
qu'il ne se doivent pas fier 100
en lor fames, n'en lor mesnies,
se li nes ont ainz essaïes
que plaines soient de vertuz.
Mains hom a esté deceüz
par fame et par lor trahison. 105
Cil fu moines contre reson,
qui ja en sa vie nel fust,
se sa fame nel deceüst.
        La seconde a molt grant envie
de l'anel; ne s'oublia mie, 110
ainz se porpensse comment l'ait;
molt fu plaine de grant agait.
Il avint a un vendredi,
tout ainsi com vous orrez ci.
Ses sire ert au mengier assi, 115
anguilles avoit jusqu a .VI.;
les anguilles erent salees
et sechies et enfumees.
"Dame," dist il, "quar prenez tost,
ces anguilles cuisiez en rost." 120
"Sire, ceenz n'a point de feu."
"Et ja en a il en maint leu
ci pres. Alez i vistement!"
La dame les anguilles prent,
et trespassa outre la rue; 125
chiés son ami en est venue.
Quant il la vit, molt ot grant joie,
com se il fust sire de Troie,
et la dame grant joie maine.
Iluec fu toute la semaine, 130
et l'autre jusqu'au vendredi.
Quant vint a eure de midi,
la dame apela un garçon:
"Gars," dist ele, "va en meson,
et saches que mon seignor fait." 135
Li gars molt tost a l'ostel vait.
La table ert mise, et sus .II. pains,
et li preudom lavoit ses mains;
asseïr devoit maintenant.
Li gars vint arriere corant, 140
et dist: "Vostre mari menjue."
Cele ne fu mie esperdue.
Chiés son voisin en est entree,
et le preudom l'a saluee,

Where she found her lover.
Many a good man has been betrayed
By a woman and her lust.   95
The man became a monk in the abbey,
Where he stayed a very long time.
Therefore I warn all people
Who hear this fabliau,
That they must not trust   100
Their wives or their servants
If they haven't put them to the test
Of whether they are full of virtue.
Many a man has been deceived
By women and by their treachery.   105
He was a monk, against all reason,
And never would have been one in his life
If his wife hadn't deceived him.
  The second lady greatly desired
To have the ring. She didn't lose her head,   110
But she thought to herself how she might have it;
She was full of tricks.
It happened on a Friday,
Just as you will hear right here.
Her husband was sitting down to eat.   115
He had as many as six eels;
The eels were salted
And fired and smoked.
"Lady," he said, "get going.
Roast these eels."   120
"Sir, there's no fire in here."
"There's still some in plenty of places
Nearby. Go on, quickly!"
The lady took the eels,
Went out onto the street,   125
And went to her lover's house.
When he saw her, he was as happy
As if he had been lord of Troy,
And the lady acted very joyful.
She was there the rest of that week   130
And the next until Friday.
When the noon hour came around,
The lady called a boy.
"Boy," she said, "go to the house,
And find out what my husband is doing."   135
The boy went at once to the house.
The table was set, with two loaves of bread on it,
And the gentleman was washing his hands;
He must have been getting ready to sit at the table.
The boy came back running   140
And said, "Your husband is eating."
She was not at all at a loss.
She went to her neighbor's house,
And the good man greeted her,

141

et la dame le resalue,   145
"Sire," dist el, "je sui venue
anguilles cuire a mon seignor.
Nous avons juné toute jor;
jel laissai or molt deshaitié
qu'il n'avoit encore hui mengié."   150
Les anguilles rosti molt tost.
Quant il fu droiz que on les ost,
si les a prises en son poing.
Son ostel n'estoit gueres loing,
et ele i fust molt tost venue;   155
tres devant son mari les rue.
"Huis," dist el, "je sui eschaudee!"
Et li preudom l'a regardee;
sor ses piez saut comme dervé.
"Pute, ou avez vous tant esté?   160
Vous venez de vo puterie."
Et la dame a haute voiz crie:
"Harou, aïde, bone gent!"
Et il i vindrent esraument,
et li preudom i fu venu,   165
chiés qui la pautoniere fu
por les .VI. anguilles rostir.
"Sire," dist el, "venez veïr!
Me sire est de son sens issu,
ne sai quel mal il a eü;   170
je me parti ore de ci..."
"Voire, pute, des vendredi!"
Cil entendirent qu'il a dit
qu'ele au vendredi s'en partit.
Cil de toutes pars l'ont saisi.   175
Li preudom fu si esbahi
que il ne sot qu'il peüst dire.
Chascuns le desache et detire,
les mains li lient et les piez,
bien est matez et cunchiiez.   180
Puis s'en issirent de l'ostel,
quar la pute ne queroit el.
L'en lor demande ou ont esté:
"Chiés dant Jehan, qui est dervé:
si est grant duel et grant domage,   185
quar orendroit li prist la rage
qu'il voloit sa fame tuer."
Cele ne se volt oublier,
ainçois a mandé son ami,
et il vint maintenant a li;   190
en sa chambre l'en a mené,
par un pertuis li a moustré
com li vilains estoit liié;
bien l'a maté et cunchiié,
et bien vaincu par son barat.   195
Li vilains reproche du chat

And the lady greeted him.   145
"Sir," she said, "I came
To cook some eels for my lord.
We've fasted all day;
I left him just now very much upset
Because he hasn't eaten yet today."   150
She cooked the eels quickly.
When they were ready to be taken out,
She took them in her hand.
Her house was not far,
And she soon arrived there;   155
She threw them right before her husband.
"Whew!" she said. "I'm hot!"
And the gentleman looked at her;
Then he jumped to his feet like a madman.
"Whore! Where have you been so long?   160
You've just come from your whoring."
And the lady cried out in a loud voice:
"Hey! Help, good people!"
They came in a hurry,
And the gentleman from the house   165
Where the wench had gone to cook
The six eels arrived.
"Sir," she said, "come see!
My lord has gone out of his mind.
I don't know what sickness he has caught;   170
I had just gone out..."
"Oh yeah, whore! Last Friday!"
They heard what he said:
That she had left on Friday.
Then they grabbed him from all sides.   175
The gentleman was so stunned
That he didn't know what to say.
Everyone pulled and yanked him.
They tied his hands and feet.
He was really trapped and duped.   180
Then they went out of the house,
Because the wench wanted nothing else.
Then people asked them where they had been:
"At Mr. John's, who's gone crazy.
And it's a great sorrow and a great shame,   185
Because he just now went raging mad
And wanted to kill his wife."
She didn't want to get side-tracked.
Instead, she sent for her lover,
And he came to her at once;   190
She led him into her bedroom
And showed him, through a peephole,
How the clod was tied up;
She really trapped and deceived him well
And conquered him by her trick.   195
The clod resembled a cat

qu'il set bien qui barbes il leche;
cestui a servi de la meche!
Mes, s'il eüst cuer de preudomme,
il s'en vanjast a la parsomme.   200
     Or oiez de la daerraine,
qui nuit et jor fu en grant paine
en quel guise l'anel aura.
Son ami ot que molt ama;
sachiez point n'en remest sor lui: 205
molt s'entr'amerent ambedui.
Un jor l'ot la dame mandé.
Quant il sot qu'el l'ot commandé,
si vint a li tout sanz demeure,
et la dame en meïsmes l'eure   210
li dist: "Biaus amis, longuement
vous ai amé molt folement.
Toz jors porroie ainsi muser;
bien porroie mon tens user
en fole vie et en mauvaise.   215
Se vous de moi avez mesaise,
molt seroie fole et musarde;
maus feus et male flambe m'arde
se vous jamés o moi gisez
se vous demain ne m'espousez."   220
"Dame," dist il, "por Dieu merci,
ja avez vous vostre mari!
Comment porroit ce avenir?"
"De grant folie oi plet tenir,"
dist ele; "j'en pensserai bien.   225
Ja mar en douterez de rien,
mes vous ferez a mon talent."
"Dame, a vostre commandement
ferai. Ja n'en ert desdaignie."
Lors li a la dame enseignie   230
qu'au soir viegne por son mari,
et si le maint avoeques li
chiés dant Huistasse le fil Tiesse,
ou il a une bele niece,
"que volez prendre et espouser,   235
se il a vous voloit doner.
Et g'irai la sanz demorer;
ja tant ne vous saurez haster,
que je n'i soie avant de vous.
Iluec nous troverez andous,   240
ou j'aurai mon afere fait
a Huistasse tout entresait,
en tel guise que vous m'aurez,
se Dieu plest, et me recevrez   245
tres pardevant nostre provoire.
Mon seignor ne saura que croire,
qu'il m'aura aprés lui lessie.
Je serai si appareillie

Because he knew very well whose moustache he licked;
He was forced to hold the candle!
But if he had had the heart of a true man,
He would have gotten vengeance in the end.   200
    Now hear about the last woman,
Who night and day was in great pain
Plotting how she would get the ring.
She had a lover, whom she loved very much.
She certainly didn't leave it all up to him: 205
They both loved each other very much.
One day the lady called him.
When he knew that she had summoned him,
He came to her right away,
And at once the lady   210
Told him: "Dear friend, for a long time
I have loved you desperately.
I might go on like this forever;
Indeed I might always waste my time
In a foolish and a wicked life.   215
If you had any grief over me,
I would be very foolish and trifling.
May the evil fire and the evil flame burn me
If you ever lie with me again,
Unless you marry me tomorrow."   220
"Lady," he said, "for the love of God,
You already have a husband!
How could this happen?"
"I hear you argue very foolishly,"
She said; "I will plan it all out.   225
You won't have anything to fear,
But you will do my will."
"Lady, I will act according to your command.
It will not be scorned."
Then the lady instructed him   230
To come for her husband in the evening
And to take him with him
To the home of Mr. Eustache, the son of Tiesse,
Where he had a fair niece,
"Whom you want to take and marry,   235
If he would give her to you.
And I'll be going there right now;
You won't be able to go so fast
That I won't get there ahead of you.
There you will find us both,   240
And I will have settled the affair
Already with Eustache
In such a way that you will have me,
God willing, and you'll take me
Right in front of our priest.   245
My lord won't know what to think,
Because he'll have left me behind him.
I will be fixed up in such a way

145

que je aurai chancgiez mes dras
que il ne me connoistra pas,   250
et me fiancerez demain
tres pardevant no chapelain.
A mon mari direz: 'Biaus sire,
el non Dieu et el non saint Sire,
ceste fame me saisissiez.'   255
Il en sera joianz et liez,
et bien sai que il me donra
a vous, et grant joie en aura,
et, s'il ainsi me veut doner,
je di que ce n'est pas prester."   260
Issi fu fet, issi avint.
Toute sa vie cil la tint
a cui son mari la dona;
por ce que il ne li presta
ne la pot onques puis r'avoir.   265
    Mes or vueil je par vous savoir
laquele doit avoit l'anel.
Je di que cele ouvra molt bel
qui moine fist de son seignor;
et cele r'ot el grant honor   270
qui le suen fist prendre et loier
et par estavoir otroier,
et toz les .VIII. jors mesconter;
ceste se refist espouser
en tel maniere a son ami.   275
Or dites voir, n'i ait menti,
et si jugiez reson et voir
laquele doit l'anel avoir.

That I will have changed my clothes
So that he won't know me,   250
And you will wed me tomorrow
Right in front of our chaplain.
And you'll tell my husband, 'Good sir,
In the name of God and in the name of St. Cyril,
Get this woman for me!'   255
And he will be joyful and delighted,
And I will know that he will give me
To you, and great joy he will have from it.
And if he wants to give me this way,
I say it's not for a loan."   260
That's how it was done. That's how it happened.
All her life the one to whom
Her husband had given her kept her;
Since he didn't lend her to him,
He never could get her back again.   265
      But now I would like to know from you
Which one ought to have the ring.
I say that she managed very well
Who made her lord into a monk;
And she also had great honor   270
Who had hers taken and bound
And had him give his consent by force
And miscount the whole week;
The other one had herself married,
The way you heard it, to her lover.   275
Now tell the truth. Let there be no lie,
And so judge by reason and truth
Which one should have the ring.

9.

En la conté de Dant Martin
avint entor la saint Martin
le boillant, que gibiers aproche,
uns chevaliers qui sans reproche
vesqui ou païs son aage.   5
Molt le tenoient cil a sage
qui de lui estoient acointe.
Une dame mingnote et cointe,
fame a un riche vavassor,
proia cil et requist d'amor,   10
et tant qu'ele devint s'amie.
Entor .II. liues et demie
avoit entre lor .II. osteus.
Li amis a la dame ert teus
qu'il erroit par toute la terre,   15
por honor et por pris conquerre,
tant que tuit le tindrent a preu.
Et li vavassors por son preu
entendoit a autre maniere,
qu'il avoit la langue maniere   20
a bien parler et sagement,
et bien savoit un jugement
recorder: c'estoit ses delis.
      Por aler aus plais a Senlis,
Apresta un matin son oirre.   25
Et la dame manda bon oirre
son ami par un homme sage
qui bien sot conter son message.
Et quant cil oï la novele,
robe d'escarlate novele   30
a vestu, forree d'ermine.
Comme bacheler s'achemine,
qui amors metent en esfroi;
montez est sor son palefroi,
ses esperons dorez chauciez,   35
mes por le chaut ert deschauciez
et prist son esprevier mué
que il meïsmes ot mué,
et maine .II. chienés petiz,
qui estoient trestoz fetiz   40

148

THE KNIGHT WITH THE SCARLET ROBE

9.

In the county of Dammartin
It happened around the feast of St. Martin,
The burning saint, whom the beasts befriend,
That a knight without reproach
Was living in that country.   5
Those who knew him considered
Him very wise.
He begged and requested love
From a darling and pretty lady,
The wife of a rich fief-holding vassal,   10
For so long that she became his beloved.
There were about two and a half
Leagues between their houses.
The lady's lover was one of those
Who wandered throughout the earth   15
To conquer honor and glory,
Until all held him in high esteem.
But the vassal meant something
Different by his esteem,
For he had a tongue which was skilled   20
In speaking well and wisely,
And he knew how to record
A judgment well; that was his delight.
    One morning he got ready to make his journey
To go to the court at Senlis,   25
And the lady quickly sent for
Her lover through a wise man
Who well knew how to deliver his message.
And when he heard the news,
He put on a new scarlet robe, lined   30
With ermine.
He rode like a young man
Whom love makes eager;
He was mounted on his palfrey,
His golden spurs on his feet,   35
But he had no shoes on because of the heat.
And he took his molted sparrow hawk,
Which he himself had molted,
And brought two little bitch dogs
That were well trained   40

149

por fere aus chans saillir l'aloe.
Si com fine amor veut et loe,
s'est atornez. D'iluec s'en part,
et est venuz droit cele part
ou il cuida trover la dame   45
mes n'i trova homme ne fame,
qui de nis une rien l'aresne.
Son palefroi tantost aresne
et mist son esprevier seoir:
en la chambre cort por veoir   50
ou il cuidoit trover s'amie.
Et cele ne se dormoit mie,
ainçois se gisoit toute nue,
et si atendoit la venue
de son ami, et il vint la   55
droit au lit ou il la trova.
Il la vit crasse, et blanche et tendre.
Sanz demorer et sanz atendre,
se voloit toz vestuz couchier.
Et la dame, qui molt l'ot chier,   60
i mist un poi de contredit,
debonerement li a dit:
"Amis, bien soiez vous venuz!
Lez moi vous coucherez toz nus,
por avoir plus plesant delit."   65
Sus une huche aus piez du lit
a cil toute sa robe mise;
ses braies oste et sa chemise,
et ses esperons a ostez.
Maintenant est el lit entrez,   70
ele le prist entre ses braz.
D'autre joie, d'autre solaz
ne vous quier fere menssion,
quar cil qui ont entencion
doivent bien savoir que ce monte: 75
por ce ne vueil fere lonc conte,
mes andui firent liemant
tel deduit com font li amant
en ce qu'il se jouent ensamble.
    Li plet furent, si com moi samble,   80
contremandé au vavassor:
ainçois qu'il fust prime de jor,
est il a l'ostel revenuz.
"Dont est cis palefroiz venuz?"
Fet il, "Cui est cis espreviers?"   85
Lors vousist cil estre a Poitiers,
qui dedenz la chambre enclos iere.
Entre le lit et la mesiere
est coulez, mes tant fu sorpris
qu'il n'a point de sa robe pris,   90
fors ses braies et sa chemise.
Assez a robe[s] sor lui mise

For flushing larks in the fields.
He was dressed in the way that courtly love
Desires and approves. He left
And came directly to where
He thought he would find the lady, 45
But he found no man or woman
Who had anything to say to him.
He reined his palfrey,
Settled his sparrow hawk,
And ran to take a look in the bedroom, 50
Where he expected to find his beloved,
And she was not sleeping,
But was lying all naked
And awaiting the arrival
Of her lover, and he came 55
Straight to the bed, where he found her.
He saw her plump and white and tender.
Without pause and without delay,
He wanted to lie down all dressed.
And the lady, who held him very dear, 60
Contradicted him a little here.
She politely told him,
"Welcome, friend!
You must lie beside me completely naked
So that your delight may be all the more pleasant." 65
He put his robe
On a chest at the foot of the bed;
He took his shirt and pants off
And took off his spurs.
Then he got into bed. 70
She took him in her arms.
I don't want to go into
The rest of their joy or the rest of their solace,
Because those who understand
Ought to know what that amounts to. 75
Therefore, I don't want to make a long story,
But both enjoyed
The kind of pleasure that lovers have
When they play together.
      The vassal's law cases,
I recall, were cancelled: 80
Before the break of day
He returned home,
"Where did this palfrey come from?"
He asked. "Whose sparrow hawk is this?"
Then the one who was closed up in the bedroom 85
Would have rather been in Poitiers.
He slipped down between the bed and the wall,
But he was so startled
That he didn't put on his robe,
Just his shirt and pants. 90
The lady put a lot of dresses,

la dame, mantiaus, peliçons.
Li sires ert en granz friçons
du palefroi que il remire.   95
Encore ot au cuer greignor ire
quant il est entrez en sa chambre;
quant voit la robe, tuit li membre
li fremissent d'ire et d'angoisse.
Lors destraint la dame et angoisse,   100
et dist: "Dame, qui est ceenz?
Il a un palefroi leenz!
Cui est il? Cui est cele robe?"
Et la dame, qui biau le lobe,
li dist: "Foi que devez saint Pere,   105
n'avez vous encontré mon frere,
qui orendroit de ci s'en part?
Bien vous a lessié vo part
de ses joiaus, ce m'est avis!
Por tant seulement que je dis   110
que tel robe vous serroit bien,
ainc plus ne li dis nule rien,
ainz despoilla tout maintenant
cele bele robe avenant
et prist la seue a chevauchier.   115
Son palefroi qu'il ot tant chier,
son esprevier et ses chienés,
ses esperons cointes et nés,
freschement dorez, vous envoie.
Par poi que je ne me dervoie   120
et juroie trop durement,
mes onques por mon serement,
ne por rien que seüsse dire
ne poi je son voloir desdire.
Des qu'il li plest, prenez cest don;   125
bien l'en rendrez le gueredon
encor, se Diex vous done vie."
Et li vavassors, qui envie
avoit du biau present avoir,
li dist: "Dame, vous dites voir;   130
du palefroi m'est il molt bel,
et des chienés et de l'oisel,
mes un petit i mespreïtes
quant vous sa robe retenistes;
quar ce samble estre covoitise."   135
"Non fet, sire, mes grant franchise,
que l'en doit bien, par saint Remi,
prendre un biau don de son ami:
quar qui de prendre n'est hardiz
de doner est acouardiz."   140
      Atant lessierent la parole,
et la dame, qui biau parole
a son seignor par tel reson,
qu'il n'i puet trover achoison,

Mantles, and furs over him.
Her husband was trembling all over
Because of the palfrey he had seen;
He was even angrier   95
When he entered the bedroom.
When he saw the robe, all his limbs
Trembled with anger and anguish.
Then he seized the lady and tormented her
And said, "Lady, who is in here?   100
There's a palfrey out there.
Whose is it? Whose is that tunic?"
And the lady, who was skillfully deceiving him,
Told him, "By the faith I owe Saint Peter,
Didn't you meet my brother,   105
Who left here just now?
He really left you your share
Of his treasures, I think!
And only because I said
That a robe like that would fit you well.   110
I didn't say a thing besides that,
But right away he took off
That beautiful, fine-looking robe
And left with only his riding tunic.
His palfrey, which he valued so highly,   115
His sparrow hark, and his bitches,
And his neat, pretty spurs,
Freshly gilded, he sends them all to you.
I almost went crazy,
And swore very sternly,   120
But not by my oaths
Nor by anything else I could say
Could I dissuade him from his will.
Since it pleases him, take this gift;
You will reward him generously for it   125
Later, if God gives you life."
And the vassal, who desired
To have some fine presents,
Said to her, "Lady, what you say is true.
I'm very pleased with the palfrey   130
And with the bitches and with the bird,
But you were a little at fault
When you kept his robe,
For that seems to be covetousness."   135
"No, it isn't, sir, but great generosity,
For by Saint Remi, a person really should
Accept a fine gift from his friend:
For one who isn't bold in receiving
Is cowardly in giving."   140
    After a while they stopped talking,
And the lady, who spoke so well
To her husband with such fine discourse
That he couldn't find any way

153

par qoi i mete contredit,   145
la dame a son seignor a dit:
"Sire, vous levastes matin.
Foi que vous devez saint Martin,
venez vous delez moi gesir,
si vous reposez a loisir: 150
l'en appareille le mengier."
Et cil n'en fist onques dangier,
ainz s'est toz nus les li coulez.
Si vous di qu'il fu acolez,
et besiez .II. tans qu'il ne seut.   155
La dame a tastoner l'aqueut
si souef que il s'endormi.
Lors bouta un poi son ami,
et cil tout maintenant se drece
vers la huche tantost s'adrece   160
ou il avoit sa robe mise.
N'i a pas fete grant devise
a lui crespir, ainçois s'atorne
et au plus tost qu'il puet s'en torne,
et atout son harnois s'en vait,   165
et le vavassor dormant lait,
qui dormi jusques vers midi.
Quant il s'esveilla, si vous di
qu'a la dame n'anuia point.
Li vavassors qui en biau point   170
estoit de son riche presant,
dist c'on li aportast avant
a vestir sa robe vermeille.
Son escuier li apareille
une robe vert qu'il avoit,   175
et, quant li vavassors la voit,
se li a dit isnel le pas:
"Ceste robe ne vueil je pas,
ainz vueil m'autre robe essaier,
dont richement me sot paier   180
mon serorge, que je molt pris."
Lors fu li vallés entrepris,
qui de tout ce riens ne savoit,
quar toute jor esté avoit
aus chans les soieors garder.   185
Lors prist la dame a regarder
son seignor, et se li a dit;
"Biaus sire, se Diex vous aït!
Or me dites, se vous volez,
quele robe vous demandez: 190
Avez vous donc robe achatee,
ou se vous l'avez empruntee
de la ou vous avez esté?
Quele est ele? Est ele a esté?"
"Je vueil," fet il, "ma robe chiere,   195
qui hui main sor cele huche iere,

To contradict it,   145
Said to her lord:
"Sir, you got up early.
By the faith you owe Saint Martin,
Come lie beside me.
Rest here at leisure: 150
The meal is being prepared,"
And he made no objection,
But slipped in beside her completely naked.
And I tell you that he was hugged
And kissed twice as much as he was used to.   155
The lady set about caressing him
So gently that he went to sleep.
Then she poked her lover a little,
And he got up at once.
He went to the chest   160
Where he had put his robe.
He had no great desire
To primp and curl; instead, he got dressed
And as soon as possible left,
Going away with all his gear   165
And leaving the vassal sleeping,
Who slept until about noon.
When he woke up, I tell you
That the lady was not worried.
The vassal, who was in a good mood   170
Because of his rich present,
Said that his scarlet robe
Should be brought for him to get dressed.
His squire laid out for him
A green robe which he owned,   175
And when the vassal saw it,
He immediately said:
"I don't want that robe;
I want to try on my other robe,
The one my brother-in-law, whom I value dearly,   180
So considerately gave me."
Then the servant, who knew nothing about
All this, was surprised,
For all day he had been
Guarding the harvesters in the fields.   185
Then the lady began to look at
Her husband and said to him,
"Good sir, God help you!
Now tell me, if you wish,
What robe are you asking for?   190
Have you bought a robe then?
Or did you borrow it
From where you were today?
What is it like? Is it a summer robe?"
"I want," he said, "my fine robe,   195
The one that was on that chest this morning,

que vostre frere m'a donee.
Bien m'a s'amor abandonee,
et bien doi estre ses acointes,
quant veut que du sien soie cointes.   200
Et de ce l'aim je encore miex,
qu'il despoilla, voiant voz iex,
les garnemenz qu'il m'a lessiez."
"Certes forment vous avilliez,"
fet la dame, "ce m'est avis.   205
Bien doit estre vavassors vils
qui veut estre menesterez!
Miex voudroie que fussiez rez
sans eve, la teste et le col,
que ja n'i remainsist chevol!   210
Ce n'apartient mie a vostre oes
d'avoir garnement s'il n'est nues;
c'apartient a ces jougleors
et a ces bons enchanteors,
que il aient des chevaliers   215
les robes, que c'est lor mestiers.
Devez vous donc robe baillier
s'el n'est a coudre ou a taillier
et soit fete a vostre mesure?
Se je vous di sens et droiture,   220
creez moi! Si ferez savoir!"
Lors ne puet il apercevoir
que cele robe est devenue,
si cuide il bien qu'en sa venue
l'eüst veüe sor la huche.   225
Maintenant son escuier huche,
mes tuit furent si enseignié
que ja n'i aura gaaingnié
a son oes vaillant une poire.
Si cuide il bien et espoire   230
vraies enseignes en orra,
mes ja par aus rien n'en saura;
ainçois sera toz bestornez.
Tels les a la dame atornez
que toz les a trez a sa corde: 235
chascuns du tout a li s'acorde.
    Lors ist li sires de la chambre,
et dist: "Dame, dont ne vous membre,
quant je fui hui main arivez,
c'uns palefroiz fu ci trovez,   240
et un esprevier et dui chien,
et disiez que tout estoit mien
cest present, de par vostre frere?"
"Sire," dist ele, "par saint Pere!
Il a bien .II. mois et demi,   245
ou plus, que mon frere ne vi.
Et, s'il estoit ci orendroit
ne voudroit il en nul endroit

The one your brother gave me.
He has really been loving to me,
And I must indeed be his friend,
Since he wants me to be handsome in his own belongings.   200
And for this I love him even better:
That right before your eyes he took off
The clothes which he left for me."
"You certainly are lowering yourself a great deal,"
Said the lady; "that's what I think.   205
A vassal must really be low
Who wants to be a minstrel!
It would be better if you had
Your head and the neck shaved without water,
So that not one hair remained!   210
It's not fitting for you
To get a garment that isn't new.
It's for jugglers
And those fine mountebanks
To get clothes from knights--   215
That's their trade.
So, then, should you take a robe
If it hasn't been sewn or tailored
And made according to your measurements?
If what I'm telling you makes sense,   220
Believe me and act wisely!"
Then he couldn't figure out
What had become of that robe.
He really believed that when he had come in
He had seen it on the chest.   225
Now he called his squire,
But everybody had been so well instructed
That he couldn't get anything
Worth a pear from them.
And he really believed and hoped   230
That he would get correct information,
But he would learn nothing from them;
He would be completely befuddled first.
The lady prepared them so well
That she pulled them all along on her string: 235
Every one of them agreed with her.
     Then the lord went out of the bedroom
And said, "Lady, don't you remember
When I came in this morning,
That a palfrey was found here,   240
And a sparrow hawk and two dogs,
And you were saying that it was all mine,
This gift from your brother?"
"Sir," said she, "by Saint Peter!
It's been a good two and a half months   245
Or more since I saw my brother.
And if he were here now,
He would by no means want

qu'en vostre dos fust embatue 250
robe que il eüst vestue:
ce deüst dire uns fols, uns yvres!
Ja vaut plus de .IIII^{xx}. livres
la grant rente que vous avez
et la terre que vous tenez. 255
Querez robe a vostre talant,
et palefroi bel et amblant,
qui souef vous port l'ambleüre:
de vous ne sai dire mesure,
quar vous estes tels atornez 260
que toz les iex avez troublez.
J'ai paor de mauvés encontre,
qui hui vous venist a l'encontre,
de fantosme et de mauvés vent.
Vous muez color molt sovent, 265
que je m'en esbahiz trestoute;
ice sachiez vous bien sanz doute.
Criez a Dame Dieu merci,
et a monseignor saint Orri
que vostre memoire vous gart: 270
Il pert bien a vostre regart
que vous estes enfantosmez.
Par la rien que vous plus amez,
cuidiez vous ore, au dire voir,
la robe et le cheval avoir?" 275
"Oïl, dame, se Diex me saut."
"Diex," dist la dame, "vous consaut,
et de sa destre main vous saint!
Quar vous vouez a un bon saint,
et si i portez vostre offrande 280
que Diex la memoire vous rande."
"Dame," dist il, "et je me veu
a Dieu et au baron saint Leu,
et s'irai au baron saint Jaque,
et saint Eloy, et saint Romacle." 285
"Sire, Diex penst de vous conduire!
Revenez vous en par Estuire,
par monseignor saint Sauveor;
iluec vont li bon pecheor,
et si revenez par la terre 290
monseignor saint Ernoul requerre.
Vous deüssiez des l'autre esté
avoir a son moustier esté
o chandoile de vostre lonc.
Por ce que vous n'i fustes onc, 295
vouez li, sire, a fere droit."
"Dame, volentiers, orendroit
ferai, se Dieu plest, ceste voie."
Ainsi la dame l'en envoie,
qui li a fet de voir mençonge, 300
et se li a torné a songe

A robe which he had worn
To cover your back:
Only a fool, a drunkard, would say that!   250
The great income which you have
And the land which you hold
Is now worth more than eighty pounds.
Get a robe to your liking   255
And a beautiful, ambling palfrey,
Which will carry you gently at an amble.
I can't talk sensibly with you,
Because you're so turned around
That your eyes are all troubled.   260
I'm afraid of some evil apparition
You encountered today,
A ghost and an evil wind.
You keep changing color,
And that really worries me;   265
You can be sure of that without a doubt.
Cry out to the Lord God for mercy,
And to my lord Saint Orri
That he protect your memory.
It's quite obvious from your looks   270
That you are bewitched.
By the thing you love best,
Did you think, honestly,
That you had the robe and the horse?"
"Yes, Lady, so help me God."   275
"Well, God help you," said the lady,
"And make you whole with his right hand!
Go dedicate yourself to a good saint,
And carry your offerings there
So that God may give you back your memory."   280
"Lady," he said, "I pledge myself
To God and to good Saint Leu,
And I will go to good Saint James,
And Saint Eloy and Saint Romacle."
"Sir, may God decide to lead you!   285
Come back through Estaires
And the shrine of my Lord the Holy Savior
(Which is where good sinners go)
And then come back by land
To seek out my lord Saint Ernoul.   290
Last summer you should have
Gone to his church
With a candle as long as yourself.
Since you have never been there,
Vow to him, sir, to act rightly."   295
"Lady, willingly, right away,
If it pleases God, I will make this trip."
Thus the lady, who had turned the truth
Into a lie for him, sent him off.
And indeed she transformed into a dream   300

ce qu'il ot veü a ses iex.
Encore esploita ele miex
qu'el le fist pelerin a force,
et tant se paine, et tant s'esforce,
qu'el le fet movoir au tiers jor: 305
onques n'i quist plus lonc sejor.
    Cis fabliaus aus maris promet
que de folie s'entremet
qui croit ce que de ses iex voie.
Mes cil qui vait la droite voie   310
doit bien croire sanz contredit
tout ce que sa fame li dit.

What he had seen with his eyes.
She succeeded even better
In that she compelled him to become a pilgrim,
And she took such pains and worked so energetically,
That she had him leave on the third day: 305
He didn't delay any longer.
    This fabliau promises husbands
That anyone who believes what he sees with his eyes
Is committing folly.
But whoever goes on the right path   310
Must truly believe without contradiction
Everything that his wife tells him.

10.

Qui d'Aloul veult oïr le conte,
si com l'estoire nous raconte,
sempres en puet assez oïr
s'il ne le pert par mesoïr.
    Alous estoit uns vilains riches,   5
mes molt estoit avers et ciches,
ne ja son vueil n'eüst jor bien.
Deniers amoit seur tote rien,
en ce metoit toute s'entente.
Fame avoit assez bele et gente,   10
novelement l'ot espousee,
c'uns vavassors li ot donee
por son avoir d'iluec entor.
Alous l'amoit de grant amor.
Ce dist l'escripture qu'Alous   15
garde sa fame com jalous.
Male chose a en jalousie!
Trop a Alous mauvese vie,
quar ne puet estre asseürez.
Or est Alous toz sos provez,   20
qui s'entremet de tel afere.
Or a Alous assez a fere,
s'ainsi le veut gaitier toz jors.
Or escoutez comme il est lors.
Se la dame va au moustier,   25
ja n'i aura autre escuier
comment qu'il voist, se Aloul non,
qui adés est en soupeçon
qu'ele ne face mauvés plet.
A la dame forment desplest,   30
quant ele premiers l'aperçoit.
Lors dist que s'ele nel deçoit,
dont sera ele molt mauvaise,
se lieu en puet avoir et aise.
Ne puet dormir ne jor ne nuit,   35
molt het Aloul et son deduit.
Ne set que face, ne comment
ele ait pris d'Aloul vengement,
qui le mescroit a si grant tort:
peu repose la dame et dort.   40

ALOUL

10.

Whoever wishes to hear the tale of Aloul,
The way the story tells us,
Can always hear enough
If he doesn't lose it by mishearing.
    Aloul was a rich commoner,   5
But he was very miserly and stingy;
There wasn't a day that he didn't have his way.
He loved money more than anything
And dedicated himself entirely to it.
He had a very beautiful and well-bred wife.   10
He had married her recently,
For a nobleman from nearby had given
Her to him for his money.
Aloul loved her with a great love.
The writings say that Aloul   15
Guarded his wife like a jealous man.
This jealousy he had was bad!
Aloul had an extremely tough life,
Because he could not be sure of anything.
Now Aloul was a complete fool,   20
Getting involved in such a business.
Now Aloul had more than enough to do
If he wanted to be always watching her like that.
Now listen to how it went for him then:
If his lady went to church,   25
She would never have any other escort,
No matter how it happened, except Aloul,
Who was always suspicious
That his wife might be making some evil assignation.
This greatly displeased the lady   30
When she first noticed it.
Then she said that if she didn't deceive him,
She would be very unworthy,
If she could find the time and place.
She could sleep neither night nor day.   35
She very much hated Aloul and his loving
And didn't know what to do or how
She might take vengeance on Aloul,
Who was so unjustly suspicious of her.
The lady could hardly rest or sleep.   40

Longuement fu en cel escil,
tant que li douz mois fu d'avril
que li tens est souez et douz
vers toute gent, et amorouz.
Li roxingnols la matinee   45
chante si cler par la ramee
que toute riens se muert d'amer.
La dame s'est prise a lever,
qui longuement avoit veillié,
entree en est en son vergié   50
nus piez en va par la rousee,
d'une pelice ert afublee,
et un grant mantel ot deseure.
Et li prestres en icele eure
estoit levez par un matin;   55
il erent si tres pres voisin,
entr'aus .II. n'avoit c'une selve.
Molt ert la matinee bele,
douz et souez estoit li tens,
et li prestres entra leenz,   60
et voit la dame au cors bien fet.
Et bien sachiez que molt li plest,
quar volentiers fiert de la crupe;
ainz i metroit toute sa jupe
que il n'en face son talent.   65
Avant s'en va tout sagement,
com cil qui n'est pas esmaiez.
"Dame," fet il, "bon jor aiez;
por qu'estes si matin levee?"
"Sire," dist ele, "la rousee   70
est bone et saine en icest tans,
et est alegemenz molt granz,
ce dient cil fusicien."
"Dame," dist il, "ce cuit je bien,
quar par matin fet bon lever.   75
Mes l'en se doit desjeüner
d'une herbe que je bien connois.
Vez le la pres, que je n'i vois!
Corte est et grosse la racine,
mes molt est bone medecine;   80
n'estuet meillor a cors de fame."
"Sire, metez outre vo jambe,"
fet la dame, "vostre merci,
si me moustrez si ele est ci."
"Dame," fet il, "iluec encontre."   85
Atant a mise sa jambe outre,
devant la dame est arestez.
"Dame," dist il, "or vous seez,
quar au cueillir i a mestrie."
Et la dame tout li otrie,   90
qui n'i entent nule figure.
Diex, c'or ne set cele aventure

She endured this torment for a long time,
Until it was the sweet month of April
When the weather is mild and sweet
And amorous for all people.
The nightingale throughout the morning   45
Sings so clearly in the branches
That everything is dying to make love.
The lady, who for a long time had
Lain awake, got up.
She went into her orchard   50
And went barefoot through the dew.
She was dressed in fur
And had a great mantel on.
And the priest at that time
Had gotten up in the morning;   55
They were very close neighbors.
Between the two of them, there was only a hedge.
The morning was very beautiful.
The weather was pleasant and sweet.
And the priest went in   60
And saw the lady with the shapely body.
And believe me, she was so pleasing to him
That he would have very much liked to mount her;
Thus he would bet his whole tunic
That he would have his way with her.   65
He stepped forward very discreetly,
Like one who was not dismayed.
"Lady," he said, "good day!"
Why have you gotten up so early?"
"Sir," she said, "the dew   70
Is good and healthful now,
And its comfort is very great.
That's what those doctors say."
"Lady," he said, "I really believe it,
For it's good to get up in the morning.   75
But one ought to have breakfast
On an herb that I know well.
Look at it closely, for I can't go there!
The root is short and fat,
But the medicine is very good;   80
There is no better for a woman's body."
"Sir, climb over,"
Said the lady, "would you please,
And show me if it's here."
"Lady," he said, "I'll meet you there."   85
And then he climbed over the hedge
And stopped in front of the lady.
"Lady," he said, "now sit down,
Because you need to gather something."
And the lady, who did not infer any   90
Figure of speech, agreed to this.
(Oh God, may Aloul, who is lying in his bed,

165

Alous, qui en son lit se gist!
La dame isnelement s'assist.
Ses braies avale li prestres,   95
qui de ce fere estoit toz mestres,
la dame enverse, si l'encline,
bien li aprent la medecine,
et ele vuisque sus et jus.
"Sire," fet ele, "levez sus,   100
fuiez de ci! Diex! Que ferai?
Jamés prestre je ne croirai."
Et li prestres resaut en piez,
qui molt estoit bien aaisiez.
"Dame," dist il, "or n'i a plus.   105
Vostre amis sui et vostre drus,
des or vueil tout vostre gré fere."
"Sire," dist ele, "cest afere
gardez que soit cele molt bien,
et je vous donrai tant du mien,   110
que toz jor mes serez mananz.
Foi que doi vous, bien a .II. anz
qu'Alous me tient en tel destrece,
qu'ainc puis n'oï joie ne leece.
Et si est tout par jalousie,   115
si en haz molt, sachiez, sa vie,
quar mainte honte m'en a fete.
Fols est qui fame espie et guete.
Desor mes porra dire Alous,
si dira voir, que il est cous.   120
Des or vueil estre vostre amie.
Quant la lune sera couchie,
adonc venez sans demoree,
et je vous serai aprestee   125
de vous reçoivre et aaisier."
"Dame, ce fet a mercier,"
fet li prestres, "vostre merci.
Departons nous huimés de ci,
que n'i sorviengne dans Alous.
Penssez de moi et je de vous."   130
    Atant s'en partent enés l'eure:
chascuns s'en va, plus n'i demeure.
Cele revint a son mari,
que molt avoit le cuer mari.
"Dame," fet il, "d'ont venez vous?"   135
"Sire," fet el, "de la desous,"
dist la dame, "de cel vergié!"
"Comment," fet il, "sanz mon congié?
Poi me doutez, ce m'est avis."
Et la dame se test toz dis,   140
que de respondre n'avoit cure.
Et Alous se maudist et jure
s'une autre foiz li avenoit,
honte et ledure li feroit.

Not know about this episode!)
The lady sat down at once.
The priest, who was a master at   95
Doing this, dropped his pants.
He tipped the lady over and bent her down.
He really taught her about the medicine,
And she slipped out and jumped up.
"Sir," she said, "get up!   100
Get out of here! God! What shall I do?
Never will I believe a priest!"
And the priest, who was very much
Relieved, jumped to his feet again.
"Lady," he said, "that's it!   105
I am your friend and lover.
From now on I want to do all your will."
"Sir," she said, "make sure that
This business is a very well-kept secret,
And I will give you so much of what is mine   110
That you will be rich forever.
By the faith I owe you, for two whole years
Aloul has kept me in such misery
That never since have I had joy or delight.
And it's all because of jealousy.   115
So know this: I really hate his life,
Because he has done me many indignities.
A man is a fool who spies and watches over his wife.
From now on Aloul will be able to say
(And he will speak the truth) that he is a cuckold.   120
From now on I want to be your lover.
When the moon has gone down,
Then come at once,
And I will be ready
To receive you and relieve you."   125
"Lady," said the priest,
"Your kindness is appreciated.
Let's leave here now,
In case Sir Aloul arrives.
Think of me and I of you."   130
    And now they left at once.
Each went off. They didn't stay there any longer.
She came back to her husband,
Whose heart was greatly irked.
"Lady," said he, "where are you coming from?"   135
"Sir," she said, "from down there,"
Said the lady, "from the orchard!"
"What," said he, "without my permission?
You have little respect for me; that's what I think."
And the lady kept quiet the whole time,   140
Because she didn't care to answer.
And Aloul cursed and swore to himself
That if it happened again,
He would do her shame and harm.

Atant remest. S'est sallis sus, 145
trestoz penssis et irascus.
Molt se doute de puterie,
bien le demaine jalousie,
qui de lui fet tout son voloir.
Ça et la vait par son manoir 150
savoir s'il i avoit nului
a cui sa fame eust mis lieu,
tant qu'il s'en entre en un jardin.
Douz tens fesoit et cler matin,
et garde et voit que la rousee 155
i estoit auques defoulee
de lieu en lieu par le vergié;
s'en a son cuer forment irié.
Avant en vait en une place,
iluec endroit li piez li glace, 160
que sa fame fu rafetie.
Por son pié qui ainsi li glie,
il esgarde tout environ
et vit le leu ou li talon
erent hurté et li orteil. 165
Or est Alous en mal trepeil
quar il set bien tout a fiance,
et li leus li fet demoustrance,
que sa fame a esté en oevre.
Ne set comment il se descuevre 170
quar n'en veut fere renommee,
s'ert la chose miex esprovee,
et plus apertement seüe.
Or est la dame deceüe,
s'ele ne se set bien gaitier. 175
    Atant est pris a anuitier:
Alous en sa meson repere;
ne veut sa fame samblant fere
que de rien l'ait aperceüe.
La mesnie est au feu venue, 180
si se sont au mengier assis.
Aprés mengier ont fet les lis,
si sont couchié tuit li bouvier,
et Alous s'en revait couchier,
il et sa fame maintenant. 185
"Dame," fet il, "couchiez devant,
dela devers cele paroit,
quar je leverai orendroit
por ces bouviers fere lever,
ja sera tans d'en champ aler 190
por noz terres a gaaignier."
"Sire, vous i irez premier,"
fet la dame, "vostre merci,
quar je me dueil certes ici
sor ceste hanche ci endroit. 195
Je croi que clous levez i soit,

Then he stopped. He jumped up 145
Very worried and angry.
He greatly suspected whoring.
Jealousy, which worked all its will
With him, was leading him along completely.
He went here and there throughout his estate 150
To learn if there was anyone
With whom his wife had had a meeting,
Until he went into a garden.
It was pleasant weather and a clear morning,
And he looked and saw that the dew 155
Was a little trampled down here
From place to place throughout the orchard;
In his heart he was greatly enraged because of it.
He went forward to one spot,
And his foot slid on that very place 160
Where his wife had been laid.
Because of his foot's sliding like that,
He looked all around
And saw the place where
The heels and the toes had hit. 165
Now Aloul was in bad torment,
For he knew well and for sure,
And the place gave him proof,
That his wife had been handled.
He didn't know how to deal with this, 170
Because he didn't want to spread it around,
As he would if the thing were better proved
And more apparent.
Now the lady was in trouble
If she couldn't keep a careful watch. 175
  Then night began to fall.
Aloul went back to his house;
He didn't want to give his wife any indication
That he had noticed anything.
The servants came to the fire 180
And sat down to eat.
After eating, they made their beds,
And all the cowherds went to sleep,
And Aloul went back to his bed,
Both he and his wife at once. 185
"Lady," he said, "lie down first,
Over there beside that wall,
Because I'll be getting up soon,
To wake those cowherds up.
It will soon be time to go to the fields 190
To plow our lands."
"Sir, you get in first,"
Said the lady, "please,
Because it really hurts me
On my hip right here. 195
I think a nail has rammed me here,

quar je en sui a grant malaise."
Atant Alous la dame apaise,
que couchiez est et ele aprés:
mes ne l'a or guetié si pres,   200
que l'uis ne soit ouvers remez.
Or est Alous molt enganez,
quar il s'en dort isnel le pas.
Et le prestres vient, pas por pas,
tout droit a l'uis, desferm le trueve,   205
puis boute un poi, et puis si l'uevre,
de toutes pars bien le compisse.
Or avoit el mez une lisse
qui fesoit grant noise et grant brait;
et li prestres el n'en a fait,   210
la charniere va compissier,
quar n'a cure de son noisier.
Quant le prestre aperçoit et sent,
vers lui lest corre, si destent,
si le sesist par son sorcot;   215
se li prestres n'esrast si tost
dedenz la chambre, a icele eure
defors fust male la demeure.
Tout souef oevre l'uis et clot,
et la lisse dehors reclot,   220
quar n'a cure de son noisier.
Molt het la lisse et son dangier,
qu'ainc ne fist bien gent de son ordre.
Adés le veut mengier et mordre.
Or est li prestres derrier l'uis,   225
mes il est plus de mienuis.
Si s'est un poi trop atargiez,
quar Alous se r'est esveilliez,
qui longuement ot traveillié
por un songe qu'il ot songié.   230
S'en est encor toz esbahis,
quar en sonjant li est avis
c'uns prestre en la chambre est entrez,
toz rooingniez et coronez,
s'avoit sa fame si sorprise,   235
et si l'avoit desouz lui mise
qu'il en fesoit tout son voloir,
et Alous n'avoit nul pooir
qu'il li peüst aidier ne nuire,
tant c'une vache prist a muire,   240
qui Aloul gete de s'error.
Mes encore ert en grant freor.
Sa fame acole, si l'embrace,
n'a cure que nus tort l'en face:
par la mamele prent s'amie,   245
et sachiez qu'ele ne dort mie,
desor mes en veut prendre garde.
Et li prestres pas ne se tarde;

And I'm in great discomfort because of it."
At last Aloul yielded to his wife:
So he went to bed first and she next.
But he didn't keep close enough watch   200
To make sure the door hadn't been left open.
Now Aloul was very much deceived,
Because he went to sleep at once.
And the priest came, step by step,
Straight to the door. He found it unlocked.   205
Then he pushed it a little and opened it.
He pissed all over it.
Now there was a bitch in the house
That was making a lot of noise and much barking.
And the priest didn't do anything about it;   210
He went on pissing on the hinge,
Because he wasn't worried about her noise.
When she noticed and smelled the priest,
She made a run for him and leaped
And seized him by the top coat;   215
If the priest hadn't gone so quickly
Into the room at that very moment,
The stay outside would have been troublesome.
Very quietly he opened and closed the door
And closed the bitch out,   220
For he didn't care for her noise.
He fiercely hated the bitch and her attacks,
For she never treated people of his order well.
She was always wanting to eat and bite them.
Now the priest was behind the door.   225
But it was past midnight,
And he took a little too long,
For Aloul, who had been tormented for a long
Time, had awakened
Because of a dream that he had dreamed.   230
He was still very disconcerted by it,
Because while dreaming he had the impression
That a priest had entered his room,
All tonsured and crowned,
And had surprised his wife so much   235
And put her underneath him in such a way
That he got all his will from her.
And Aloul had no power
To help or harm her,
Until a cow began to moo   240
And dispel Aloul from his illusion.
But he was still in great terror.
He hugged his wife and embraced her.
He didn't want anyone to wrong her.
He took his wife by the breast,   245
And believe me, she was not sleeping at all.
From now on she wanted to be careful.
And the priest didn't dawdle;

171

vait, pas por pas, tout droit au lit,
ou Alous et sa fame gist.   250
Ele est forment en grant tormente;
fet ele: "Comme gis a ente;
ostez vo braz qui seur moi gist;
traiez en la; j'ai poi de lit,
a paine puis r'avoir mes jambes."   255
"Diex!" dist Alous, "Qu'estuet ces fames?"
Par mautalent est trais en sus,
et li prestres est montez sus;
tost li a fet le ravescot.   260
Et Alous se retorne et ot
que li lis croist, et crisne, et tramble:
avis li est que on li amble.
De sa fame est en grant soloit,
quar ainsi fere ne soloit.   265
Sa main gete desus ses draz,
le prestre sent entre ses braz.
Atant se va atapissant,
et par tout le va portastant,
quar a grant paine se puet tere.   270
Le prestre prent par son afere,
et sache, et tire, et huche et crie:
"Or sus," fet il, "or sus, mesnie;
fil a putain, or sus, or sus!
Ceenz est ne sai qui venus   275
qui de ma fame m'a fet cop."
Et la dame parmi le cop
Saisi Aloul, et par la gueule:
li prestres de sa coille veule
les dois par force li dessere,   280
et sache si qu'il vint a terre
enmi la chambre sor un aistre.
Or a le prestre esté a maistre,
molt a souffertes granz dolors.
Cui chaut, quant c'est tout par amors,   285
et por fere sa volenté?
Atant sont li bouvier levé.
L'uns prent tinel, l'autres maçue,
et li prestres ne se remue,
semprés aura le col carchié,   290
a ce que il sont molt irié
por lor seignor qui ainsi crie.
Toute est levee la mesnie
cele part corent et vont tuit.
Or n'a li prestres de reduit,   295
fors tant qu'il entre en un toitel
ou brebis gisent et aignel.
Iluec se tapist et achoise.
Or fu au lit grande la noise
de la dame et de son mari,   300
qui molt avoit le cuer mari

He went step by step right to the bed
Where Aloul and his wife were lying.   250
She was suffering extremely great anxiety;
She said, "How uncomfortable it is lying here.
Take away your arm that's sprawled across me.
Get back. I don't have enough bed.
I can hardly have my legs to myself."   255
"God!" said Aloul. "What do these women need?"
He pulled back in a huff,
And the priest climbed up
And roused her completely back to life.
And Aloul turned over and heard   260
The bed crack and creak and shake.
He felt like someone was riding horseback on it.
He was very much concerned about his wife,
Because it usually didn't do this.
He threw his hand above her sheets   265
And felt the priest between her arms.
Then he kept on feeling about,
And he went groping all over,
For he could hardly keep still.
He got the priest by his thing   270
And pulled and yanked and shouted and cried:
"Get up," said he, "get up, my servants!
Sons of whores! Get up, get up!
Someone's come in here--I don't know who!--
Who has made me a cuckold with my wife."   275
And the lady seized Aloul
Around the neck and by the jaw.
The priest was trying to force loose
The fingers from his balls.
And he pulled so hard that he landed   280
In the middle of the room on the fireplace.
Now the priest had been taught a lesson:
He had greatly suffered mighty griefs.
What did it matter to him, when it was all for love
And for doing his will?   285
By now the cowherds had gotten up.
One took a stick; the other, a club,
And the priest didn't move.
He would soon have his neck beaten,
Because they were so enraged   290
By their lord, who was shouting like this.
The whole household was up.
They all came there on the run.
Now the priest had no hiding place
Until he came to a lean-to   295
Where sheep and lambs were lying.
There he hid and kept quiet.
Then in the bed there was very loud quarreling
Between the lady and her husband,
Whose heart was very much chagrined   300

173

de ce qu'il a perdu sa paine:
a paine puet r'avoir s'alaine,
tant orent hustiné ensamble.
Mes la mesnie les dessamble,
si est remese la meslee.   305
Et Alous a trete s'espee,
celui quiert avant et arriere;
n'i remest seille ne chaudiere,
que li bouvier n'aient remut.
Or sevent bien et voient tuit   310
que par songe est ou par arvoire,
ne tienent pas la chose a voire.
"Sire," font il, "lessiez ester.
Alons dormir et reposer;
songes fu ou abusions."   315
"Vois por les vaus, vois por les mons,"
fet Alous, qui ne mariroit,
"quant je le ting orains tout droit
a mes .II. mains, et vous que dites?
Comment! S'en ira il donc quites?   320
Alez le querre en cel mestier,
et sus et jus en cel solier,
et si gardez soz cel degré:
molt m'aura cil servi a gré
qui premiers le m'enseignera.   325
.II. sestiers de forment aura,
au Nöel, outre son loier."
Quant ce entendent li bovier
qui molt covoitent le forment,
ça et la vont isnelement: 330
tout par tout quierent sus et jus.
S'or n'est li prestres bien repus,
tost i puet perdre du chatel.
      Or avoit il enz en l'ostel
Hersent, une vieille bajasse,   335
qui molt estoit et mole et crasse.
En l'estable s'en vient tout droit
ou li prestres repuz estoit,
tous sanz lumiere et sanz chandeille.
Les brebis eschace et esveille,   340
et va querant et assentant
ou li prestres ert estupant.
S'avoit ses braies avalees,
et les coilles granz et enflees,
qui pendoient contre val jus: 345
or est li cus entor velus,
si sambloit ne sai quel figure.
Hersens i vint par aventure,
ses mains geta sor ses coillons,
si cuide que ce soit moutons   350
qu'ele tenoit iluec endroit
par la coille qui grosse estoit;

Because his trouble had been wasted.
He could hardly get his breath back
Because they had quarreled together so much.
But the servants separated them,
And the melee started again.   305
And Aloul drew his sword
And searched up and down;
No bucket or kettle was left
Which the cowherds hadn't moved.
Then they all knew and saw   310
That it was because of a dream or an illusion.
They didn't consider all this to be true.
"Sir," they said, "let it be.
Let's go to sleep and rest;
It was a dream or an illusion."   315
"Look through the valleys; look through the mountains!"
Said Aloul, who would not be distracted.
"I had him right here
In my two hands, so what do you say?
What? Will he get off scot-free?   320
Go look for him in the workshop,
High and low and in that loft,
And look beneath that step.
The one who shows him to me first
Will earn my gratitude by his service.   325
He'll get two gallons of wheat
In addition to his salary at Christmas."
When the cowherds, who coveted
The wheat very much, heard this,
Right away they went back and forth.   330
They searched up and down all over the place.
If the priest was not well hidden now,
He could lose his goods.
     Now there was in the house
Hersent, an old servant,   335
Who was very flabby and fat.
She went straight to the stable
Where the priest was hidden,
Completely without light and without candle.
She chased and awakened the sheep   340
And went looking and feeling
Where the priest was hiding.
He had his pants down,
And his big, swollen balls
Were hanging all the way down.   345
Now his ass was hairy all around,
And it seemed like some sort of face.
Hersent happened to come on him there.
She thrust her hands upon his balls
And thought that this was a sheep   350
Which she was holding there
By the balls, which were big,

et un poi met ses mains amont,
velu le trueve et bien roont
en un vaucel en le moiere.   355
Hersent se trest un poi arriere.
Si se merveille que puet estre.
Et cil, qui veille, c'est le prestre,
Hersent saisi par les timons,
si pres de li s'est trais et joins   360
qu'au cul lui a pendu sa couple.
Or est Hersent merveille souple,
ne set que fere; s'ele crie,
toute i vendra ja la mesnie;
si sauroient tout cest afere;   365
dont li vient il miex assez tere
qu'ele criast, ne feïst ton.
Hersent, ou ele vueille ou non,
sueffre tout ce que li a fait,
sanz noise, sanz cri et sanz brait: 370
fere l'estuet, ne puet autre estre.
"Hersent," fet il, "je sui le prestre.
A vo dame ere ci venuz,
mais j'ai esté aperceüz;
si sui ci en grant aventure,   375
Hersent, gardez et prendez cure
comment je puisse estre delivres,
et je vos jur sor toz mes livres
que toz jors mes vous aurai chiere."
Hersent, qui fet molt mate chiere,   380
"Sire," fet ele, "ne cremez,
quar, se je puis, bien en irez."
Atant se lieve, si s'en part
Hersens, qui auques savoit d'art.
Samblant fet qu'ele soit iree,   385
a haute voiz s'est escriee:
"Fil a putain, garçon, bouvier,
que querez vous? Alez couchier,
alez couchier, a pute estraine.
Comme a or emploié sa paine   390
ma dame, qui tant bien vous fet!
Molt dit bien voir qui ce retret:
qui vilain fet honor ne bien,
celui het il sor toute rien.
Tel loier a qui ce encharge.   395
Ma dame n'a soing de hontage,
ainz est certes molt bone dame;
bon renon a de preude fame,
et vous li fetes tel anui.
Mes, se j'estoie com de li,   400
ceenz n'auriez öes ne frommage
s'auriez restoré le domage:
des pois mengerez et du pain.
Bien vous nomma a droit vilain

And she put her hands a little further up
And found it hairy and very round,
With a little valley in the middle.   355
Hersent drew back a little
And wondered what it could be.
And the priest was watching her.
He seized Hersent by the thighs.
He pulled and joined her so close to him   360
That his pair hung down from her ass.
Now Hersent was terribly humiliated.
She didn't know what to do. If she cried out,
The whole household would come down at once,
And they would know about this whole business.   365
So it would be better for her to keep quiet
Than to cry out or make a sound.
Hersent, whether she liked it or not,
Endured everything he did to her
Without noise, without crying out, and without uproar.   370
She had to do it; she couldn't do anything else.
"Hersent," he said, "I am the priest.
I came here to your lady,
But I was noticed,
And I'm in great trouble now.   375
Hersent, be on the lookout and take care
So that I may be saved,
And I swear to you on all my books
That from now on I will always hold you dear."
Hersent make a mournful face: 380
"Sir," said she, "don't be afraid,
For if I can see to it, you will get out of here all right."
Then Hersent, who was fairly cunning,
Got up and left.
She pretended to be angry   385
And cried out in a loud voice:
"Whoresons, boys, cowherds,
What are you looking for? Go on to bed!
Go on to bed on your filthy straw.
How has my lady used her energy,   390
Doing so much good for you!
He speaks the truth who says this:
A churl will hate above all things
Whoever does him honor or good.
That's the wages a person gets for doing this.   395
My lady doesn't care for shameful deeds,
But she is certainly a very good lady;
She has a good reputation as a respectable wife,
And you are disturbing her very much.
But if I were she,   400
You would never get eggs or cheese in here,
And you would pay the damages!
Peas and bread you will eat!
Whoever first gave you your name

177

cil qui premiers nomma vo non,   405
par droit avez vilain a non,
quar vilain vient de vilonie.
Que querez vous, gent esbabie?
Que menez vous tel mariment?"
Quant li bouvier oient Hersent   410
et il entendent la manace,
s'ont grant paor que li frommage
ne voist chascun de fors le ventre.
Tout maintenant vienent ensamble
por eus desfendre et escondire.   415
"Hersent," font il, "ce fet no sire,
qui nous fet fere son talant,
mes ce sachiez d'ore en avant,
n'i a celui qui s'entremete.
No dame done sanz prometre,   420
et si est molt et preus et sage,
et noz sire fet grant outrage
qui a si grant tort la mescroit;
or entend bien avoec, et voit
que il a tort; si va couchier."   425
        Recouchié sont tuit li bouvier,
et Alous molt sa fame chose,
et dist que ne face tel chose,
dont il ait honte en mi la voie.
"Diex, com puis ore avoir grant joie,"   430
fet la dame, "de tel seignor
qui me porte si grant honor!
Honis soit or tels mariages,
et honis soit li miens parages
qui a tel homme m'ont donee.   435
Ne jor, ne soir, ne matinee,
ne puis avoir repos ne bien,
et si ne set ne ne voit rien
porqoi il me mescroit issi.
Molt aura lonc afere ci,   440
s'ainsi me veut adés gueter.
Des ore a molt a espier:
assez a encarchié grant fais."
"Dame," fet il, "lessiez me en pais;
a mal eür, aiez repos."   445
Atant li a torné le dos,
et fet semblant que dormir doie.
        Et li prestres, qui ne s'acoie,
qui en l'estable estoit repuz,
de rechief est au lit venuz: 450
si se couche avoeques s'amie.
Et Alous, qui ne dormoit mie,
sent que li prestres est montez,
et lui meïsme est porpenssez
que il sont dui, et il est seus: 455
si n'est mie partiz li geus,

Was right in naming you *churl*.
You rightly have *churl* for a name,   405
For *churl* comes from *churlishness*.
What are you looking for, you confused people?
Why are you acting so angry?"
When the cowherds heard Hersent,
And they understood the threat,   410
Then they were greatly afraid that the cheese
Wouldn't get through to their stomachs.
They all came together now
To defend themselves and deny.
"Hersent," they said, "our lord is doing this.   415
He makes us obey his will.
But know this: from now on
There is no one who will interfere.
Our lady gives with no strings attached,   420
And besides, she is very decent and wise,
And our lord is committing a great outrage
When he so wrongfully suspects her;
Now he is getting along fine with her and understands
That he is wrong. So, go to bed!"   425
     All the cowherds went to bed,
And Aloul scolded his wife very much
And told her not to do that kind of thing
That would make him ashamed in public.
"God! How can I now have great joy,"   430
Said the lady, "with such a lord
Who brings me such honor!
Now shame on such marriages,
And shame on my family
For giving me to such a man.   435
No day or evening or morning
Can I have rest or satisfaction.
And I don't know and I can't see
Why he is suspecting me.
He's going to have a long drawn-out affair   440
If he wants always to be watching over me like this.
From now on he'll have a lot to spy on.
He has taken a big burden upon himself."
"Lady," he said, "leave me in peace!
Damn you, get some rest."   445
Finally he turned his back on her
And pretended that he needed to sleep.
     And the priest, who had not calmed down
And who was hidden in the stable,
Immediately went to the bed   450
And lay down with his beloved.
And Aloul, who was not sleeping a bit,
Felt that the priest had mounted,
And he himself was grievously aware
That they were two and he was alone.   455
The game was not at all fair,

quar il est seus et il sont dui;
tost il porroient fere anui
s'il commençoient la meslee.
Tout coiement a pris s'espee,   460
d'iluec se lieve, si les lait,
a ses bouviers iriez revait.
"Dors tu," fet il, "va, Rogelet?
Foi que doi ti, revenuz est
cil qui ma fame m'a fortret;   465
estrange honte m'aura fet.
Esveille tost tes compaignons,
s'alons a lui, si l'assaillons,
et se par force prendons l'oste,
chascuns aura ou chape ou cote,   470
et son braioel a sa mesure."
Si s'afiche chascuns et jure,
quant il entendent la promesse,
que maus cus lor chantera messe,
se le puent tenir aus poins.   475
    Hersent, qui n'estoit mie loins,
qui n'ert encore recouchié,
s'estoit a un huis apoïé;
d'iluec entendoit tout le fet,
et tout l'afere et tout le plet,   480
comment Alous porquiert sa honte.
Au prestre vient, et se li conte
mes or se liet, et si se gart.
Et li prestres d'iluec se part,
mes trop se tarde a destorner.   485
Ce li porra sempres peser,
qu'Aloul en mi sa voie encontre.
"Diex," fet li prestres, "bon encontre."
Et Alous saut et si le prent
par les cheveus ireement.   490
"Or ça," fet il, "fil a putain,
or i metez chascun sa main,
Esforciez vous du retenir."
Qui lors veïst bouviers venir,
se li uns fiert, li autres boute,   495
comme cil qui n'i voient goute.
Por le prestre ont Aloul a(i)ers,
les os li froissent et les ners,
del retinir s'esforcent tuit;
et li prestres saut, si s'enfuit,   500
ne set quel part, quar il est nuis,
si ne set assener a l'uis.
Molt volentiers vuidast l'ostel,
tant que il trueve un grant tinel,
et taste a terre et trueve un van;   505
fez ert en meïsme cel an.
Li vans ert molt et granz et lez,
apoiez ert a uns degrez.

Because he was alone and they were two;
They could soon do him harm
If they began the fight.
Very quietly he took his sword.   460
He rose from there and left them.
Enraged, he went again to his cowherds:
"Are you sleeping?" he said. "Well, Roger?
By the faith I owe you, the man who
Led my wife astray has come back;   465
He is about to shame me dreadfully.
Quickly wake up your companions,
And let's go get him, let's attack him,
And if we take the enemy by force,
Everyone will get either a hat or a coat   470
And a belt to fit him."
Then they all promised and swore,
When they heard the promise,
That a sorry asshole would sing mass for them,
If they could get their hands on him.   475
     Hersent, who was not far off,
Who had not yet gone back to bed,
Had leaned against a door;
From there she was hearing the whole affair
And the whole business and the whole contract,   480
How Aloul sought his own shame.
She went to the priest and told him
To get up and take care of himself.
And the priest got out of there,
But he took too long leaving.   485
He would always have to regret this,
For he met Aloul on the way.
"God!" said the priest, "well met!"
And Aloul leapt up and grabbed him
Angrily by the hair.   490
"There now!" said he. "Son of a bitch!
Now everybody lend a hand.
Make an effort to hold him."
You should have seen the cowherds come!
One of them hit; the other pushed,   495
Like people who couldn't see at all.
They attacked Aloul instead of the priest.
They broke his bones and his nerves.
They all worked hard to hold him;
And the priest jumped up and ran away--   500
He didn't know which way, because it was night,
And he couldn't find the door.
He would have very willingly left the house,
Until he found a big stick
And groped along the ground and found a winnowing basket.   505
It had been made that very year.
The basket was very big and wide.
It was leaning against a step.

Le van a pris et si l'enporte
sus les degrez, et s'en fet porte.   510
Illuec vaudra estal livrer:
bien saura son parrin nommer
qui la vaudra a lui venir,
tant comme il se porra tenir.
Or ert li prestre en forterece,   515
et Alous est en grant destrece,
que li vilain ont entrepiez;
vilainement fust ja tretiez,
s'il ne se fust si tost nommez.
Ours ne fu onques miex foulez,   520
que li vilains prist au broion,
s'il ne nommast si tost son non.
Quant il sevent que c'est lor sire,
si ne sevent entr'aus que dire,
que molt en est chascuns iriez.   525
"Sire," font il, "estes bleciez?"
"Naie," fet il, "j'ai pis eü;
mes or tost alumez le fu,
et si fetes au couvenant."
Le feu alument maintenant,   530
par la meson quierent le prestre.
Rogiers, qui ert toz li plus mestre,
son seignor veut servir a gré.
Contremont puie le degré
dont li prestres l'entree garde,   535
mes Rogiers, qui ne s'en prent garde,
sempres aura une cacoute.
Le van qu'il tint enpaint et boute
si qu'il le perce et qu'il l'eslosche
et li prestres vers lui s'aproche,   540
tele li paie sor l'eschine,
de son tinel, que tout l'encline
jus del degré en mi la place.
Or a Rogiers ce que il chace;
se Rogiers a riens qui li poist,   545
ce m'est avis, c'est a bon droit:
qu'aloit il querre la? Folie?
Ez vous Aloul et sa mesnie!
"Diva," fet il, "es tu hurtez?"
"Sire," fet il, "mal sui menez;   550
tout ai froissié et cors et vis,
que je ne sai quels Antecris
m'a si feru seur cel degré;
pres va que n'ai le cuer crevé;
mestier auroie de couchier."   555
Sor les degrez vont li bouvier:
"Par le cul bieu, qui est ce dont?"
Lor buissons lievent contremont,
savoir vuelent ce que puet estre,
et gardent, et voient le prestre   560

He took the basket and he carried it
Up the steps and made a shield out of it.   510
There he would want to give battle.
As long as the priest held his own,
Any man who was good enough to get up to him
Would learn what real fighting was.
Now the priest was in a fortress,   515
And Aloul was in great distress,
For the churls had trampled on him.
He would have been handled churlishly by now
If he hadn't identified himself.
A bear which a churl had caught in a trap   520
Would never have been better beaten,
If he hadn't identified himself.
When they knew it was their lord,
Not one of them knew what to say,
Because each of them was all worked up.   525
"Sir," they said, "are you wounded?"
"Naw," said he, "I've had worse;
But now light the fire quickly
And do your duty."
They lit the fire at once   530
And looked for the priest throughout the house.
Roger, who was by far the most competent,
Wanted to please his lord with his service.
He climbed up the stairway
Whose entrance the priest was guarding,   535
But Roger, who didn't notice him,
Would soon be wounded.
He pushed and shoved the winnowing basket which he held,
Until he put a hole in it and dislodged it,
And the priest approached him.   540
He gave him a whack so hard on the spine
With his stick that he thrust him all the way
Down the steps and onto the floor.
Now Roger got what he was asking for.
If Roger had anything to grieve him,   545
In my opinion, it served him right.
What was he seeking? Foolishness?
Here came Aloul and the servants!
"Hey!" he said, "are you hit?"
"Sir," he said, "I've been badly treated;   550
My body and my face are all beaten,
And I don't know what Antichrist
Hit me on that stair;
My heart almost burst;
I need to lie down."   555
The cowherds went up the steps:
"By Gar's ass, who is it then?"
They raised their torches.
They wanted to know what this could be,
And they looked, and they saw the priest,   560

qu'est apoiez deseur la porte,
et voient le tinel qu'il porte;
si se traient chascuns ariere,
quar paor ont que il nes fiere.
Et Alous saut, s'espee trait,   565
hardiement vers lui en vait,
com cil qui molt est aïrez.
Contremont puie les degrez,
monte .IIII. eschaillons ou .III.;
le prestre escoute, s'est toz cois.   570
Fet il: "Qui estes vous la sus?"
"Li prestres sui, estez en sus,
qui fortune grieve et demaine.
Est il ore jors de quinsaine?
Je cuidoie qu'il fust Nöel,   575
s'ai grant paor que cest tine[l]
ne vous viengne parmi le col;
bien se porra tenir por fol
qui sentira combien il poise."
Dont recommença la grant noise   580
entre le prestre et les bouviers.
Alous, qui auques estoit fiers,
tant a alé qu'il vint au van,
si en abat le meillor pan
a s'espee qui bien trenchoit.   585
Li prestres, quant il l'aperçoit
que on abat sa forterece,
cele part son tinel adrece,
et fiert Aloul par tel vigor
qu'il li fet prendre un si fet tor[t]   590
qu'ainc tant comme il mist a descendre,
ne trova point de pain a vendre.
Quant a terre par fu venuz,
s'est si dolenz, s'est si confuz,
qu'il ne pot dire un tout seul mot.   595
"Aloul, ceenz sont li malot,"
fet li prestres, "en ce tinel;
ne vous vuelent en lor ostel,
ce m'est avis, acompaignier.
Mes, se leenz eüst bouvier   600
qui en eüst meillor eür,
viegne ça sus tout aseür,
molt bien puet estre de l'ostel;
mes, s'il i pert de son chatel,
de rien n'en revendra a moi,   605
quar cist chastiaus est en defoi;
dont i fet il mauvés monter."
Qui donc oïst bouviers jurer
les mons, les tertres et les vaus,
ainz i sera chascuns si chaus,   610
et si matez, et si delis,
c'on les porra escorchier vis,

Who was leaning on the door,
And saw the stick that he was carrying;
And each one drew back,
For they were afraid that he would strike them.
And Aloul leapt up. He drew his sword   565
And went bravely toward him,
Like someone who is very angry.
He climbed the stairs.
He climbed three or four steps;
The priest listened; he was very quiet.   570
Aloul said, "Who are you up there?"
"Stay there! I am the priest,
Whom fortune grieves and mistreats.
Is it Easter season?
I thought it was Christmas.   575
And I'm very much afraid that this stick
Will come crashing down on your neck;
Whoever feels how much it weighs
Will be able to call himself a fool."
Then the great uproar between   580
The priest and the cowherds began again.
Aloul, who was now quite fierce,
Made it all the way up to the winnowing basket,
And he chopped off the best piece from it
With his keenly slicing sword.   585
The priest, when he perceived
That the fortress was being knocked down,
Brought up his stick in that direction
And struck Aloul with such force
That he made him take such a knock   590
That once he started to fall down
He found no time to sell bread.
When he reached the ground,
He was so sorrowful and so confused
That he couldn't even say one single word.   595
"Aloul, there are hornets in here,"
Said the priest, "in this stick.
They don't want you spending time
In their house--that's what I think.
But if there's a cowherd here   600
Who thinks he'd have better luck,
Let him come right up here!
He can be lodged here very well.
But if he loses any of his goods,
He won't come back complaining to me about anything,   605
Because this castle is being defended,
Which makes it hard getting up to."
You should have heard the cowherds swear
By mountains, hills, and valleys.
But they would all be so heated up   610
And so frustrated and so confounded
That they could be skinned alive,

185

ainz qu'il ne l'aient mis a terre.
Lors recommence la granz guerre
entre le prestre et les bouviers: 615
molt i sera li assaus fiers.
Au degré sont tuit assamblé
li bouvier, qui molt sont troublé,
por lor seignor sont coroucié.
Ja ont tant fet et tant drecié   620
tout environ et bans et perches,
seles, eschieles, eschamperches,
qu'au prestre vienent a delivre.
Et il si bien d'aus se delivre
qu'il n'i a si hardi, ni tel,   625
ne un, ne autre, enz en l'ostel,
tant soit garnis ne bien couvers,
qu'il ne le trebuche a envers
jus de l'eschiele, maugré sien.
Quar il entent et voit tres bien   630
que, s'il le tienent a delivre,
a deshonor le feront vivre,
a grant vergoingne et a grant honte.
Atant ez Robin qui i monte,
un des plus fors de tout l'ostel.   635
En sa main tient un si grant pel
qu'a grant paine le soustient il.
La ou en a .IIIᶜ. ou mil,
n'i a il plus hardi qu'il est.
Cil passe d'auques Rogelet,   640
quar molt est plus entremetanz;
molt se tendra por recreanz
se il ne venge son seignor!
C'est cil qui porte le tabor
le Diemenche a la carole.   645
De rien le prestre n'aparole,
ainz vient avant, si l'empaint outre,
et le prestre de son pel boute
si qu'il le fet torner seur destre;
puis vint avant, s'aert le prestre   650
par les cheveus; a lui s'acouple,
et cil, qui crient perdre sa couple,
se dresce, s'a estraint les denz,
Robin sesi parmi les lenz;
a ses .II. mains a lui le tire,   655
et cil resache par grand ire;
se s'entretienent vivement
c'on les peüst sus un jument
porter ans .II., se il fust qui.
Et li bouviers lievent li cri.   660
"Seignor," font il, "montons la sus!
Prenons bastons, tineus et fus,
s'alons no compaignon aidier!"
Quant assamblé sont li bouvier

Before they had put him down.
Then began the great war
Between the priest and the cowherds.   615
The assault would be very fierce.
The cowherds, who were very much disturbed,
Were all assembled at the stairs.
They were enraged because of their lord.
Now they had done so much and gotten up so many   620
Benches and poles all around,
Scaffolds, ladders, and vine poles,
That they came quickly to the priest.
And he performed so well against them
That there was none so hardy in any way--   625
Not one or another of the household,
No matter how well armed or well covered--
That he did not fling backward
Down off the ladder against their will,
For he understood and saw very well   630
That if they got a good hold of him
They would make him live in dishonor,
In great disgrace, and in great shame.
Finally here came Robin climbing up there,
One of the strongest in all the house.   635
He had such a big stick in his hand
That he could hardly hold it.
Among three hundred or a thousand,
There was not a man more bold than he.
He excelled Roggie somewhat,   640
For he was much more aggressive.
He would really consider himself a coward
If he didn't avenge his lord!
He was the one who carried the drum
On Sundays in the carole dance.   645
He didn't talk about anything with the priest,
But came forward and shoved him out
And pushed the priest with his stick
So that he made him turn to the right;
Then he came up and grabbed the priest   650
By the hair and grappled himself to him,
And the other, who was afraid of losing his balls,
Straightened up, gritted his teeth,
And seized Robin by the sides.
He pulled him toward him with his two hands,   655
And the other pulled back angrily.
They held to each other so vigorously
That if someone wanted to do it, he could have
Carried them on a mare for two years.
And the cowherds raised a cry.   660
"Lords," they said, "let's climb up there!
Let's take sticks and clubs and logs,
And let's go help our friend!"
When the cowherds were assembled,

187

si montent tuit communaument,   665
et li prestres, quant il entent
que Robins doit avoir aïue,
si se resforce et esvertue.
Tant a Robin a lui tiré,
que desouz lui l'a enversé   670
toz le degrez outre son vueil,
si qu'il li samble que li oeil
li soient tuit du chief sailli.
Mes or sont il si mal bailli
qu'il ne se pueent retenir,   675
ainz les couvint aval venir.
Les degrez ont toz mescontez,
et si les a toz enversez
cil qui aloient a l'assaut,
tant ert ja chascuns montez haut,   680
que sempres se tendront por fol.
Li degré chieent seur lor col,
si les trebuchent et abatent,
les pis, les testes lor debatent,
les braz, les flans, toz les costez,   685
bien ont toz les degrez contez.
Quant a terre par sont venu,
si cheïrent ensamble el fu,.
qui molt estoit alumez granz.
Molt soufrirent cil granz ahanz   690
qui desouz furent, ce sachiez,
qui plaint ses braz, et qui ses piez,
et qui son cors, et qui sa teste.
Or vous dirai comment le prestre
est mal baillis et deceüz.   695
Quant a terre fu parvenuz,
si le saisi dans Berengiers:
c'est uns vilains, c'est un bouviers,
les jumenz seut chacier devant.
Ainc ne veïstes son samblant: 700
l'un oeil a lousque, et l'autre borgne,
toz diz regarde de clicorgne.
L'un pié ot droit, et l'autre tort.
Cil tint le prestre si tres fort
par un des piez qu'il ne li loist   705
a reperier la ou soloit,
ainz huche et crie hautement:
"Que fetes vous, mauvese gent?
Venez avant, et si m'aidiez
que cis prestres soit escoilliez.   710
Par les nons Dieu, s'il nous eschape,
chascuns aura perdu sa chape
que nous promist, et no cotele."
Quant li prestres ot la novele,
sachiez que point ne li agree.   715
Tant a sa jambe a soi tiree

They all climbed together,   665
And the priest--when he heard
That Robin was going to have help,
Gathered his strength and made a great effort.
He pulled Robin to himself so hard
That he spilled him willy-nilly   670
All the way down the stairs beneath him,
So that it seemed that his eyes
Jumped completely out of his head.
But now they were so out of control
That they couldn't keep themselves up,   675
But they all had to come down.
They couldn't keep count of the steps as they came.
And he whom they had gone attacking
Routed every one of them.
All of them had climbed so high   680
That they would later call themselves fools.
The steps fell upon their necks
And knocked them and beat them
And hit their chests and heads
And arms and flanks and all their sides.   685
They had the steps counted right by now.
When they reached the ground,
They fell into the fire,
Which was well lit and large.
Believe me, the ones who were underneath   690
Suffered very great anguish.
Some moaned about their arms and some about their feet
And some about their bodies and some about their heads.
Now I will tell you how the priest
Was defeated and disappointed.   695
When he reached the ground,
Mr. Berengier seized him.
He was a churl. He was a cowherd.
He was used to herding the mares before him.
You've never seen the like: 700
He had one squinty eye and the other was out.
He always looked askance.
He had one foot straight and the other bent.
He held the priest so hard
By one foot that he didn't let him   705
Get back up to where he had been,
And he shouted and cried out loudly:
"What are you doing, wicked people?
Come on and help me
So that this priest can be castrated.   710
In God's name, if he escapes,
Everyone will lose his hat,
Which he promised us--and our jackets!"
When the priest heard this news,
Believe me, it didn't please him.   715
He pulled his leg back so hard

que des mains dant Berengier l'oste,
mes il i a lessié sa bote,
et son sorcot por son ostage.
Miex li vient il lessier son gage　　　　　　　　720
que de lessier son autre afere.
Bien voit qu'il n'a leenz que fere,
d'iluec se lieve, si les lesse,
et chascuns aprés lui s'eslesse;
qui rue fust, et qui tinel.　　　　　　　　725
Li prestres entre en un chapel,
si se pent la sus contremont,
ses genouz met tout en un mont,
si se quatist que on nel truist.
Cil i vienent, si font grant bruit;　　　　　　　　730
el chapel sont trestuit entré,
mes il n'ont nule rien trové,
ne un ne el, neïs le prestre;
molt se merveillent que puet estre,
ce lor samble estre faerie.　　　　　　　　735
Li plus sages ne set que die,
si dont dolant et abosmé,
tuit cuident estre enfantosmé
del prestre, qui les a brullez.
Forment en est chascuns irez.　　　　　　　　740
Del chapel sont tuit fors issu,
a lor seignor en sont venu,
se li ont les noveles dites
que li prestres en va toz quites.
"Quites, deable," fet Alous,　　　　　　　　745
"et je remaindrai ci si cous.
N'en serai vengiez par nului!
Desor me torne a grant anui
li acointance de ce prestre.
Se vos volez mi ami estre,　　　　　　　　750
si le m'aidiez a espier
une autre foiz. Alons couchier,
que je suis molt bleciez es costes.
Maudiz soit ore si fez ostes
qui cop me fet et si me blece!　　　　　　　　755
N'aurai mes joie, ne leece,
si me serai de lui vengiez."
Atant se r'est Alous couchiez.
"Seignor," fet il, "prenez escout
en cele cort et tout par tout,　　　　　　　　760
car il me samble tout por voir
qu'il soit ancor en cest manoir.
Por ce, s'en cest manoir estoit
nul lieu repuz, trover seroit."
"Sire, a bon eur," font li bouvier,　　　　　　　　765
"mes il nous covendra mengier,
que nous avons anuit veillié;
si sommes auques traveillié,

That he released it from Mr. Berengier,
But he left his boot
And his coat as a hostage.
It was better for him to leave them pawned   720
Than to leave his other business.
He clearly saw there was nothing else to do there.
He got up from there and left them,
And they all threw themselves after him;
Some carried logs, and some, sticks.   725
The priest went into a threshing barn,
And he hung there upside down.
He put his knees up
And hid so that no one would find him.
They came in and made a lot of noise;   730
All of them crowded into the barn,
But they didn't find a thing,
Not one thing or another, and not the priest;
They were amazed that this could be.
It seemed like magic to them.   735
The wisest didn't know what to say.
They were sad and downhearted.
They all thought they had been spellbound
By the priest, who had tricked them.
Everyone was very angry.   740
They all went out of the threshing barn
And came to their lord
And told him the news,
That the priest had gotten completely away.
"Got away? Damn it!" said Aloul,   745
"And I am left here a cuckold.
I will not be avenged by anybody!
From now on, the acquaintance of this priest
Turns me to great pain.
If you want to be my friends,   750
Help me find him
Some other time. Let's go to bed,
For I am very wounded in the sides.
Cursed be such a guest
Who makes me a cuckold and wounds me!   755
I will never again have joy or pleasure
If I am **not** avenged of him."
At last Aloul had gone back to bed.
"Lords," he said, "keep your ears open
In the yard and all over,   760
Because I really think
That he's still on this manor.
Therefore, if he's hidden anywhere
On this manor, he will be found."
"Sir, if we are lucky--" said the cowherds,   765
"But we will have to eat,
Because we've been up all night;
And we have worked quite a bit.

n'i a celui ne soit lassez!"
"Ce vueil je," fet Alous, "alez,   770
mengiez, et si veilliez trestuit.
N'i a mes gueres de la nuit;
de legier le poez veillier."
      Lors se departent li bouvier,
si font grand feu por aus chaufer.   775
Entr'aus commencent a parler.
Du prestre et de s'aventure
li uns a l'autre si murmure.
Quant assez orent murmuré,
et dit, et fet et raconté,   780
si reparolent du mengier;
c'est la costume du bouvier,
ja n'il ert liez s'il ne menjue.
Rogiers, qui porte la maçue
desus toz cels de la meson,   785
commande c'on voist au bacon
et aporce on des charbonees,
mes qu'eles soient granz et lees,
si que chascuns en ait assez.
Entrues est Berengiers levez   790
par le Rogier commandement.
Un coutel prist isnelement,
qui d'acier est bien esmoluz.
Tant a alé qu'il est venuz
droit au chapel, ou li bacons   795
estoit penduz sus les bastons.
Berengiers va par tout tastant
le plus cras a son esciant,
quar il set bien que el plus cras
est tout adés li mieudres lars.   800
Endementiers que il le taste,
le prestre saisi par la nache,
Par leus le trueve mole et dure,
si cuide que ce soit presure,
c'on i seut prendre en tel maniere.   805
Avant retaste, et puis arriere,
tant qu'il encontre les genous,
si cuide avoir trové os cors
c'on i ait mis por le sechier.
Forment se prist a merveillier   810
de ce qu'il trueve tel harnas.
Sa main a mis de haut en bas,
s'a encontré le vit au prestre.
Or ne set il que ce puet estre,
por ce que il le trueve doille,   815
se c'est chauduns, ou c'est andoille
c'on i ait mis por essuer.
Celi voudra, ce dist, coper,
por ce que c'est uns bons morsiaus.
Li prestres ot que li coutiaus   820

There's not one of us who is not tired out!"
"I agree," said Aloul; "go on,   770
Eat, and then all of you stay awake.
The night is almost over;
You can easily stay awake."
    Then the cowherds left,
And they made a large fire to warm themselves.   775
They began to whisper among themselves.
Each to the other, they talked
About the priest and his adventure.
When they had whispered and talked
And spoken and related a great deal,   780
They talked about eating.
(That's the way it is with a cowherd:
He will never be happy if he doesn't eat.)
Roger, who carried the club
Over all the others in the house,   785
Ordered someone to go get the side of bacon
And bring some slices of smoked bacon back,
Saying that they should be big and thick
So that everyone would have enough.
So Berengier got up   790
To obey Roger's order.
He immediately took a knife,
Which was made of well-sharpened steel.
He went until he came straight to the barn,
Where the sides of bacon   795
Were hung on the sticks.
Berengier went groping all over
For the one he thought was fattest,
For he knew for sure that the fattest
Bacon is always the best.   800
While he was groping for it,
He grabbed the priest by the buttocks.
He found them both soft and hard,
And thought it was a rennet
Which was often hung there that way.   805
He groped up further and then back down,
Until he found the knees,
And he thought he had found the front legs
That were put there to dry.
It surprised him very much   810
To find that kind of equipment.
He put his hand high and low,
And found the priest's prick.
Now he didn't know what this could be,
Because he found it soft,   815
As if it were tripe or sausage
That had been hung there to dry.
He said he would like to cut this,
Because it was a good morsel.
The priest realized that the knife   820

li vait si pres des genetaires,
si ne mist au descendre gaires.
Seur Berengier chiet a un fais,
les os li a brisiez et frais,
pres va qu'il n'a percié le col.   825
Or se tient Berengiers por fol,
quant il i vint sanz le craisset.
Au retorner arrier se met;
au feu en va toz esmanchiez,
"Seignor bouvier," fet il, "aidiez,   830
que cil bacons soit rependuz!
La hars est route, s'est cheüz;
par pou ne m'a le col tout frait
parmi le col. Ait mal dehait
li machecliers qui le dut pendre!"   835
Qui donc veïst lumiere prendre
et alumer par le meson.
Berengiers les maine au bacon
por esgarder et por veïr
comment ce fut qu'il pot cheïr.   840
Quant il parvindrent el chapel,
n'i troverent ne un ne el.
La sus estoient les bacons,
si com devant, sor les bastons,
tout .XX.; n'en ert nes un a tire.   845
Lors commencierent tuit a rire.
Li un dient que Berengier
n'osa le bacon aprochier,
li autres dist que bien puet estre
que il avoit paor du prestre   850
por ce fu il si effraez.
"Seignor," fet il, "or est assez!
Bien puet huimés ce remanoir;
mes je di bien, et si di voir,
que je senti que uns bacons   855
cheï sor moi o les jambons.
Encore i avoit il presure,
que je senti et mole et dure;
or esgardons que ce puet estre."
"Je cuit," font il, "que c'est le prestre,   860
dont Berengiers senti les piez.
Por nous estoit la sus muciez,
gardons partout que il n'i soit."
Et Berengiers garde, si voit
le prestre ester devers un huis,   865
mes li obscurtez et la nuis
li desfent molt a raviser.
Le prestre prent a portaster,
et li prestres, quant il entent
que Berengiers le voit et sent,   870
si set tres bien que trovez iert;
entre col et chapel le fiert

194

Was getting close to his genitals,
And it didn't take him long to come down.
He fell in a lump on Berengier.
He snapped and cracked his bones.
He almost broke his neck.   825
Now Berengier thought he had been crazy
To come there without the oil lamp.
He headed back
And ran to the fire with one arm hurt.
"Sir cowherds," said he, "help   830
Me hang this bacon up again!
The rope broke, and it fell down;
It almost completely broke my neck
In half right here. Damn
The butcher who was supposed to hang it up!"   835
You should have seen them take the light
And light up all the house.
Berengier led them to the side of bacon
To look and see
How it could have fallen down.   840
When they came to the threshing barn,
None of them could find it there.
The sides of bacon were up there,
Just as before, on the beams,
All twenty. Not even one was out of place.   845
Then they all began to laugh.
Some said that Berengier
Didn't dare get close to the bacon.
Others said it was very likely
That he was afraid of the priest.   850
That's why he was so frightened.
"Lords," said he, "enough of that now!
This can very well remain as it is;
But I say well and I say true
That I felt one side of bacon   855
Fall on me along with the hams.
Besides, it had a rennet
Which I felt to be both soft and hard;
Now let's think about what this could be."
"I think," they said, "that it's the priest,   860
Whose legs Berengier felt.
He was hidden up there because of us.
Let's look everywhere to see if he isn't here."
Then Berengier looked and saw
The priest standing by a door,   865
But the darkness and the night
Prevented him from recognizing him.
He started to feel around on the priest.
And the priest, when he realized
That Berengier saw him and felt him,   870
Knew very well that he would be found out;
He hit him between his neck and his hat

del poing, qu'il ot gros et quarré,
si qu'a ses piez l'a enversé.
"Alez," fet il, "dant Berengier!   875
Avez vous tost vostre loier?
Destornez vous, et levez sus,
cuites estes et absolus,
ne sai doner autres pardons.
Fetes venir voz compaignons,   880
si auront part en ceste offrande.
Fols et qui fol conseil demande;
ne vous tieng mie trop a sage,
quant de fere si fet message.
Aviez seur toz pris le baston,   885
adés vuelent cil viez bordon
lor talent fere et acomplir.
Fetes voz compaignons venir,
s'auront de ce bienfet lor pars."
Qui donques veïst de toutes pars   890
venir bouviers a grant foison,
sempres aura male leçon
li prestres, s'il ne se desfent.
Et Rogiers saut premierement,
si le saisi par la main destre,   895
et li prestres de sa senestre
l'a si feru arriere main
que tout le fet doloir et vain.
Molt fust en males mains Rogiers,
ne fust la torbe des bouviers   900
qui molt l'angoisse et molt l'apresse.
Des bouviers i avoit tel presse
que tout emplissent le chapel;
mes il ont doute du tinel,
dont il avoit devant servi.   905
Tel noise mainent et tel cri
que Alous lor sire s'esveille,
qui de la noise s'esmerveille;
tantost comme il la noise entent,
aperçoit il tantost et sent   910
que c'est li prestres ses amis,
qui de rechief s'est leenz mis.
Il saut en piez, si trait l'espee,
si s'en vint droit a la meslee.
Quant parvenuz fu a l'assaut,   915
parmi trestoz ses bouviers saut,
s'aert le prestre par derriere,
et cil le fiert parmi la chiere,
si qu'il l'abat sor un bouvier.
Mes que vaudroit a detrier?   920
De toutes pars chascuns l'assaut,
et sa desfense poi li vaut.
Retenu l'ont et pris entr'aus:
par tant si est remez l'assaus.

196

With his fist, which was big and square,
So that he threw him down at his feet.
"Go," said he, "Sir Berengier! 875
Have you all your wages?
Turn over and get up.
You are forgiven and absolved.
I can't give you any other pardons.
Have your friends come here 880
And they will take part in this offering.
A fool will ask for foolish advice;
I don't think that you were very wise,
When, to deliver such a message,
You--of all people--took up a stick. 885
These old hornets always want
To accomplish and achieve their pleasure.
Have your friends come,
And they will have a part in this blessing."
You should have seen the cowherds come 890
In a great gathering from all directions.
The priest would soon have a cruel lesson
If he didn't defend himself.
And Roger jumped up first
And seized him by the right hand, 895
And the priest, with his left hand,
Gave him such a backhand swipe
That it made him hurt and useless all over.
Roger would have been in a bad way
If it hadn't been for the crowd of cowherds 900
Who greatly harassed and pressed him.
There was such a crowd of cowherds
That they completely filled the barn;
But they were terrified of the stick,
Which he had used before. 905
They raised such a hue and cry
That their master, Aloul, awoke
And was amazed by the noise;
As soon as he heard the noise,
He immediately perceived and felt 910
That it was his friend the priest,
Who had gotten in again.
He jumped to his feet, drew his sword,
And went straight to the brawl.
When he arrived at the assault, 915
He jumped into the very midst of his cowherds
And grabbed the priest from behind,
And the priest hit him in the face
And knocked him back on top of a cowherd.
But why should I go on longer? 920
Everyone attacked him from all sides,
And his defense was not much use.
Together they got hold of him and took him.
Finally the attack was completed.

197

Alous a ses bouviers demande   925
s'il l'ocirra, ou il le pande.
Il respondent communement
qu'il n'en puet fere vengement,
de qoi on doie tant parler,
comme des coilles a coper.   930
"Coper," fet Alous, "mes noier.
Et ne porquant soit au trenchier,
quar vous dites parole voire;
vostre conseil vueil je bien croire.
Or alez, le rasoir querez   935
dont cil prestres sera chastrez!
Fetes isnelement et tost!"
Quant li prestres entent et ot
c'on dit de lui itel parole,
doucement Aloul aparole.   940
"Aloul," dist il, "por Dieu merci,
ne me desfigurez issi!
De pecheor misericorde!"
"Ja voir n'en sera fete acorde,"
fet Alous, "a nul jor, ne paie!"   945
Se li prestres des lors s'esmaie,
de legier le puet on savoir.
Il ont aporté le rasoir,
le prestre enversent et abatent;
molt le laidengent et debatent   950
ainz qu'il le puissent enverser;
un taiseron font aporter
por les jambes miex eslaisier:
"Liquels s'en saura miex aidier
viegne, si praingne le rasoir."   955
"Je, sire," fet Berengiers, "voir!
Je li aurai molt tost copees."
Les braies li ont avalees,
et Berengiers jus s'agenoille,
si prent le prestre par la coille.   960
Ja fust le prestre en mal toeillé,
quant la dame, le feu toeillé,
vint acorant a sa baisselle.
Devant li trueve une grant sele,
qui molt estoit et fors et granz.   965
A ce qu'ele est fors et pesanz,
fiert Berengier si sor l'eschine
qu'ele l'enversa et encline;
pres va que n'a perdu la vie.
Et Hersens prent une hamie,   970
si le fiert si parmi les rains
que li craissés li est estains,
et li bouvier tout se departent
por les granz cops qu'eles departent.
Chascune tel estor i livre   975
que le prestre tout a delivre

198

Aloul asked his cowherds 925
If he should kill him or hang him.
They all replied with one voice
That he could exact no other vengeance
Which would be spoken of so well
As to cut off his balls. 930
"To cut," said Aloul, "or to drown.
Nevertheless, let it be to slice,
Because you are telling the truth;
I really will take your advice.
Now go get the razor 935
To castrate the priest with!
Do it quickly and soon!"
When the priest heard and realized
That they had said this about him,
He spoke sweetly to Aloul. 940
"Aloul," he said, "for God's sake,
Don't disfigure me here!
Have mercy on a sinner!"
"In truth, no truce or treaty will ever be made
On any day," said Aloul. 945
If from that point the priest was stunned,
You could easily tell it!
They brought the razor.
They turned the priest over and beat him.
They abused and roughed him up a great deal 950
Before they could get him turned over.
They had a log brought
To bind his legs better.
"Whoever can help out best,
Come and take the razor." 955
"I will, sir," said Berengier, "yes indeed!
I'll have them cut off him soon."
Then they took off his pants,
And Berengier knelt down
And took the priest by the balls. 960
By now the priest was in a bad position,
When the lady, holding a shimmering light,
Came running with the servant woman.
In front of her she found a big stool,
Which was very strong and stout. 965
With all her strength and weight,
She hit Berengier so hard in the back
That she threw him over and knocked him down;
He almost lost his life.
And Hersent took a hook 970
And struck him so hard in the kidneys
That the oil lamp was blown out,
And the cowherds all got out
Because of the great blows the women were dealing.
Each of the women put up such a fight 975
That they easily caught hold of the priest

ont mis et jeté du manoir.
Et il s'enfuit, si fet savoir,
lassez et traveilliez et vains.
Bien ert cheüs en males mains,   980
quar si cheveil contremont tendent
et les pesques contreval pendent
de son sorcot et de sa cote;
en gage i a lessié sa bote.
Eschapez est de grand peril: 985
molt a esté en grant escil.

And threw him out of the manor.
And he fled--and that was the smart thing to do--
Tired and overworked and spent.
He really had fallen into the wrong hands,   980
For his hair stood straight up,
And the rags hung straight down
From his overcoat and from his coat;
He had left his boot as a token
And had escaped from great danger.   985
He had been in great torment.

11.

Metre vueil m'entente et ma cure
a faire un dit d'une aventure
qu'avint a Orliens la cité.
Ce tesmoingne par verité
cil qui m'en dona la matire.   5
Il avint, si com j'oï dire,
c'uns clers amoit une borgoise
qui molt estoit sage et cortoise.
Molt savoit d'engin et d'aguet:
a feme, qui tel mestier fait   10
et qui veut amer par amors,
covient savoir guenches et tors,
et engien por soi garantir.
Bien covient que sache mentir,
tele eure est, por couvrir sa honte.   15
La borgoise dont je vous conte
fu bien de cel mestier aprise,
comme cele qu'amors ot mise
et molt enlacié en ses laz.
Molt amast d'un clerc le solaz;   20
molt vousist bien et li pleüst
qu'entre ses braz toz nus geüst,
et ele o lui en un biau lit,
por avoir du clerc le delit.
Li sires, qui riens ne savoit   25
quel corage sa feme avoit,
a dit au soir, aprés mengier,
qu'au point du jor sanz atargier
l'esveillast, qu'el nel lessast mie,
et qu'el ne fust trop endormie   30
s'ele de riens son preu amoit:
au jor lever le covenoit
por aler a Meün sor Loire,
ou il avoit marchié ou foire.
    La borgoise s'en esjoï   35
forment, quant la parole oï
que se[s] sires li commanda.
Tout maintenant au clerc manda
qu'il fust la nuit bien esveilliez,
et qu'il fust bien appareilliez   40

202

THE FRANCISCAN'S BRITCHES

11.

I want to put my mind and my care
Into a poem about an adventure
Which took place in the city of Orleans.
The man who told me about it
Testifies to its truth. 5
It happened, as I heard tell,
That a clerk loved a bourgeois' wife,
Who was a very wise and courtly woman
Who knew a lot about deceit and cleverness.
A wife who carries on that way 10
And who wants to love romantically
Needs to know tricks and turns
And cunning to keep herself safe.
She really has to know how to lie
(Such is her lot) in order to cover up her shame. 15
The wife I'm telling you about
Was well skilled at this business,
Like a woman whom love had taken
And bound up in its snares.
She greatly enjoyed the pleasures of a clerk 20
And very much desired and wanted
Him to lie completely naked in her arms,
And she with him in a fine bed,
So as to have her pleasure with the clerk.
The husband, who knew nothing 25
Of what kind of heart his wife had,
Said one evening, after eating,
That at daybreak, without delay,
She should wake him up, and not forget,
And that she shouldn't sleep too long 30
If she valued her reputation as a wife!
He had to get up at dawn
To go to Meung sur Loire,
Where there was a market at the fair.
The wife rejoiced 35
Greatly when she heard the words
Of her husband's orders.
Immediately she sent word to the clerk
To stay wide awake that night,
To stay well dressed, 40

203

d'entrer comme bien avertiz
leenz, quant en sera partiz
li sires devant l'ajornee.
Que vous feroie demoree?
Que li borgois couchier s'en vait   45
et la dame fu en aguet
et en grant porpens du preudomme
d'esveillier au premerain somme!
    Il dormi, et cele veilla.
Et quant li sires s'esveilla,   50
ele li dist: "Or sus, biaus sire!
Certes molt ai au cuer grant ire
que nous avons si longuement
dormi. Je sai certainement
que trop avez fet grant demeure.   55
A paines vendrez mes a eure
huimés a Meün au marchié."
Lors s'est li preudom descouchié,
si s'est vestuz et atornez.
De son ostel s'en est tornez,   60
et la borgoise le convoie
sanz plus jusqu'a l'uis de la voie.
    A l'issir de leenz li dist:
"Je vous commant a Ihesucrist,
qui soit garde de vostre cors."   65
Atant li preudom s'en ist fors
quar d'errer avoit grant besoing.
Il ne fu pas d'ilueques loing,
quant li clers ot passé le sueil,
qui onques n'ot dormi de l'ueil   70
de toute la nuit por atendre,
si comme vous poez entendre.
Quant li preudom s'en fu alez,
lors fu li clers plus acolez
et .IIII. tenz besiez adonques,   75
que li borgois n'ot esté onques,
qui or s'en vait en sa besoingne.
Que vous feroie longue aloingne?
Mes je vous di que la borgoise
et li clers, a cui point n'en poise,   80
firent molt lie contenance.
Ne firent pas grant demorance
ne grant dolor au despoillier:
li clers toz nuz o la moillier   85
au borgois qui s'en va se couche.
Braz a braz jurent sus la couche.
La borgoise ama le complot
du clerc, si fist ce que lui plot.
    Et li borgois qui fu levez   90
trop tost, si comme oï avez,
ala son voisin apeler
qui devoit avoec lui aler

And, being warned ahead of time,
To come in there when her husband
Had left before dawn.
Why should I make a long story?
The bourgeois went to bed,   45
And the wife was on the watch
And very careful to wake
The good man when he first dozed off!
    He slept, and she stayed awake.
And when the husband woke,   50
She told him, "Get up, good sir!
My heart is sorely distressed
That we've been asleep
So long. I know indeed
That you've tarried too long.   55
You'll hardly arrive on time
For the market today at Meung."
Then the bourgeois got out of bed.
He quickly got dressed and ready
And left his house,   60
And his wife accompanied him
No farther than the door.
    Upon leaving, he told her:
"I commend you to Jesus Christ,
That he may protect your body."   65
At last the bourgeois set out,
Because he really needed to get going.
It wasn't long after that
When the clerk crossed the threshold.
He hadn't slept a wink   70
During the night from waiting,
As you can understand.
With the husband gone off,
The clerk was embraced more
And kissed four times as much   75
As the bourgeois had ever been,
Who was now going off on his business.
Why should I make a long story?
But I tell you that the wife
And the clerk, who did not mind all this,   80
Had very happy faces.
They didn't take much time
Or much trouble getting undressed:
The clerk lay down completely naked
With the wife of the absent bourgeois.   85
They lay in each other's arms in bed.
The wife liked the arrangement
With the clerk and did what pleased her.
    And the bourgeois, who had been awakened
Too early, as you have heard,   90
Went to call his neighbor,
Who was supposed to go with him,

205

et li dist: "Or sus, biaus compains,
tant avons dormi, par toz sains,
que por fols nous poons tenir.   95
Ainz qu'a Meün puissions venir,
sera il bien pres de midi."
Et li autres li respondi:
"Compains, estes vous forsenez?
Vous n'estes mie bien senez,   100
qui volez errer a tele eure!
Biaus amis, se Diex me sequeure
et il me gart de toz anuiz,
il n'est pas encor mienuiz."
"Compains," fait cil qui s'esbahist,   105
"dites vous voir?" Et cil li dist:
"Je vous di voir, par saint Richier."
"Je m'en vois donc," fait il, "couchier."
    Atant s'en est d'iluec tornez;
a son ostel s'en est alez,   110
dont fiert a l'uis, et si apele.
"Diex, com ci a pesme novele,
biaus douz amis, ç'a dit la dame.
Me[s] sires est a l'uis par m'ame,
malement sommes assené,   115
maufé l'ont si tost ramené,
qui li puissent le col brisier."
Et cil ne fine de huchier,
et dist: "Or sus, levez vous tost!"
Maintenant li clers se repost   120
et prist quanques du sien i a
fors ses braies qu'il oublia,
dont tuit troi orent puis grant ire.
Tant apela a l'uis ses sire
qu'entrez i est, couchier se vait,   125
et la dame l'endormi fait.
Cil l'apela; bien fist le sourt
icele qui molt sot de hourt.
Li borgois delez li se couche,
et cele, qui molt fu farouche   130
por tenir le vilain a sot,
sailli du lit sanz dire mot,
ausi com se fust forsenee.
A haute voiz s'est escriee:
"Sainte Marie, aïe! Aïe!   135
Or sui je morte et mal baillie,
se vous n'avez de moi merci.
Qui est ce couchiez delez mi?
Qui est entrez dedenz mon lit?
Ja nus hom solaz ne delit,   140
fors mon seignor, n'aura de moi!"
Lors fu li sires en esfroi
que sa fame du sens n'issist.
Au plus souef qu'il pot li dist:

And told him, "Get up, good friend!
We've slept so long, by all the saints,
That we should consider ourselves fools.   95
Before we can get to Meung,
It will be almost noon."
And the other answered,
"Friend, are you out of your mind?
You're not at all sane,   100
Wanting to go at such a time!
Good friend, as God may help me
And protect my body from all harm,
It's not yet midnight."
"Friend," he answered, astonished,   105
"Are you telling the truth?" And the other told him:
"I am telling you the truth, by Saint Richier."
"Then I'm going," said he, "back to bed."
      Then he turned around,
Went back to his own home,   110
Knocked on the door, and called out.
"God! What bad news this is,
My dear, good friend," said the lady;
"By my soul, my husband's at the gate.
We've come together at a bad time.   115
Devils have brought him back this soon--
I wish they would break his neck."
The man didn't quit shouting,
But called, "Get up! Get up right away!"
Right away the clerk hid   120
And took whatever belonged to him
Except his britches, which he forgot and which
Would later cause great distress to all three of them.
The husband knocked so hard at the door
That he got in. He was going to go to bed,   125
And the lady acted as if she were sleeping.
He called to her, and she acted deaf,
Like someone who knew a lot about trickery.
The bourgeois lay down beside her,
And she, who was very fierce,   130
In order to keep the clod foolish,
Jumped up from bed without saying a word,
As if she were out of her senses.
She cried out in a loud voice,
"Saint Mary, help, help!   135
I'm betrayed and ruined
If you don't have mercy on me.
Who has lain down beside me?
Who has gotten into my bed?
Never will any man except my lord   140
Have comfort or pleasure from me."
Then the husband was afraid
That his wife had gone out of her senses.
As gently as he could, he said:

207

"Bele tres douce chiere amie,   145
por Dieu ne vous marissiez mie!
Je sui vostre leal espous
qui m'estoie couchiez lez vous."
Et ele l'en a desmenti:
"Vos avez," fet ele, "menti.   150
Me[s] sires est fors de la vile.
Alez vous en, ou, par saint Gile,
je crierai ja a tel bruit
que no voisin i vendront tuit.
Il n'a mie ceenz bordel!"   155
Molt fist bien le putain lordel
la dame, qui bien le sot fere
"Me[s] sires est a son afere,"
fet ele, "Alez! Alez vous en!
Vous estes fols et hors du sen,   160
qui me cuidiez fere mauvese."
"Dame," fet il, "ne vous desplese,
preude fame estes et veroie.
Certes trop tost levez estoie,
il n'est pas plus de mienuit.   165
Si vous pri qu'il ne vous anuit
se je sui arriere venuz,
delez vous me couchai toz nus,
com cil qui l'ai fet maintes foiz,
si m'aït Diex et sainte Croiz.   170
Miex vous aim c'onques mes ne fis."
"Sire," fet ele, "or m'esbahis
de ce qu'ançois ne vous connui.
Je vous ai fet molt grant anui,
et si m'en tieng or molt por fole.   175
Or vous connois a la parole!
Certes ge m'en esbahis toute."
Maintenant delez lui se boute
si l'acole, et li dist: "Biaus sire,
por Dieu, pardonez moi vostre ire   180
se je de vous joieuse soie
que je pas ne vous connoissoie.
Et sachiez, se vous conneüsse,
ja du lit levee ne fusse.
Mes j'avoie d'autre paor!   185
Si en estoie en grant fraor,
ne vous en devez merveillier.
N'avez mestier de plus veillier,
dormez vous, si ferez que sage."
Et cil, qui en ot grant corage,   190
dormi jusques au point du jor.
Au matin, sanz plus de sejor,
se vesti et appareilla,
et la borgoise qui veilla,
commanda a Dieu son seignor.   195
Mes ne set pas la deshonor,

"Beautiful, sweet, dear friend,   145
For God's sake, don't be distressed!
I am your loyal husband,
Who has lain down beside you."
And she contradicted him:
"You have lied," she said;   150
"My lord is out of town.
Get out, or by Saint Giles,
I'll cry out so loudly
That our neighbors will all come here.
This isn't any bordello here!"   155
The lady, who knew how to do it well,
Made him out to be a vile pervert.
"My lord is going about his business,"
She said. "Go! Get out!
You're mad and out of your senses,   160
Trying to do me harm."
"Lady," said he, "don't be upset.
You're a decent wife and true.
Indeed you got up too early.
It's not past midnight.   165
I beg you not to be annoyed
Because I came back.
I lay beside you all naked,
As I have done many times,
So help me God and the Holy Cross.   170
I love you more than I ever did."
"Sir," she said, "now I am amazed
That I didn't recognize you.
I did you great wrong,
And now I feel like a real fool.   175
Now I recognize you by your speech!
Really I am completely confused."
Then she cuddled beside him
And kissed him and said, "Dear lord,
If I may have joy from you again,   180
For God's sake, spare me your anger,
Since I didn't recognize you.
And know, if I had recognized you,
I would never have gotten out of bed.
But I was very much afraid!   185
I was in a great fright;
You shouldn't be amazed at that.
You don't need to stay awake any longer.
Go to sleep. That would be the wise thing to do."
And he, who wanted very much to do it,   190
Slept until the break of day.
In the morning, without waiting any longer,
He got dressed and all ready,
And his wife, who was awake,
Commended her lord to God.   195
But she didn't know the dishonor

ne la tres grant descouvenue,
que cel jor li est avenue,
que ses sires a si mespris
que les braies au clerc a pris,   200
n'il meïsme ne le set pas.
    Et li clers vint isnel le pas
a la dame, se li a dit:
"Bele amie, se Diex m'aït,
orendroit m'en covient aler: 205
qui aime, il doit s'amor celer.
Por ce m'en vueil aler matin
que ne me voient li voisin
issir fors de vostre meson."
"Biaus amis, vous dites reson,"   210
dist la dame, "ce m'est avis."
La bouche li bese et le vis,
et il a li, puis s'entrefont
le geu por quoi assamblé sont,
et, quant il orent fet lor gieu   215
si s'entrecommandent a Dieu.
Lors prist li clers les autres braies,
puis dist: "Ce ne sont pas les moies,
ainz sont les braies au vilain."
Bien fu la dame prise a l'ain.   220
Quant ele a la parole oïe,
molt fu dolente et esbahie.
Sa robe a en son dos vestue,
puis s'en est de son lit issue.
Au clerc autres braies baillie[e]s,   225
qui furent blanches et delie[e]s,
par amor le requiert et prie
que toz ses garnemenz li die,
qui pendoient a son braier.
Et cil n'en fist mie dangier,   230
ce m'est avis, trop longuement,
ainz li a dit molt doucement.
Lors dist qu'ele n'en doute rien
qu'ele s'en chevira molt bien,
bien en saura venir a chief.   235
Lors s'entrebaisent de rechief.
    Atant li clers d'iluec s'en part.
La dame sot molt de renart:
engingneuse fu de toz tors.
Quant il fu grant eure de jors,   240
por chacier sa honte a honor
s'en vint a un Frere menor,
se li dist et li regehi
tout ce que vos avez oï
et li prie por Ihesucrist   245
qu'il l'i aït, et il li dist:
"Dame," dist il, "et je comment?"
"Dites," fet ele, "seulement

Or the great misfortune
That had come to her that day,
For the husband made a mistake
And put on the clerk's britches
Without even realizing it.   200
        Then the clerk came at once
To the lady and told her:
"My dear friend, so help me God,
I must be going now.
One who loves must hide his love.   205
Therefore, I want to leave early
So that the neighbors don't see me
Leave your house."
"Good friend, you are right,"
Said the lady, "in my opinion."   210
She kissed his mouth and face,
And he hers; then they played the same game
With each other that they had gotten together to play.
And when they had played their game,
They commended each other to God.   215
Then the clerk took the other britches
And said, "These aren't mine;
They are the clod's britches."
The wife was really caught on a hook.
When she heard those words,   220
She was very sorry and dismayed.
She put her robe on
And got out of bed.
She gave him a pair of britches
Which were white and loose-fitting.   225
Out of love she asked him and begged him
To describe completely for her
The pants that had hung from his belt.
And he didn't balk at that,
It seems to me, for very long,   230
But he told her very nicely.
Then she said she wasn't worried
And that she would get out of it all right.
She would know how to come out ahead.
Then they kissed each other again.   235
Then the clerk left.
The lady was well versed in the ways of Renart the Fox:
She was clever with all the tricks.
When it was later in the day,
In order to turn her shame to honor,   240
She went to see a friar
And told him and admitted to him
Everything that you have heard,
And begged him for the sake of Jesus Christ
To help her, and he said to her: 245
"Lady," he said, "how can I do that?"
She said, "Only say

a mon seignor, quant il vendra,
qui por mauvese me tendra, 250
que vos braies en ai portees
et desouz ma coute boutées,
por filz ou fille concevoir.
Quar j'avoie songié por voir
que cele nuit conceveroie 255
un enfant qu'en mon lit auroie
les braies d'un Frere menor.
Sire," dist ele, "a mon seignor
dites que j'ai ainsi songié."
"Sachiez bien que si ferai gié 260
de molt bon gré et volentiers."
Atant s'en va la dame arriers,
qui de ce fu molt esjoïe.
        Or est reson que je vous die
du borgois qui toz fu jeün 265
venuz au marchié de Meün
et d'autres o lui ne sai quanz.
Li borgois comme marcheanz
ala o les autres mengier.
Quant ce vint a escot paier, 270
si cuida prenre son argent,
si com tesmoingnent mainte gent,
si a trové une escritoire
ou li canivet au clerc ere,
et son parchemin, et sa pene. 275
Par poi li borgois ne forsene
quant il n'a sa borse trovee.
Lors (l')apele putain provee
[sa feme. Ce me reconnurent
aucun qui en la place furent.] 280
Que vous diroie de ce plus?
Molt fu esbahiz et confus
de ce qu'ilueques li avint.
Celui jor meïsme s'en vint
a son ostel; quant vit sa fame, 285
"Dites moi," fet il, "bone dame,
vous savez bien comment il vait.
Enpirié avez vostre plait."
Et la dame, qui fu hardie,
qui ne fu pas trop esbahie, 290
li dist hardiement: "Biaus sire,
n'aiez en vostre cuer grant ire.
Je sai molt bien que vous avez.
La verité pas ne savez
de ce que vous avez trové. 295
Bien vous sera por voir prové
que de chose qu'aiez trovee
ne doi estre de riens blasmee.
Or venez o moi en ma chambre."
Et il i vait, et li remambre 300

212

To my husband, when he comes
Thinking I'm a wicked woman,   250
That I borrowed your britches
And stuffed them under my pillow
In order to conceive a son or a daughter.
For I had truly dreamed
That that night I would conceive   255
A child when I had
A friar's britches in my bed.
Sir," she said, "tell my husband
That that is what I dreamed."
"Rest assured that I will do it   260
Gladly and willingly."
Then the lady went back,
Very much pleased about this.
        Now I should tell you
About the bourgeois, who, not having eaten,   265
Came to the market of Meung,
And others with him--I don't know how many.
The bourgeois, being a merchant,
Went with the others to eat.
When he came to pay his check,   270
He reached for his money.
As many people testify,
He found a writing bag
With the clerk's knife in it
And his parchment and his pen.   275
The bourgeois almost went out of his mind
When he didn't find his purse.
Then he called his wife a proven
Whore. Some people who were at
The place remembered that for me.   280
What more should I say to you?
He was greatly astonished and confused
By what was happening to him there.
That very day he went back
To his house; when he saw his wife,   285
He said, "Tell me, good wife,
You know very well how it goes.
You've spoiled your case."
And the lady, who was bold
And who was not dismayed,   290
Boldly answered him, "Good sir,
Don't hold such anger in your heart.
I know well what's the matter with you.
You don't know the truth
About what you have found.   295
You will have certain proof
That I should be blamed for nothing
On account of anything you have found.
Come with me into my bedroom."
And he went in, and she told him   300

213

tout ce que je vous ai retret.
Et cil les braies au clerc tret
d'entor lui, et les seues chauce.
Maintenant la dame li hauce
et lieve les panz de sa robe,   305
comme cele qui bien le lobe,
et fet assez male aventure:
li a mises a la çainture
les braies au clerc et pendues,
qu'il porta a Meün vestures: 310
"Portez les, sire, au cordelier
tout maintenant sanz delaier."
Si tost comme il entra leenz
si dist: "A il nului ceenz
qui m'enseignast tel cordelier?"   315
Et cil, qui devoit deslier
la borgoise de cele honte
dont vous avez oï le conte,
s'est levez et commence a rire.
Maintenant d'une part le tire,   320
trestout ce li dist et conseille
tout coiement dedenz l'oreille
que la borgoise li ot dit,
"Sire," fet il, "se Diex m'aït,
grant joie m'avez ou cuer mise.   325
Par poi que n'ai m'a fame ocise,
par mon pechié, et a grant tort.
Sire, voz braies vous aport,
vez les ci!" Et cil les a prises,
en une aumaire les a mises.   330
Puis a dist, que li borgois l'oie:
"Que Diex li doint avoir a joie
conceü ce qu'ele a songié."
"Amen," fet cil. Lors prent congié   335
li borgois au frere menu.
    A son ostel en est venu.
Lors acole sa fame et bese.
"Dame," dist il, "ne vous desplese
se je vous ai fete marrie.
Foi que je doi sainte Marie,   340
tele amende vous en ferai
que jamés de vous ne serai
en soupeçon de jalousie."
Or est bien la dame aaisie
de fere au clerc sa volenté,   345
qui por s'amor a grant plenté
ot mis du sien et despendu.
Bien a la borgoise rendu
au borgois le sac aus besaces.
En toz lieus et en toutes places   350
porra mes venir et aler,
que ja n'en estovra parler

Everything that I have told you.
And he took off the clerk's britches
From around him and put on his own.
Now the lady lifted
And raised the flaps of his tunic,   305
Being very deceitful,
And did a pretty, evil trick:
She attached and hung from his belt
The clerk's britches,
Which he had worn to Meung: 310
"Take them, sir, to the Franciscan
This moment, without delay."
As soon as he arrived there,
He said, "Is there anyone here
Who will show me to a certain friar?"   315
And he, who was supposed to release
The wife from this shame
Which you have heard the story of,
Got up and started laughing.
Now he drew him aside   320
And told and whispered
In his ear very quietly
Everything which the wife had told him.
"Sir," he said, "as God may help me,
You have put great joy in my heart.   325
I came close to killing my wife
Out of my own sin and wrong.
Sir, I bring you your britches.
Here they are." And he took them
And put them into a closet.   330
And then he said for the bourgeois to hear:
"May God grant her
To conceive joyfully what she has dreamed."
"Amen," said he. Then the bourgeois
Took his leave of the friar.   335
He went back to his house.
Then he hugged and kissed his wife.
"Lady," he said, "don't be upset
If I wronged you a little.
By the faith I owe Saint Mary,   340
I will make such amends to you
That I will never be suspicious
Or jealous of you again."
Now the lady was secure
In doing what she wanted with the clerk,   345
For whose love she gave and spent
Abundantly from what she had.
The wife acted well
In paying the bourgeois back.
Everywhere and in every place   350
From now on she would be able to come and go,
For the cuckold would never dare mention it

li cous jamés jor de sa vie.
Bien s'est la borgoise chevie
qui bien et bel son plet define.
Atant mon fablel ici fine.

355

Ever again in his life.
The wife got out of it well,
And carried her case to a good conclusion.   355
Now I have finished my fabliau.

1. D'ESTORMI

Text

420. A: lieu du daarain p. *(See* Ménard, *Fabliaux français,*
p. 40, for rationale of manuscript correction.)

Translation

16. Literally: which was beating her openly.

22. *covine:* situation.

64. *hamoingnier:* to carry something through.

90. *entre chien et loup:* between dog and wolf: the time
dogs go to sleep and wolves appear; at sunset. The first priest
comes at sunset (90); the second at the beginning of night when
the bells ring (103); the third during early night (122).

105. Note the pun: *Amant,* lover.

116-117. Or: who pursued her shamefully and in an evil
manner. (*Sa* could refer to the lady; see 198-199.)

122. *prinsoir (prime soir):* early evening.

171. *cibole* (from the Latin *caepula,* onion): head of an
onion or knobby end of a stick.

186. *si pert:* He loses [the power of] speech. Silence,
here, is very important; see 189.

253. There are only two priests because Jehan had put one
aside, propped up, for Estormi; see 336-337.

256. Literally: Jehan would have his ass ill set.

417. *juer de bondie:* to trick or dupe.

471. Literally: He did not carry him.

480. Literally: My bread is baked.

586-587. Ménard, *Fabliaux français,* links this proverbial
expression to proverb 2034 in Morawski.

588-591. Ménard, *Fabliaux français,* considers these lines
not to be part of Jehan's remarks but as the author's observations
(p. 45).

2. DE SAINT PIERE ET DU JOUCLEUR

Text

Variant manuscript: B.N. 19152 (D), fol. 45 ro. -47 ro.,
entitled "D'Un Jugleor qui ala en enfer et perdi les ames as dez."
Several faulty lines exist in D: 6, 87, 181, 199, 282. *In addi-*
tion, D *has some faulty or poor rhymes:* 117, 118, 235, 236, 267,
268.

After 6. Ne sai comment on l'apela,/ mais sovent as dez se
pela;/ sovent estoit sanz sa viele,/ et sanz chauces et sanz
cotele, (cf. A's 15-16)/ si que au vent et a la bise/ estoit
sovent en sa chemise./ Ne cuidiez pas que ge vos mente,/ n'avoit
pas sovent chaucemente;/ ses chauce avoit forment chieres,/

de son cors naissent les lasnieres/ (cf. A's 17-18).
       14. fiertez
       19. par estoit molt de grant a.
       After 22. mais ne sai que plus vos en die/ taverne amoit et
puterie.
       26. A: en la foule.
       39-42. *Omitted.*
       50. li autre usurier ou l.
       51. vesques, prestres, moines a.
       63-64 *and* 67-68. *Inverted.*
       76. Diva, fait il, comment t'esta.
       86. que d'a. arc v. covenra t.
       After 114. Mais ce saiches tu sanz mentir,/ quant nos
revenron a loisir,/ ge te ferai molt bien servir/ d'un gras moine
sor un rotir,/ a la sauxe d'un usurier/ ou a la sauxe d'un hoilier.
       117-118. En enfer est remés toz seus/ Seignor, un petit
m'entendez.
       135-136. *These lines are placed after* 138.
       137. Laissiez m'en pais, alez. . . .
       150. Ge t'en d. a. c. s. f.
       151. *Omitted.*
       After 152. sachiez molt li vint a talent.
       153-154. *Inverted.*
       171. Cil a gité, que qu'il anuit.
       177. V.," dist il, "ge sui honiz.
       181. A: .XII.
       193. par les elz beu.
       203. s. huimais a.
       204. ces .XXI. a. et tant a.
       207. .XV. p.
       209. "Ge l'otroi.
       214. que je v. sines en .II. d.
       218. a duel me tornera cist g.
       After 232. mal dahaiz qui sus le me mist/ et mal dahez qui
les assist.
       233. gloton.
       235. s. Michel.
       236. doing sus le chief.
       239. qui noz ames volez trichier.
       241. A: le mes.
       After 242. savoir se il vos remenroient/ par ceste teste non
feroient!"
       248-249. *Inverted.*
       253-256. quant il voit sa cheveceüre/ passer jusc'outre sa
ç./ m. par ont entrax .II. luitié/ feru, bouté et desachié.
       After 256. Li uns saiche, li autres tire/ la robe au jugleor
descire.
       267. s'a gré vos vient et atalent.
       268. "M. m'atalent.
       271. S. ge dis grant vilenie.
       272. or me r. de ma folie.
       278. Adonc s'acorderent ainsi.

280. .LXIII. a.

284. ou s. .VI., .XX. ou n.

285-286. "Ge le ferai par tel couvent/ que tu me feras ensement."/ Li jogleres dit: "N'en doutez/ que ja vos i soit deveez."

287. Or me di donc b.

289. sanz maltalent.

290. pranez ames a vo talent.

292-294. volez ch., 1. m./ cortois, volez v./ v. princes ou chastelains.

302. d. gie**x** m'a trahi.

307. A: .XXII., f.

309. tox les .XII. .XX. vaille bien. A: .XXII.

310. "Getez, de.

312. s. en .II. et el tiers as.

313. "Compaiz," fait il, "ge la joë.

317-319. Diex, com ge sui maleüreus/ c'onques ne fui aventureus/ et sui toz et sui jors molt m.

After 328. por vos giter de cest torment,/ mis ge au gieu tot mon argent.

333-334. Adonc fu li joglerres mus:/ "Sire," fait il, "or n'i a plus./ Ou ge du tot m'aquiterai,/ ou ge trestot par perderai,/ et les ames et ma chemise."/ Ne sai que plus vos en devise.

341. qui durement fu esperduz.

348. "Vassal," fet il, "com as ouvré".

352. .I. vielz hons vint çaiens a mi.

After 356. si me gita d'un dez toz fax/ li traïstres, li desloiax:/ ainc n'en ting dez, foi que doi vos,/ si ai perdu voz genz trestoz."/ Quant li maistres l'a entendu,/ par poi ne l'a gité el fu.

357. p. lierres trichierres.

After 358. honi soit vostre joglerie/ dont j'ai perdue ma mesnie.

361. Au malfé en viennent.

After 362. tant le batent, froissent et fierent,/ et tant forment le lesdengierent,/ et si li ont fait fiancer/ que jamais ribaut ne holier/ ne jogleor n/aporteront,/ n'ome qui a dez joeront.

After 370. vuidiez l'ostel, gel vos commant,/ ge n'ai cure de tel sergant;/ jamais jogleor ne querrai,/ ne lor lignier ne tenrai./ Ge n'en vueil nul, voisent lor voie,/ mais Diex les ait qui aime joie.

371. Vuidiez l'ostel! De vos n'ai cure!"

377-382. cil entre enz, or est garant./ Adonc retornent li tirant./ Or faites feste, jogleör/ ribaut, houlier et joëor/ que cil vos a bien aquitez/ qui les ames perdi as dez.

Translation

22. *le cembel:* an arrogant life style.

44. i.e., for the jongleur's soul.

49. Johnson and Owen (hereafter referred to as J.O.) translate *champions* as "professional fighters" who suffered from a very bad reputation (p. 105).

103. *sor:* "on pain of" (J.O., p. 106).

167. J.O. (p. 106) give a succinct description of the rules of the dice game; they are playing at *hasard* (173), here called *tremerel* (erroneously, it would appear): "Any one of the totals 18, 17, 16, 15, 6, 5, 4, or 3 constitutes a throw called *hasard*, and if this appears as the first throw of a round it is a winning one. If any one of the remaining totals from 14 to 7 inclusive appears at the first throw it is called a *chance* and is apportioned to the opponent. The thrower then throws again, and this time if he throws a *hasard* (technically called *re-hasard*), it is a losing throw, the opponent wins the round and handles the dice for the next round. Should the thrower after throwing one chance to his opponent, throw another *chance*, this is credited to himself [the thrower], and the round continues either his own number comes up, in which case he wins, or his opponent's number, in which case the thrower loses. . ."

169. The jongleur will throw the entire round of this game.

172. The jongleur throws 8, a *chance* given to St. Peter, who wins 3 souls after his opponent throws 6 (*re-hasard*) (175). St. Peter will be throwing the next round.

180. Second round, double stakes (178). A erroneously has .XII. (181), which is a *chance*, but here St. Peter is clearly the winner (182), totalling 9 souls: 3 souls from the first round and 6 from the second.

183. Third round. St. Peter, as winner, continues to throw for a double stake of 12 (187). St. Peter again throws a *hasard* (191) and is now owed 21 souls (192).

188. *qui l'ait:* "who gives up. . ." (J.O., p. 107).

198. *a plus poinz:* the higher total wins, in one stroke of three dice (203). The jongleur loses 15 (*quisnes*) to 17 to St. Peter, who has now won 42 souls, double stake. A has 43 (216); we have kept that apparently erroneous number because of the rhyme, because of the possibility that St. Peter might be cheating the hapless jongleur, or, also likely, because of forty (204) added to the initial stake of three.

279. They play again at *a plus poinz*. St. Peter already has 43 souls (280). The stakes having been raised to 40, the jongleur, complaining about his bad luck (282), asks to triple it to 120 (284). They tie (299 and 304). St. Peter is so thankful for the tie (305: *bon encontre*, "good meeting") that he proposes to double the stakes from 120 to 240. This figure (307, 309) comes from D: .XII. .XX. (twelve times twenty). A, incomprehensibly, has .XXII., either due to a scribal error or to a total miscomprehension of the reckoning of the game. As J.O. point out, the rule for the tie-breaker must be that if the first thrower exceeds 12, he wins (109). St. Peter throws 13 (312).

306. Either St. Peter sees this tie as a good omen for further luck, or he states that they will have to play another round.

331-332. Parody of the words said by Christ to the thief on the cross (?)

358. *jonglerie:* trickery, pranks; obvious pun on *jongleur*.

365. *nis un:* not even one.

3. DE SIRE HAIN ET DE DAME ANIEUSE

Text

Variant manuscript: Hamilton 257 (C), fol. 5 vo. -7 vo.

24. encendrer et bruler (*no rhyme*).
29. m. desaudeluie.
30. huiseus.
After 30. et li enfant bien a son conte/ quant un poi de noise sormonte.
38. q. maugré sien.
42, 44. vieillart.
53. si s'en revient inellement.
54. H. debonerement.
84. ma honte.
107. s. du mien et du vostre;
126. volenteuse.
182. ja ne me verras en sus trere.
189. treborner.
207. de c. (+1).
212. p. le tigier.
223-224. *Inverted.*
223. Se je t'ateing une autre enpeinte.
282-284. *Illegible in A, supplied by* C.
297. l'estonne.
298. aupoing li vet, e. h. l'en done.
304, 309, 310. *Omitted.*
322. de Bertran.
323. *Omitted.*
332. n'i touchier mie.
345. "Je ne sui mie si novices.
346. "A. que tu t'en isses.
348-349. que tu seras en la merci/ dist (?) dire H. a toz jors mes.
365. servir Haimon a.
379-380. *Inverted.*
380. et li feras tot son afere/ si com.
397. s'abandonoit.
404. veulent b.
405. demener sor vos p.

Translation

10. *estre a chavestriaus:* to insult one another (*chavestrel:* halter).
16. *seur le pois:* in spite of, against the will of. Literally: and it was against his will; or, it was all in spite of herself, she couldn't help it, such was her nature; see 50.
20. *porcuite:* (fem. adj.) plotting, scheming.
29. *l'auleluye:* the hallelujah, the main point.
44. *c'est du mains:* it is in the morning, good morning.
Or: it is obvious! This is it! (showing exasperation at her hus-

band's unusual request of a bony, tough fish, difficult to prepare; see 48.)

45. *epinoches:* small, spiny-backed fish.

60. will you stop that! (Action of finishing, of tying up the sheaf).

124. Literally: it is very near for me to begin.

165: b. from which the quarrel arose.

208. *chanter d'autre martin:* to play another tune, to be more humble.

229. Depreciatory formula: I do not value you two whitings. (Note the continuous references to sea fish.)

300. *choisir:* to perceive, to notice.

321. *Bertram:* nephew of the epic hero Guillaume d'Orange.

322. *Tristran:* well-known hero of the romance.

4. DE BOIVIN DE PROVINS

Text

Variant manuscript: B.N. 24432 (P), fol. 49 vo. -52 ro.

1. Un b. l. fu de vins.

9. chauces d'un gros b.

After 14. Et ses cheveus avoit merlés/ ne voult que pingne i fust boutés/ le jour ne .III. fois ne trois/ bien contrefist le vilenois.

15-16. *Inverted.*

After 28. et comment il se goulousa/ et le moquois qu'il recorda.

35. .XXXII.

39-42. *Omitted.*

43-44. *Inverted.*

49-50. *Omitted.*

51. Brunel .L. s.

55-56. *Omitted.*

59. .LII. et .XIX.

61-74. *Omitted.*

75-76. *Inverted.*

After 80. Mes je nel savroie des mois/ s'en avoie feves ou pois/ a chascun pois prendre un sost/ ainsi le savré je bien tost.

87-88. *Omitted.*

90. ne faites pas noise ne ples.

91-92. *Omitted.*

103. que les estuie.

105. de Mabile m. d. n.

107-108 and 109-110. *Inverted.*

111. Mes un clerc l'en mena par guille.

113-114. Comment eüs si fol courage/ qui estïez de bon parage.

115-122. *Omitted.*

124. Or orrez qu'il avint en l'eure.

After 124. Mabile issi de sa maison.

126. le vostre nom quar me fust dit.

After 126. Et cil respont sanz contredit.

130-135. *Omitted.*

136-137. Aprés ce le vilains respont/ com s'il fust marriz et plain d'ire.

157-158. *Inverted.*

157. et il vous amer s. r.

158. et lui servir du.

159. sire preudon.

After 165. et puis en un banc assis (-1)/ Mabile les mist a raison.

166. "Or ça, mi gentil compaignon.

After 166. querez moi öés et poucins/ et si pourchaciez de bons vins.

167. et si querés de gras ch.

After 167. Adont parla un des gloutons.

170. Qu'avez-vous dit (elle), ribaut failli.

After 170. vous semblez mouton acueilli.

173-174. *Inverted.*

173. ce mengier.

175-181. Adont s'en vont sans demorance/ et aporterent sanz doutance/ .IIII. chapons a tout .II. oies.

After 185. rire molt fort et eschiniez/ et si aprestent le mengier.

193 *and* 195. *Omitted.*

197-199. "En vo p. vostre v./ m'en iré o vous," dit Mabile./ Par pou ne faitez pleurer (-1).

202-203. *Replaced by:* et Ysanne haste forment/ le mengier tant que tout fu prest/ et les tables metre s'en vest/ pour ce qu'au preudomme n'ennuit.

207-209. Qui veïst ces tables guarnir/ et apareiller a plesir/ de sel, de coutiax, de bons vins;/ au brouet furent les poucins/ dont chascun ot grant escüelle,/ si ot un ribaut qui öeille/ qui souvent fet au vilain corne.

210. A *lacks a verb in this clause.*

212-214. *Omitted.*

215-218. Devant lui met on un chapon/ et demie öé par delez/ et si ot de bons pastez/ et oublees et chanetiaus./ Bien fu serviz li vileniaus.

227-228. *Inverted.*

232-238. Mabile ne c'est plus teü:/ "Seigneurs, alez en la hors (-1)/ grant bien vous fera li essors,/ et si repensez du souper,/ quar molt bien vous va du disner."/ Adonc s'en vont en mi la rue./ Mabille ne c'est arrestue;/ aprés eulz leur a bien l'uis clos,/ bien a fermé, non pas esclos.

After 239. qui molt savoit de barat et guille.

241-242. s'onques eüstez part en fame.

245-246. soulas de f. qui est faille/ nient plus ne vault que ne fet paille.

247-249. Belle niece par saint Germain/ bien a .III. anz, j'en sui certain/ qu'a fame n'oy ne part ne hart;/ de tiex chose ne m'est pas tart,/ et si n'ai de tout ce que faire.

254. a ces amis la fortrei gié.

255-256. *Inverted.*

260-280. Et celle en fu toute apensee;/ Ysanne ala avant couchier;/ aprés lui ala dant Fouchier./ Li vilains ne s'oublia mie/ pour parfaire la lecherie;/ copa sa bource de sa main/ et si l'a mis(s)e dedens son sain (+1)/ et tant qu'en la chambre en entra/ et tant qu'il fu avala (-1)/ et tant a fait qu'il asouvit/ tout son talent et son delit.

287. j'ai perdu .C. soulz de deniers;/ niece, ci a maus acointiers.

288-291. Quand M. escouta Fouchier,/ si se commance a escrier.

292. "Or hors, filz a putain, larron/ issies tost hors de ma maison.

295-297. se vous de ceenz n'issiez hors,/ je vous feré moudre les os."/ "Ge l'iré dont au prevost dire.

305-306. si l'a dit tretout par guille:/ "Or ça," dit elle, "douce amie/ celle grosse bource farcie."/ "Dame, comment vous bailleray"/ dit Ysanne, "ce que je n'ay.

Translation

1. allusion to his craftiness and to his merry life. Note the name *Boi-vin* (wine-drinker).

12 and 22. warn us that two master tricksters will be confronting each other; see also 136.

66-68. Boivin laments, for Mabel to hear, the fact that he is not smart enough to add without the help of a coarse abacus.

127. Mabel does not perceive the obscenity contained in Boivin's alias.

142. Literally: I have been a long time without having comfort on account of you.

177. Literally: however they may have furnished.

200. This remark must be due to Mabel's own superstition about receiving good news before dinner.

254. Literally: that I have cheated her from her parents. Ménard, *Fabliaux français,* (p. 143) prefers P's version: "I have kidnapped her from her friends," on the grounds that A's *trechié* does not mean "to take away fraudulently."

Notes on Variant Ending from P:

1. The verb *is* is missing from this line, which is one syllable short.

19. In view of A's line 345, we assume that it is Mabel's dress that is ripped and not the pimp's robe.

5. DES .III. AVUGLES DE COMPIEGNE

Text

Variant manuscripts: B.N. 1593 (E), fol. 105 ro. -106 vo.; B.N. 12603 (F), fol. 240 vo. 242 vo. *Fragment, Troyes* (151-293), *follows E and F. E and F have several faulty lines in addition to*

the ones cited: E: 52 (-1), 57 (-1), 75 (+1), 78 (-1), 87 (-1),
157 (+1), 209 (-), 238 (-1), 287 (-1), 290 (-1); F: 2 (-1),
10 (-1), 27 (-2), 98 (-1), 248 (-1) 251 (+1), 277 (-1), 317 (-1).

5. E: quant il dit fabliaus et contes (-1); F: dont on fait.

6. E: devant rois et d. (+1); F: devant rois, dus et c.

14. E: E. .III. nul g.; F: E. .III. .I. g.

24. E: e. et garson.

29. A: a. n'en v.

39. E: a. faunoient; F: a. ambousant.

55. A, F: Savez, fet il.

59. E: b. garnie (*faulty rhyme*).

63. E: et si fuciens ataverné.

71. E, F: huchoit p.

73. E: d'Auvergne.

74. A: et vin et p.; F: cha char d'oissons et poissons (-1).

77. E, F: si puet on aise h.

85. *from* F; A *lacks* 85 *and adds, incomprehensibly:* "ce li ont
dit et li acointe;" E: en une belle sale pointe.

90. E: D'aus aseoir f. (*line missing in* F).

91. E: en la salle qui estoit pointe.

101. A: p. et chapons; F: plais, ch., p. et capons (-1).

102. E: et v. noviaus qui furent bons.

108. E: l. c. fu biaus et b. a.; F: sages.

109. E: et fu v. molt richement; F: biaus et v. m. r.

110. E: cortoisement.

127. E, F: et ses sergens.

129. E, F: "En charité.

132. E: si m'aït Diex et saint Tiebaut.

136. F: et chius i vait s. d.

148-150. E. Li avugle sanz contredit/ en vont l'oste
araisonnant:/ "Sire. . .(A's 150 *is missing in* E).

153-156. F: et dist li ostes: "Volentiers/ Robert," fait l'uns,
"car li bailliés/ vous le vis qui veniés premiers."/ "Mais vous qui
veniés daarains/ li donnés, car je n'en euc mie."/ "Dont l'a. . . .

157 (+1), 209 (-1), 238 (-1), 287 (-1), 290 (-1); F: 2 (-1)

158. E, F: Par la cervelle Dé, non ai (F: c. bieu).

168. E: devant li metez.

175. E: .I. ligaz; F: .III. laingnars.

176. E: fu en ces biaus draz.

192. E: et legiers.

194. E: c. recite (?).

207. E, F: a l'ostel quant je r.

211. E, F: d. son sergent.

212. E: p. si qu'i montast; F: p. et son harnas.

214. *Omitted in* F.

229. E: la grant messe d.

230. E: Li c. est venus a l'autel (*faulty rhyme*).

247. *Omitted in* F.

252. E: "Molt tres volentiers, p. s. G.

259. E, F: li prestres (douz *is omitted*).

268. E: et l. c. maintenant s'avoie; F: l. c. monte si s'avoie.

277. E: p. le messel et l'e.

281-284. F: au bourgois molt forment anoie/ mais paiiés me tost ma monnoie.

288. E: Veez, fait li b., veez; F: Or, i f. li b. veés.

299-300. *Inverted in* E, F.

312. E: li païsant.

313. E: l'ont pris et lié de maintenant; F: le vont illuec tantost predant.

314. E: v. formant tordant; F: v. estroit loiant.

322. E: li prestres f.

323. E: que li borjois f.

325-330. *Omitted in* E.

334. E: Ici fenit li miens c.; F: Ensi definera son c.

Translation

3. *menestrel:* composer.

4. Do these terms point to an aristocratic audience of the fabliau?

10. Obviously, the narrator of this fabliau is not the author.

14. *nis un:* not even one.

29. Ménard, *Fabliaux français,* (p. 162) is right to correct A from E and F: the clerk suspects that at least one of the beggars is not blind (see 40), for they walk merrily (20) and without the traditional boy to guide them (28).

74. The coupling of pâté and fish has been kept (see 101) since A's wine and fish would uselessly repeat the preceding two lines.

198. *persone:* beneficiary of an ecclesiastical benefice; a priest.

233. *chiere reborse:* a glum, scowling look.

249. *deut (doloir):* to hurt; to ache.

6. LI LAIS D'ARISTOTE

Text

Variant manuscripts: B.N. 19152 (D), fol. 71 vo. -73 vo.; B.N. 1593 (E), fol. 154 ro. -156 vo.; B.N. 1104 (Q), fol. 69 vo.- 72 ro.; Arsenal 3516 (k), fol 345 ro. -347 ro. (*not cited by Nykrog*).

3-4. *Omitted in* k.

3. D: reprendre.

4. E: p. entendre.

5. k: Ains doit on volentiers oïr.

6. k: de ce c'on se puet e.

7. E: b. cors soit d.; k: c'est raisons et c.

8. E, Q, D: l'enfrume.

9. D: ausi tost com il.

10. D, E, k, Q: li bon; D: le desloent.

11. Q: adés le bien disant; E: dissant; D, k: prisant.

14. D, E, k, Q: de tel a.

17-18. *Omitted in* A, E.
22. D, E, k, Q: v. mesdit.
23. E, k, Q: t. povre e.; D: molt en ovrez vilainement.
27. D: felonnie; Q: as genz la vostre felonnie.
28. D, E, k, Q: cruex vilonie.
After 28. k: mais tex est li mons devenus/ que ne s'en set mais garder nus./ Tant soit de cortoisie entiers/ qu'il ne mesdient volentiers.
29-32. *Omitted in* A, E, Q.
31. D: demorrez.
38. D, k, Q: traitié; E: tracier.
39. D, k: a affaire.
40. D, k: d. la matere.
41. D, k: la matere; E: la verité; Q: la reson.
43. A, E: retrere; Q: retrete.
44. A, Q: retrere; E: contraire; k: s. vilain mot et.
46. D: e. escoutee a.
47-48. *Omitted in* k.
47. D: en m'uevre.
48. D: n'orroiz v. remuevre; E: nommer; Q: conter.
50. D, k: resprandrai; E: respondrei; *omitted in* Q.
53. A, E, Q: et toute r. a sa savor.
54. D: Ne ne quier estre t.
56. D, E, k, Q: arrivant.
64. E: et henorer.
66. D: q. as autres s. estre a.
68. E: et tout c. a. a. gent.
70. k: p. c. c'onors (*remainder illegible*).
71-84. *Omitted in* A, E, Q.
76. k: et repince.
78. k: que hom n'en a ne altres bien.
83. k: le fraim p. m. s. voloir f.
85. D: Li sires.
87. E: n. vice le m.
95. E: bracie m.; D, k, Q: braies.
97. *Omitted in* k.
98. *Illegible in* k.
99. D: b. com a son aidier.
102. D, k: a. et sire et m.
103. E: desmonte l.
106. D: a. obeist t. a. a.
108. E, Q: h. pris; D, k: h. sorpris.
112. D: quant sor trestout le plus preudome.
114. *Omitted in* E.
120. D, E, k, Q: amender.
121-136. *Omitted in* A, E, Q.
122. k: argant.
128. D: garde q.
129. D: qu'est la.
143. D, k: bachelers.
144. D: d'une feme baude; k: u. seule dame; Q: p. u. seule estrange f.

145-146. *Omitted in* D, k.

146. Q: qui autrement ne s'escondi.

152. D, k: ce le roi r.

154. D: a. en son cuer t.

167. E: b. en proie.

168. E: s. fors de voe.

173. Q: que guerpissiez si fet u.

175-176. *Omitted in* k.

175-180. *Omitted in* A, E, Q.

180. k: car bien set qu'il li est mestiers.

188. "ore" *omitted in* E, Q.

190-216. A, E, Q: Honte et mesdis et esmes (A: mesfes)/
l'en fet tenir (A: couvrir) tant qu'a celi/ reva qui tant li abeli.

195. k: s. gent cors, sa cler f.

198. k: plus blanc de.

199. k: ex, nés et bouche et col et c.

204. "sogist" *omitted in* k.

211. k: mais n'avrai bien ce.

217. k: car ele estoit loial amie; D: la pucele; Q: la bele.

231. D, k: estoient sovent a; E, Q: a. joer a.

235-236. *Omitted in* A, E, Q.

235. D: defis amis.

239-240. *Inverted in* E.

240. D: s'arz et enging ne.

242. D: reproschier.

243. D, k, Q: d'uevre; E: de mute.

246. D, k: abandone.

249. A, D, k: ne clergie.

250-251 *and* 255-264 *omitted in* D, E, Q.

261-262. *Omitted in* k.

267. D: s'esbahi.

269-270. Q: Si en comença a noter/ et ceste chanson a chanter,
omitted in A, E.

271-272. Q: "Main se levoit bele Erembours./ Mout estes
vaillanz biaus cuers douz./ D'autre ne quier avoir regart.

273. D, k, Q: m. escueil.

279. D: la bele, la blonde se.

After 280. k: Blanceflor s'est apareillie/ comme sage et bien
enseignie.

284. "ert" *omitted in* Q.

285-286. *Omitted in* A, E, Q.

287. A: si fesoit douz et qoi oré.

299-300. *Omitted in* A, E, Q.

303-308. *From* D, k. *For the varying forms this chanson takes
in* A, E, Q, *see* Delbouille, *Le Lai*, p. 77. *The reasons for his
choices are given on* pp. 21-28.

316. k: l. et saines.

317. D: sont molt bones a raproschier.

320. D, k: tant savra de folie en lui.

332. A: de ma folie.

335-336. *Omitted in* D.

336. E. Q: outrage; k: ostage.

340. D. Q, k: en filosofie plus aigres; E: en filorpes et a.
345. *Omitted in* k.
After 346. k: e tot ensi m'est il avis.
349-353. *Omitted in* A, E, Q.
354. k: p. escondire.
After 354. Q: ne son voloir pas escondire.
355. A, E: Ainsi li mestres se detire.
After 355. A, E: et molt durement se demente.
356. D: un chapel de.
357. Q: i assembla de plusors f.
360-362. *Omitted in* k.
361. *Omitted in* A, E, Q.
362. A, Q: Douce; E: Doucetes.
364. k: Ci entroit ou; E: t. m'amiate.
366. E: m. s'esmoie.
374. *Omitted in* E.
375. D: son blon c.
377. D, k: que maistre Aristote a.
381. E: c. descuevre.
382. E: se cuevre; D: quar n'a cure que cil se cueille.
383. *Omitted in* E, k.
384. A: Lez un.
385. *Omitted in* A; D: dont l'aive est bele et clere la
gravele.
386. E: Si est fille en sa main; D: roi ses dels li renovele.
388. D, E, Q: Hé biaus c.; "amis" *omitted in* A, D, E, Q.
389. D: a. solaz et.
392. D: que maistre A. l'aert.
394-397. *Omitted in* D.
394. E, k, Q: a merveille.
395. A, E, Q: chei l'estincele (Q: chandeille).
396. A: vil.
398. D, k: Bien fait senblant d'estre marrie (k: esbahie).
399. D, k: cele, puis a dit: "Diex aïe!
417. D, k: arestant; E, Q: deportant.
418. D, k: Dist A.: "Or laissiez.
422-423. *Omitted in* A, E, Q.
436. D: s'irai; D, E, k, Q: honorablement.
437. D, k: Li viellarz; D, E, k, Q: liement.
After 439, 444, and 469. k *adds 40, 32, and 12 lines
transcribed in* Delbouille *on pp.* 83-86.
440. D: a amors mis en; D, E, k, Q: en effroi.
443-446. *Omitted in* A, E, Q.
447. D, k: d'un viel rados.
457. D, k: et Alixandre; E, Q: la damoisele.
457-461. *Omitted in* A, E, Q.
462-463. *Omitted in* A; *inverted in* E, Q.
464. D: ch. haut; E: v. sainne.
466. *Omitted in* E, Q, *and* k; A: Pucele blanche que laine.
468. *Omitted in* E, k.
469. E: *follows* 466; D: Et qui bone amor m.
470-471. *Omitted in* D, k.

472-473. *Omitted in* D, E, k, Q.

485. D, E, k, Q: honteusement.

486-487. *Omitted in* A, E, Q.

497-510. D: Li rois fu liez en iceste eure.

497. k: qui tote science d.

498-499. k: puis qu'ele s'en velt entremetre./ Et se ge vueil dont paine metre/ a vos oster de sa prison,/ nel tenez mie a mesprison,/ car bien savoie la doutance/ et l'anui et la mesestance/ qui de Nature vient et muet./ Puisque par force m'en estuet.

507-509. Q: Miex velt estre sanz compaingnie/ qu'avoir compaingnon a amie./ Par cest lai vos di en la fin:/ Tez cuide avoir le cuer molt fin/ et molt sachant tot sanz essoine/ qui l'a molt povre a sa besoigne.

507. D, k: Alixandres molt l'.

520, 524-525. *Omitted in* D.

524. E: a force a.

525. D, k: p. qu'il i a mal et.

526. D: dont est repris et qui; k: c'est vilonie, et qui.

528. E: qu'Alixandre b.

529. E: Aristotes et m.; D, k: son seignor et.

534-535. *Omitted in* D.

537. D, k: et v. qui la force a.

541. D, k: quant ne mesprit par apresure.

544. k: mais mostrer vos voil en.

546 579. *Omitted in* D.

547. k: entalenté.

552. k: devorer.

554-555. *Omitted in* k.

562. E: p. deduit a.

565. k: puis qu'ele a pooir et.

571. k: em patience.

573. k: l'anui.

574-579. *Omitted in* k.

576. E: que loiaument s.

Translation

23. Literally: This is too wicked an excuse.

29. *s'estancher:* to stop.

32. *Guanelons:* traitor in the *Chanson de Roland*.

59. i. e., dessert.

109. *desroi:* rebellion, revolt.

134. *sa volonté:* ambiguous; could also be *his* will.

191. *estre:* against (prep.).

196. *retraçon:* defect.

210. *m'asent:* agree, go along with.

382. *se çoile (celer):* to hide.

395-396. Allusion to the tale of Solomon and Marculf, well known at the beginning of the thirteenth century, in which a cat, trained to hold a candle with its two front paws, drops it in order to chase after a mouse. The moral of the tale is that instinct is stronger than training. On the variations and adaptations of this tale, see Delbouille, pp. 100-101.

521. From the *Disticha Catonis.* See Delbouille, p. 104.

578. From Vergil's *Eclogue X: "Omnia vincit amor."*

7. DE JOUGLET

Text

Variant manuscript: British Museum add. 10289 (Y), fol. 175 vo. -178 vo. This manuscript contains several faulty lines: 56, 129, 140, 141, 351, 381, 383. Line 444 of this manuscript names Colins Malés as the author of the tale. Since A has been fairly diligent in giving credit to authors, we consider Malés to be the author of only the variant tale.

1. J. en coste Montferrant.

9. quar ele n'avoit plus d'esfanz.

19. biau propris e bel h.

20. espia biau le m.

25. de moutons locuz et de chaz.

26. a l'ostel vint isnel le pas.

27-28. *Omitted.*

32. "Que ferés vos s. G.

35. .XL. 1.

40. Que me doisiez Mahaut v. f.

47. qu'eus en ont fet le m.

49. .I. an e.

50-53. Le voir vos dirai sanz noisier/ tout apertement sanz gloser.

56. a un m. J.

59-60. *Omitted.*

64. ainz que fussent au m.

67. puis le fet haut tout sus m.

68. et R. se prist a user.

70. Mes cil Juglet, qui le dechoit.

75-76. *Omitted.*

79-80. e si enflé e si bargié/ que por tout l'avoir de Blangié.

83-90. dit que fere li convenoit/ quar puisqu'ome a feme venoit/ c'estoit le droit et la costume./ Robins en fait molt laide frume/ mes il ne l'ose corocier./ Tant l'a fet Juglet esforcier/ que par un poi que il ne crieve/ mes encor plus assez le grieve/ ce que il nous lesse chier./ S'il peüst son ventre vier/ il ne l'eüst pas tant maumis./ "Par foi," fait Juglet, "biaus amis.

95. quar son v. li douloit mout.

103-108. espousa la, espousé fu./ A l'ostel s'en sont revenu./ Cel jor furent bien atorné/ quar il orent a grant plenté/ boen flaons e boens mortereus/ qui qu'en eüst ire ne deus.

112-116. Toz jors aloit Juglet soentre/ ou Robins tant ne sout prier/ Juglet ne tant bel esforcier.

118-119. s'a il plus angoissous d'un c./ li ventre, si grant comme il est.

233

127. vostre fiz est un poi plus pris.
128. por ce qu'il n'avoit m.
129. de f. aussi fete eure.
135-138. de cest chetif las asoté/ qui a fame de tel beauté.
140. "mes" *omitted.*
141. il ne traite ne.
145-150. il me besast et acolast/ e apreïst e ensegnast/ e m'estreinsist molt durement/ maduit soient tuit mi parent.
158. mes ele ne sot que cuidier.
162. De paor se c. a pleindre.
163. e dist: "Mon segnor.
167. votre afere ne vos querele.
171-172. Sire, devez estre hontous/ vos me semblez molt angoissous.
174-175. "Rien, damoisele, je n'ai nient."/ "Comment? Si n'en saroi le voir?
176. Moi le.
185. leaument.
187-188. *Omitted.*
191. e qu'eissi l'a Juglet servi.
197. tout droit en coste cel espuer.
199-200. fait Robins, "par seint Nicholay."/ Dou lit se lieve sans delay.
207-208. si se couche entre .II. linceus/ mes lors fu il plus angoisseus.
212. "Nay, dame, ainz.
213. e plus corocié que d.
After 214. fait cele, "biaus amis Robert/ poi goste d'autrui qui ne pert.
217. se bien ne voil c'.
221-222. tantost de son lit se leva/ au lit J. tantost s'en va.
225-230. E sachiez bien qu'il ne fu pas/ tout autretant sanz mot de gaz/ comme d'aler jusqu'a l'huis hors/ que son ventre le repreist lors.
233-234. issi soufrent males quereles/ "Robin," fet dame Mahaut, "quel es?"
246. tout coi les i out o.
256-259. Molt s'en estoit esmerveillié/ quant il se sent si borbeillier/ c'on l'oïst bien desverdellier/ d'une buce de corsin.
263-269. fait il, "aprismes me muir j'en."/ "Faites a malheür soit cen./ Maudit soit hui le cors Juglet/ quant vos avez mal gibelet/ a asaitier ceste avespree.
288-290. Il l'acole huimés; "Qu'est cen."
295-296. *Inverted.*
301. .XL. 1.
307-318. Lor afere a moi plus ne monte./ D'eus ne voil alognier le conte./ Moi ne chaut comme il lor enprengne:/ se il n'en seit, c'il si aprengne,/ e se il n'en fait, s'en ait soufrete./ A l'endemain quant le jor jete/ sa lumiere par tout li mont,/ dame Mahaut se lieve maont,/ si s'est assise sus son lit./ L'us de la cambre evre un petit/ com cele qui molt sout d'abet:/ "ha," fet ele,

"Juglet, Juglet!/ Come estrez ore endormi! (-1)/ Levez tost sus, biau doz ami."

328.　paumes s. G.

333-337.　tastez a l'esponde devant."/ Cil a bouté sa main avant,/ si n'a soing que dou soen rien perde.

339-340.　qui ne li put mie un pou./ "Vez," fet il, "por le digne clou."

343.　je chaucerai seveaus mes b.

351-352.　fait il, "qui m'a fait cen?"/ "Juglet," fet ele, "que est cen?"

358-359.　e ma chemise toute ordee/ si sunt mes braies deslavees.

368.　Juglet est cele part s.

369-372.　comme home qui molt fu ir[é]/ mes de ce fu mal atiré.

376.　toute sa main e. . .(ms. illegible).

377.　en furent toollié t.

378.　Il tresue d'aïr e t.

390.　il p. e. cel postel.

402-412.　Beginnings are illegible.

405.　. . .t avant, son sercot prent.

407-410.　Omitted.

413-415.　ce m'est avis, a un di luns/ que l'en out beneet les fons/ a une vile ou il passa.

422.　ch., bien serez paiez.

423-428.　font li vilain qui rude sont/ "Tenez," fet il, "deliez donc.

432.　toute sa main a e.

433-434.　en la merde qui jus avale./ Cele jornee fu molt male.

444.　s., ce dit Colin Malet.

446.　qui assez miez c. 1.

Translation

19.　cortiz:　one of these small gardens contains the pear tree which will later play an important role in the tale.

28.　mes:　country house.

46.　la sus bon jus:　from top to bottom.

66.　p. d'estrangleïs:　variety of pears.

68.　brouster:　to graze (like a cow).

107.　Literally:　no matter who might have anger or sorrow over it.

108.　morteruel:　mild gruel, a peasant dish.

117.　Literally:　and so it is more powerful than a boil.

125.　chiere mate:　dejected face.

136.　Literally:　(surely) he must be impatient now.

180.　Note again the ironical evocation of the saint's name.

192.　Literally:　whoever, for this one or that one; i. e., for whatever reason.

234.　Literally:　R., and in what manner?

333.　s'esploitier:　to accomplish; to hurry.

235

343. *viaus:* at least.
337. Literally: for the thought (he was) gripping his pants.
357. where I have not handled shit.
442. he could not help himself a whole year.

8. DES .III. DAMES QUI TROUVERENT L'ANEL

Text

(No variant manuscript.)

Translation

44. *essoire:* excuse.
46. *grant oire (erre):* in great haste, rapidly; *s'aparessir:* to get lazy.
70. Or: (for me) to be part of your abbey.
112. *agait:* vigilance, ruse, trick.
196. *reproche:* nears (verb).
235. Note the passage from indirect to direct discourse, picking up the lady's words in mid-sentence. (See Gérard Moignet, *Grammaire de l'Ancien Français*, Paris: Klincksieck, 1973, p. 368.)

9. DU CHEVALIER A LA ROBE VERMEILLE

Text

Variant manuscripts: Hamilton 257 (C), fol. 29 ro. -30 vo. B.N. 1593 (E), fol. 149 vo. -150 vo. Pavia 130 E. 4. (0) *also contains this tale but its text is illegible.*
3-4. C: une merveilleuse aventure/ d'un chevalier qui sanz laidure.
14. E: Li mari.
24. C, E: saint Liz.
30. E: d'e. vermeille.
31. C: de fres e.
45-50. *Omitted in E.*
57. E: belle et gresse et t.
60. *Omitted in C.*
79. E: furent (*scribal error, cf.* 80).
98. C: li membre t.
115. E: et vos lessa por ch.
117. C: et son oisel et.
120. C: deloie.
124. C: ("je" *omitted*) escondire.
128. C: li chevalier.
129. C: b. cheval apie (*faulty rhyme*).
137-138. E: leus est de prandre et de doner/ bien li saurai guierredoner.
150. E: r. un petit (*faulty rhyme*).
153. C: maintenant s'est e lit c.
155. E: a. b. tant par lobemant.

156. E: t. le prant.

After 164. C, E: son palefroi (E: espervier) prent et si monte/ de li ne veil fere long (E: ne ferai autre) conte.

165. E: mesquatant les chenez an lait.

172. E: erranmant (+1).

182. E: sergenz.

194. E: Est alé bone par esté?

197. E: mes serorges.

211-212. *Placed after 216 in* C; *omitted in* E.

214. C: b. vieleours; E: autres chanteours.

221. E: amez m.

235. E: la dame a touz mis a.

245. E: .III. m.

251. E: un malvés ivres.

252. E: .III.cc.

254. E: et les arnois.

258. E: le val ne sai de quel m.

259-270. *Omitted in* E.

After 266. C: que tot le sens avez changié/ et mauvés songe avez songié.

283. C, E: s. Jame.

284-285. C, E: "Oïl [E: Ha (-1)] sire," ce dist la dame/ "com ci a haut pelerinage/ Diex qui vos done tel corage/ que vos puist (E: vuet) mener et conduire."

After 288. E: por ce que Diex lor anvoit joe/ si devez bien en ceste voe.

289-290 *and* 293-306 *omitted in* E.

306. C: com cele qui het son seignor.

307. E: C. contes es homes.

312. E: que preudefame dit.

Translation

26. *oirre, erre:* journey.

27. *bon oirre:* rapidly.

48. *arener:* to tie one's horse up.

152. *faire dangier de:* to argue; to make difficulties.

162. *faire devise:* to make small talk; to mention.

163. *crespir:* to curl.

211. *a vostre oes:* to your profit (here: worthy of your rank); see also 227.

286. Identified by M.R. as Estaires, near Dunkerque.

10. D'ALOUL

Text

(No variant manuscript.)

17. Or: there is a bad thing in jealousy; jealousy is a bad thing.

19. i. e., of his wife's conduct, faithfulness.

63. Literally: for he is fond of striking with his rump; see 95-96.

70-73. The unintentional sexual innuendos in the lady's speech enable and encourage the priest to continue this figure of speech.

126-127. Literally: your gift is to be thanked.

259. *ravescot:* action of reviving somebody.

405. Literally: who first called your name.

497. *aers (aerdre):* assaulted; see 650, 917.

514. (512 in the French). Literally: will learn to name his own godfather.

640. This is the only use of the diminutive for *Roger*, obviously for the rhyme.

886. The wasps (the stings) which the priest claimed were in his stick (596).

11. DES BRAIES AU CORDELIER

Text

Variant manuscript: B.N. 19152 (D), fol. 120 vo. -122 ro.

2. a raconter une a.

5-6. *Inverted in* A.

6. Ilo avint (+1).

23. cele se jut en.

27. li dist un jor.

29. l'esveillast ne l'obliast mie.

40. *Omitted in* D.

46. A: en bon point.

58, 66. li borjois.

73. que li sires.

83. grant delai.

88. si fist du clerc.

90. si tost comme oī avez (-1).

91. un preudom.

102. B. compainz.

103. et gart mon cors.

110. est repairiez.

111. lor vient a.

112. male n.

115. nos somes molt mal a.

116. deables le ront amené.

119. levez l'uis.

125. tantost un poi c.

127. el fist le s.

128. com cele q.

138. et puis a dit: "Qui est ce ci.

139. Qui s'est couchiez d.
159. a l'uis ralez v.
181. que ja de vos aie joie.
184. issue ne f.
222. molt malement fu e.
225. a tex braies.
226. qui sont bones et.
227. li commande et.
230. Et il ne (se) s'en fist pas proier.
234. ele se convenra.
239. toz jorz.
240. Q. f. g. e. et grant j.
241. changer.
247. D. por Dieu et.
251. b. ai enpruntees.
260. "Dame," fait il, "molt volentiers.
273. t. a unë e.
279-280. *Omitted in A; these lines are needed to confirm the identity of "l'" of 278.*
286. Lors li a dit: "Par mon chief, Dame.
287. or sai ge bien.
After 298. Ne soiez de riens en malaise/ mais venez et ne vos desplaise.
299. ovueques moi dedanz ma.
302. clerc let.
303. de son dos les s. si ch.
310-312. Porter li fist aval les rues/ jusqu'a tant qu'il vint au moster/ la ou erent li cordelier./ Par tans orra autres noveles/ qui ne seront pas molt beles.
322. trestot belement en l'o.
339. s'un poi vos.
352. que ja n'en osera.
355-356. molt a bien son plait afiné/ atant ai mon flabel finé.

Translation

41. Literally: to enter as one who has been well warned, duly notified.
338-339. Literally: may it not displease you if I saddened you.
344. *aaise:* put at ease, contented.
348-349. Literally: the wife did well to give back to her husband a double bag for a sack.
354. *se chevir:* to manage; to tide over a difficulty.